STUDENT POLITICS

PERSPECTIVES FOR THE EIGHTIES

Edited by
PHILIP G. ALTBACH

The Scarecrow Press, Inc.
Metuchen, N.J., & London
1981

ACKNOWLEDGMENT

Most of the chapters in this volume originally appeared in two special issues of Higher Education, Volume 8, Number 2 (November, 1979) and Volume 9, Number 2 (March, 1980). I am indebted to the publisher, Elsevier Scientific Publishing Company, Amsterdam, for their kind permission to reprint these essays.

Philip G. Altbach
Buffalo, New York
October 1, 1980

Library of Congress Cataloging in Publication Data
Main entry under title:

Student politics, perspectives for the eighties.

    Essays.
    Includes index.
    1. Students--Political activity--Addresses, essays, lectures. I. Altbach, Philip G.
LB3610.S825   378'.1981   81-2725
ISBN 0-8108-1430-7   AACR2

CONTENTS

STUDENT ACTIVISM IN THE 1970s AND 1980s

by Philip G. Altbach

Unlike the large number of books dealing with student activism which appeared during the late 1960s and early 1970s, this volume stands virtually alone. The attention given by scholars and analysts to the topic of student political activism in recent years has been very modest. This is surprising because student activism, in many countries and particularly in the Third World, remains at a high level. Students have been involved in major political unrest in such nations as South Korea, Thailand, Afghanistan and Iran in the past few years. Despite newspaper accounts, virtually no scholarly or analytical attention has been paid to these significant student movements. The lack of attention is due, in large part, to the relative lack of activism in the universities of the industrialized nations. As a number of the essays in this volume indicate, the student movements of the major European nations have undergone a decline and have experienced a characteristic set of generally demoralizing events in the 1970s. The American student scene, so active in the 1960s, has changed considerably.

It is my contention that it is as important to understand the lack of activism and the changes which have occurred on the campuses of North America and Western Europe as it is to study the more "abnormal" activist period of the 1960s. As Altbach and Levine and Wilson point out in this volume, American student activism of the 1960s' variety has virtually disappeared, although a minority of students remain involved politically, but in different kinds of activities. Further, student attitudes do not seem to have changed dramatically in the United States, and this may have implications for future student activism.

The European scene, as analyzed in this volume, presents another pattern of decline in activism. In Italy and West Germany most dramatically, but also in France, it is

1

possible to observe the transformation of the mass student movements of the 1960s into the terrorist-oriented "underground" organizations of the 1970s. These groups lost most of their support in the universities, and activism in general declined. The causes for this dramatic change are complicated, but the pattern is clear. The American movement underwent a similar but less dramatic transformation with the rise and fall of the "Weatherman" underground radical organization in the early 1970s.

It is important to study the current campus situation, not only to understand the concerns and attitudes of today's student population but also to find a partial explanation of the dramatic changes which have taken place in recent years. Further, while it is impossible accurately to predict student activism or to anticipate the kinds of issues that will stimulate political interest, a careful look at recent history and contemporary reality may help us to understand not only what has happened but also what might occur in the future. Student movements themselves should be concerned with understanding their past--to discover both indications of errors and traditions worth preserving. Those involved with higher educational institutions need to be concerned with the patterns of student activism--and they should be particularly interested in their own responses to activism in the historical context. Such reflection may enable administrators and others to respond more constructively to challenges to academic order than seemed to be generally the case during the 1960s.

The Literature on Student Activism:
The Development of a Field of Study

The study of student activism is by no means an academic discipline, nor even a recognized speciality, but the literature in the field is large and varied enough to consider as a field of study. The literature on student activism is largely an artifact of the worldwide student movements of the 1960s. A bibliography published in 1970 and not considering the United States listed 1,800 books and articles on the topic of student activism (Altbach, 1970). The literature continued to grow at a rapid rate in the early 1970s as scholars caught up with the activist movements of the period. Publication on student activism abruptly stopped in the middle 1970s when the activist movements themselves came to an end. While the literature covers many countries and regions, without question the large bulk of the literature deals with the United States and to a lesser extent with Western Europe. A bibliographical volume published in 1973 features 9,000 items on the United States alone, roughly half of which are directly concerned with activism (Altbach and Kelly, 1973). Other parts of the world, and particularly the Third World, have received much less analytical attention even though student movements in these countries have been more effective in terms of inducing social or political change.

It seems clear that research and analysis on student activism was stimulated by the crises of the 1960s rather than by an intrinsic academic concern for the topic. For when the crisis was over, the large bulk of the writing stopped. For a certain limited time, a substantial amount of money from universities, government agencies and foundations was available for research on students and particularly on political aspects of student life, and these funds stimulated much research and writing. A number of large-scale surveys of student attitudes in various countries were done as part of this research effort. Liebman et al. (1972) reported on student attitudes and activism in Latin America, and Trow (1975) edited a volume which reported on the massive Carnegie-funded survey of American students and faculty. Without the funds that became available in North America and Western Europe much of the research on student activism would not have taken place.

In addition to the availability of research funds, interest from the mass media, publishers and scholarly journals was high during the late 1960s. This interest stimulated scholars and others to write about student activism and provided a wide audience for their writings. A veritable library of books on student politics was published in this period, many of which overlapped with each other. Such dramatic events as the Berkeley Student Revolt of 1964, the French "events" of 1968, the saga of the American SDS and the killings at Kent State University all received attention in a number of books, and even a film or two. The interest of the media in the topic was, not surprisingly, short lived, and it is now very difficult to find an outlet for discussion of student activism. Research funds are virtually unavailable.

Several different kinds of writers took an interest in student activism and contributed to the literature during the 1960s. A number of journalists and "pundits" wrote about student activism with varying degrees of perception. James Michener's (1971) book on Kent State was a best-seller and increased public interest in the topic. French intellectuals such as Raymond Aron (1969) wrote on student activism. Student activists themselves contributed several useful volumes to the literature and these gave a radical flavor to the discussion. Perhaps the most famous such volume, Cohn-Bendit's (1968) Obsolete Communism, was influential not only in Europe but in the United States and the Third World. Such titles as The Strawberry Statement (1968) and The Whole World Is Watching (1970) typify the flavor of this literature [1]. Probably the largest single group writing about student activism were social scientists from a variety of disciplines who brought the concerns and methodologies of their fields to research and writing on student activism. Sociologists and political scientists were particularly active in researching aspects of student activism.

It is difficult to generalize about the nature of the literature on students. Much of the analysis was unfavorable to student movements and student activism, particularly when students were critical of higher education. Lewis Feuer's Conflict of Generations (1969) was typical of the analyses of student activism from a critical perspective. Few of the social scientists who wrote about students considered the student organizations themselves. Most dealt with attitudes, motivations, or ideologies. A great deal of the writing of the 1960s is of little relevance, as it was linked to specific events and written from the perspective of the immediate crisis.

No widely accepted theoretical perspectives on student activism emerged from the massive outpouring of writing on students in the 1960s. Most authors found that national differences, academic traditions and movements were so different that adequate generalization was impossible. Those writers, such as Feuer (1969) or Miles (1971), who made overarching generalizations, were criticized for failing to take account of a sufficient number of national experiences. Despite a very substantial data base concerning student activism in different national settings and in varying historical periods, no satisfactory theoretical formulation is now available which is widely accepted by scholars in the field. The different methodological approaches and ideological predilections have made the emergence of an accepted theoretical base even more difficult, and this lack of a theoretical perspective has hampered further research, since each scholar or author must develop an original framework or begin with no existing clear framework.

The literature in the field is impressive in its bulk, for the unusually active short period of productivity, and in its diversity. The literature, which has diminished to a trickle, had added a significant amount of factual knowledge but continues to lack a theory. The social scientists who wrote on student activism when there was a ready market for books and articles and when funds were available have returned to more established research topics in their respective fields.

The Industrialized Nations and the Third World

While largely ignored in the literature, the dramatic differences between the experiences of student activists in the industrialized nations and the Third World are perhaps the key analytic variable in the study of student activism.   Indeed, if a theoretical framework is to be developed, it will have to be divided into at least two analytical categories, since these experiences are so different.   One can see many similarities among the industrialized nations of Western Europe and North America.   The movements of the 1960s developed at about the same time, in response to similar stimuli, and they declined at approximately the same period (with some variations).   There are similarities in academic traditions, the role and functions of the universities and the like (Ben David, 1977).

Third World student activism is more difficult to categorize and it is beyond the scope of this essay to provide a theoretical basis for Third World activism.   It is clear, however, that while students in the industrialized nations have never been responsible for the overthrow of a government (although they came quite close in Japan and in France in the 1960s), students have directly caused political upheavals in a number of Third World nations.   In other words, Third World students have from time to time been effective in stimulating revolutionary social change and, on a few occasions, such as the 1918 Cordoba reforms (Walter, 1968) in Latin America, major university change.   Further, students in the Third World are a consistent, important, and even legitimate part of the political equation.   Students are, in many cases, the "fourth branch" of government and the campus is a key part of the political system.   Given their crucial political and social importance, it is surprising that Third World student movements have received so little analysis from scholars.

As Levy points out in this volume, internal political conditions within a Third World nation can alter the scope and impact of student political involvement. Recent military dictatorships in Latin America, for example, have by and large kept students from playing an active political role through active repression of student movements. Nevertheless, student activism in the Third World remains an important factor, and although it is beyond the scope of this essay to analyze all the reasons for this, it is possible to point to some of the principal ones.

- Third World nations often lack the established political institutions and structures of the industrialized nations, and it is thus easier for any organized group, such as the student community, to have a direct impact on politics.
- Students have, in many cases, been involved in independence movements and from the beginnings of the state have been a recognized part of the political system. Thus, in contrast to the West, where activism is seen by most people as an aberration and an illegitimate intrusion into politics, Third World students are expected to participate directly in politics.
- Third World university students constitute an incipient elite and have, in many countries, a consciousness that they are somehow special. They are members of a tiny minority who have access to postsecondary education and their opportunities for access to positions of power and authority in society are very significantly better than the average (Barkan, 1975). The differences between those who have had postsecondary education and those who have not in the Third World are very substantial. The advantages have been somewhat diminished as unemployment of graduates has risen in a number of nations, but the generalization still holds true. These advantages, real or imagined, the small size of the student community and the historical sense of eliteness have all contributed to the possibility of student activism.
- The location of the major universities of the Third World contributes to the possibilities of activism. Many are based in the capital cities, and a large proportion of the student population is within easy reach of the centers of power. This simple fact of geography makes demonstrations easier to or-

ganize and gives the students a sense that they are at the center of power and have access to it.

• Relatively few Third World nations have effectively functioning democratic political systems. As a result of this, and of the widespread problems of illiteracy and poor communications, students are often seen as spokespersons for a broader population. They have, in a sense, authority beyond their small numbers, and those in power often take student demonstrations and grievances seriously for this reason. In many cases, seemingly small student demonstrations have been effective in quickly mobilizing larger social movements or have had a surprising impact on the authorities. In a sense, Third World students act as a "conscience" of their societies.

• Because Third World students, on the average, come from higher socio-economic backgrounds than their compeers in industrialized nations, they have an added impact. While there are significant national differences and the situation is changing as higher education systems expand in the Third World, a substantial portion of the student population in many Third World nations comes from urban elite backgrounds and they have, through their families, direct access to powerful segments of society.

These factors are a partial explanation for the relative effectiveness of student activist movements in the Third World in the past twenty years. All Third World student movements have not been effective, however, and repression has often been used and has been effective in destroying movements. Indeed, violence against students and loss of life have been much greater in the Third World than in the industrialized nations. South Korea and Thailand provide recent examples of massive repression of students.

Students in industrialized nations have, in somewhat different ways, been effective as agents of social change. When compared to direct activism and effectiveness of Third World students, they pale into insignificance, but the impact of activism in the industrialized nations should not be ignored. Perhaps the most effective role students have played has been in the cultural and social realms. Avant-garde movements, from women's liberation and civil rights to changing sexual mores and innovations in musical styles, have begun, to a considerable extent, in the universities.

Students have also had an impact on politics in some industrialized nations, but in ways which have been fairly indirect. In the United States, the movement against the war in Vietnam emerged from the campuses after being confined there for a number of years. It did, in the long run, have an impact on the societal consciousness. Students were influential in forcing President Johnson not to seek a second term in office. While the American student movement was unsuccessful in ending the war, its role as a catalyst for the anti-war movement was quite important. Similarly, the movement for civil rights for blacks and racial equality generally emerged from the universities and later became a powerful social movement in its own right.

In Western Europe, students were also influential in the 1960s. In both France and West Germany, students brought the problems of a lack of parliamentary opposition to public attention during the late 1960s. They also had an impact in stimulating reform in academic systems which were under considerable strain at the time as a result of expansion without much structural change. Students in Eastern Europe have also been important political catalysts in countries like Poland, Hungary and Czechoslovakia from time to time [2]. In the United States and in Western Europe, the period of student effectiveness was limited to the 1960s, although the American movement also flourished during the 1930s.

The Decline of the 1970s

The contrast between the high level of student political activism in many countries during the 1960s and its gradual decline during the mid-1970s is dramatic. A number of the chapters in this volume deal directly with this contrast, but relatively few analysts have attempted a full explanation of the causes for the decline. The following comments are an attempt to begin such an explanation in the context of the industrialized nations.

1. It is almost always impossible to maintain a high level of political and organizational activism for a long period of time. Mass mobilization cannot last forever, and the high level of activism of the late 1960s could not be maintained. Students felt the need to return to their studies, careers beckoned, and the leadership of the movement did not have the energy to pursue the struggle permanently.

2. In part, the "decline" of the 1970s is an artifact of the mass media. Great attention was paid to campus unrest during the late 1960s by television and other media, and this helped to bring student activism to public attention and helped to transmit it internationally. The mass media have not been especially interested in student unrest in recent years, and thus activism has not been widely publicized. In a sense, the lack of mass media attention has inhibited the rapid expansion of localized student movements since communication is now not as easy and there is less direct impetus.

3. As Arthur Levine and Raymond Boudon point out in their chapters, the focus of student political concern has changed. The topics which concern students now lend themselves less dramatically to mass movements. In France, the 1968 university reform provided students with institutional participation and an element of the student movement has concentrated on university involvement. In the United States, student concerns have become linked to personal and spiritual improvement, and to the betterment of campus conditions. Such issues are not the stuff of mass movements.

4. Most analyses indicate that student attitudes have not changed very much in recent years and that the student community remains well to the left of the general population (Lipset, 1976). Boudon supports this notion for France, Statera for Italy and Levine for the United States. Students may not be engaged in mass movements but they do remain left-of-center in their attitudes. Both Boudon and Statera are concerned about the lack of student commitment to the established political system, since this increases the potential for anti-regime activism at a future date should an appropriate issue arise. Several analysts have also pointed out that student attitudes towards "life style" questions, such as the use of drugs, music styles, divorce, are significantly more liberal than those of the mainstream of most societies. This is especially true in the industrialized nations, and may well have an impact on the future direction of society.

5. The economic situation of the 1970s has had an impact on the student population, in general tending to diminish activist movements in the industrialized nations. The 1960s were a period of impressive economic prosperity and growth in the industrialized nations. There were ample professional and other high-status positions for university graduates. The first wave of graduates from the enlarged univer-

sities encountered an expanding economy which needed their
skills. This sense of economic security encouraged students
to engage in political activism without major worry about future job opportunities. This situation changed dramatically
in the 1970s. The combination of inflation, the oil crisis,
and a general slowdown in Western economies placed professional jobs at a premium. Social science and humanities
graduates, those most active in student politics, had a particularly difficult time finding jobs. Students turned from the
social sciences and humanities to professional fields in order
to ensure brighter career prospects, and political activism
began to appear a risky undertaking. The economic downturn
brought a change in the priorities of many students, and clearly had a role in diminishing student activism.

6. The very success of the university reform efforts
of the 1960s in several countries diminished the activist thrust.
In some countries, including the United States, academic regulations seen by student activists as onerous (such as in loco
parentis) were removed and the curriculum liberalized. In
other countries, such as France and West Germany, patterns
of governance were changed and students now participate in
university affairs. This institutional participation has, according to Boudon, involved students in internal university
politics and has kept them, to some extent, away from external politics. While the results of the reform efforts differ
widely from one country to another, with the United States
and Britain ranking quite low on the scale of academic change
(Astin et al., 1975), many of the changes that have occurred
have contributed to a diminution of activism.

7. Demographic factors have helped to influence the
current of student life. In the industrialized nations, a decline in the university age population and fiscal problems in
higher education have combined to decrease substantially the
expansion which was characteristic of the 1960s. There is
less pressure for university places in many countries, and
conditions in the universities are, in some cases, less crowded than during the previous decade. During the 1960s, new
universities were being established at a rapid rate, and existing institutions expanded as well. This created strains on
both students and academic staff, and may have contributed
to the crisis. The expansion has abated in many countries
and ended in several.

8. The student movement itself perceived that it had
"failed" in the most basic respect--it did not achieve massive

social change and revolution. While the movement, in some countries, stimulated social crises and in others brought about university reform, it did not achieve its basic goals. This caused some activist organizations, in the late 1960s and early 1970s, to shift to increasingly radical tactics and ideologies, and they often alienated most students in the process. These tactics not only failed to gain the desired results; they also lost mass support and in some countries engendered repression from the political authorities. Students in several countries embarked on a period of "ultra leftism" and often turned to terrorist tactics to achieve their goals. The "Weathermen" in the United States, the Baader-Meinhof gang in West Germany and the Red Army in Japan all reflected this current. In all these cases, terrorism has the effect of weakening the movement. The terrorist thrust, according to Statera, continues in Italy, due in large part to Italy's continuing social crisis.

9. Finally, and perhaps most important, external political realities have changed. Student activist movements were primarily stimulated by societal politics rather than internal university-based matters, and changes in politics naturally have a key impact on the student movement. Where issues have changed, as in the United States, the student movement has been directly affected. In the United States, for example, the end of the Vietnam War and particularly the end of the military draft removed the major stimulating element for the activist movement. No other issue has replaced the Vietnam War for a student movement which has been historically stimulated by foreign policy-related matters (Altbach, 1974). The perceived "failures" of the parliamentary systems of France and West Germany during the de Gaulle regime and the coalition between the Socialists and Christian Democrats have not been repeated in those countries. Further, leftist ideological politics have become even more confused with the emergence of Eurocommunism, new political directions in China, and the failure of the tactics of many of the ultra-left groups.

The Future of Student Activism

Attempting to predict, in a comparative context, the future of student activism is impossible. As indicated earlier, the distinction between the Third World and the industrialized nations is a key variable. National differences in terms of educational systems, political traditions and realities, and other factors also make cross-national generalizations very difficult. Even in the national context, it is difficult to predict activism or campus unrest. Most of the student movements of the 1960s took everyone by surprise. Administrators and others responsible for universities did not expect the student movements of the period and, almost without exception, did not respond constructively to them, thereby exacerbating the difficulties. Social scientists and observers of mass movements were also caught off guard. It seems, too, that the student activists themselves did not expect the scope of the response to their protest movements. Student leaders were, in a sense, trying to keep up with their followers.

In the industrialized nations, many of the currents described in the previous section, which have contributed to the decline of activism in the 1970s, are still evident. But there are many imponderables. In the United States, for example, foreign policy has been the main stimulus for student activism. While there are no foreign policy issues at present which seem to have the potential for mobilizing large numbers of students, such issues may develop. The reestablishment of registration for selective service, which has engendered some activism, has some potential for creating further struggle.

As Levine and Wilson point out in this volume, one must define activism carefully. In the United States, new kinds of student political involvement have emerged in recent years and these deserve careful attention. The rise of student lobbying groups, the change in orientation of student governments, the growth of the Public Interest Research Groups and the anti-nuclear power and environmental movements are all indications of a new kind of student political involvement. Similar changes in the directions and orientations of activism are observable in other countries. In a sense, the militancy of the 1960s has affected the ways in which student life is analyzed. The 1960s, in the industrialized nations, were an aberration and the present period is a more normal example of student political life.

Non-political aspects of student culture deserve more careful attention. The growth, in the United States, of religious movements on campus, the revival of fraternities and sororities, the continuing impact of avant-garde cultural and musical styles, and other factors are all important. They have, almost without exception, not been carefully considered by analysts. Students, after all, are an important part of the academic enterprise whether or not they are involved in political activism and disruption.

Activism is even more unpredictable in the Third World, and at the same time is more important. It can be assumed that political regimes which have engendered the opposition of the educated groups in society and which are not effective in meeting perceived social needs will face some opposition. The universities are traditionally among the first to react to social discontent and often play an active role. Thus, while it is impossible to predict the exact nature of student unrest in a given Third World nation, it is very likely that students will continue to play a very active and at times effective role in political affairs.

The main purpose of this volume is to reflect on the dramatic changes in student political activism that have taken place in the past twenty years and to focus some attention on the contemporary situation. There is a need to understand these changes more adequately, and to expand our knowledge of student cultures generally.

Notes

1. The Strawberry Statement became a rather undistinguished motion picture, one of several dealing with campus themes.

2. For a discussion of the roles of various European student movements during the 1960s, see S. M. Lipset and P. G. Altbach (1969), John and Barbara Ehrenreich (1969), and Gianni Statera (1975).

References

Altbach, P. (1970). A Select Bibliography on Students, Politics and Higher Education (Revised Edition). Cambridge, Mass.: Harvard Center for International Affairs.

Altbach, P. (1974). Student Politics in America: A Historical Analysis. New York: McGraw-Hill.

Altbach, P. and Kelly, D. (1973). American Students: A Selected Bibliography on Student Activism and Related Topics. Lexington, Mass.: Lexington Books.

Aron, R. (1969). The Elusive Revolution: Anatomy of a Student Revolt. New York: Praeger.

Astin, A. et al. (1975). The Power of Protest. San Francisco: Jossey-Bass.

Barkan, J. (1975). An African Dilemma: University Students, Development and Politics in Ghana, Tanzania and Uganda. Nairobi: Oxford University Press.

Ben-David, J. (1977). Centers of Learning: Britain, France, Germany, United States. New York: McGraw-Hill.

Cohn-Bendit, D. and G. (1968). Obsolete Communism: The Left-Wing Alternative. London: Andre Deutsch.

Ehrenreich, J. and B. (1969). Long March, Short Spring. New York: Monthly Review Press.

Feuer, L. (1969). The Conflict of Generations. New York: Basic Books.

Gerzon, M. (1970). The Whole World Is Watching. New York: Paperback Library.

Kunen, J. S. (1968). The Strawberry Statement: Notes of a College Revolutionary. New York: Random House.

Liebman, A., Walker, K., and Glazer, M. (1972). Latin American University Students: A Six-Nation Study. Cambridge, Mass.: Harvard University Press.

Lipset, S. M. (1976). Rebellion in the University. Chicago: University of Chicago Press.

Lipset, S. M. and Altbach, P. G. (1969). Students in Revolt. Boston: Beacon Press.

Michener, J. (1971). Kent State: What Happened and Why. New York: Random House.

Miles, M. (1971). The Radical Probe: The Logic of Student Rebellion. New York: Atheneum.

Statera, G. (1975). Death of a Utopia: The Development and Decline of Student Movements in Europe. New York: Oxford University Press.

Trow, M., ed. (1975). Teachers and Students. New York: McGraw-Hill.

Walter, R. (1968). Student Politics in Argentina: The University Reform and Its Effects, 1918-1964. New York: Basic Books.

FROM REVOLUTION TO APATHY: AMERICAN
STUDENT ACTIVISM IN THE 1970s*

by Philip G. Altbach

The 1970s has been seen as a period of student political apathy in the United States. Scholars, university administrators,
and students seem just as surprised by the present period of
political quiet on campus as they were by previous waves of
activism [1]. The present decade stands in especially sharp
contrast to the "revolutionary" 1960s, clearly one of the most
active periods on campus [2]. The general public, which at
one period in the sixties labeled student activism the issue of
greatest national concern, no longer takes much interest in
campus life. While explanations of the previous wave of activism were numerous if diffuse and often unconvincing, few
social scientists have posited hypotheses concerning the current campus calm (Woodward, 1974; Lipset, 1976, pp. xxvii-
1).

     The contemporary campus scene is much more com-
plicated than is immediately apparent. Compared to the
1960s, the seventies has indeed been quiet. No major student movements have emerged, disruptive demonstrations
have been rare, and in general students have not seemed to
be politically oriented. Yet, basic student attitudes do not
seem to have changed dramatically from the sixties, according to opinion surveys. Students remained on the liberal to
radical end of the political spectrum. In the past few years,
they have grown somewhat more conservative on political issues and somewhat more liberal on life-style questions, but
without major shifts. Some sporadic student activist currents
were apparent during the decade as well. Kent State Univer-

*Reprinted by permission of the author and publisher from
Higher Education, 8:6 (November 1979), pp. 609-626. Copyright 1979 by the Elsevier Scientific Publishing Co., Amsterdam.

sity erupted briefly in 1977, resulting in almost 200 arrests.
American foreign policy in South Africa--and university in-
vestments there--stimulated demonstrations at perhaps fifty
universities, with some violence occurring in California. And
some new forms of political action, such as the environmental movement, the Public Interest Research Groups, and state-
wide student lobbying efforts emerged in the seventies. Those
involved in activism were more politically sophisticated, having learned from the mistakes of the sixties.

In many ways, the seventies are much more typical of
American student life than was the previous decade. Viewed
in historical perspective, university students have not been
notably politically active in the United States. Yet, the campus has from time to time played a role in shaping American
politics. The major political events of the seventies, such
as Watergate, the so-called "taxpayers revolts" and others
were played out basically without campus participation. Foreign policy issues, the main stimulus of major student activism, have not been a major factor in the public consciousness
during the seventies.

Student activism was also not a major political force
in most of the European industrialized nations during the seventies. The dramatic West German and French student movements of the 1960s have virtually disappeared from the scene.
Small groups of students continued to be politically active,
and the focus of the activism that remained was leftist. Italy
has been an exception to the rule of quiet, as students have
sporadically responded dramatically to Italy's continuing economic and political crisis. Students have been key political
forces in a number of Third World nations, and thus there
are relatively few cross-cultural generalizations that can be
made. Thai students helped to topple a regime, and students
constitute a key oppositional force in South Korea. Iranian
students were a key element in overthrowing the Shah, and
students in India and Latin America remain politically involved. The patterns of student activism differ substantially
around the world, although the period of relative quiet which
is observable in the United States has been repeated in most
of the European democracies.

This article will describe and analyze the current
status of student activism in the United States and will offer
some tentative explanations for the lack of political concern
on the campus. It will also seek to contrast the present situation with the period of more intense activism in the 1960s.

It is my conviction that the present lack of activism tells us much about the state of campus life.

Historical Perspectives

American student activism must be seen in historical perspective (Altbach, 1974; Altbach and Peterson, 1971, pp. 1-14). While students were involved in political and other activities at earlier periods, the history of ideologically-based activist movements and organizations stems from the early years of the twentieth century. Students were, for example, sporadically involved in political and other activism in the period following the War of 1812, and later in the anti-slavery movement of the nineteenth century, but no identifiable organizations emerged from these movements (Novak, 1977). In this century, one can see both organizational continuity and several distinct phases of activism. The Intercollegiate Socialist Society (ISS), founded in 1905, was the first self-consciously radical student organization. It survived, under various names until the 1960s. Its last incarnation, Students for a Democratic Society (SDS), was the most successful national student organization of the sixties (Sale, 1973). The saga of the SDS and its predecessors, while beyond the scope of this article, illustrates the themes of some organizational continuity and changing campus political styles and orientations over a half-century period.

The twentieth century has seen several distinct waves of student activism. The "progressive" period prior to World War I was the emergence of the first ideological student organization. The ISS and other groups, such as the Young Intellectuals, saw themselves as educational enterprises, and were not activist in orientation. They were liberal or radical in their views, and conservative student movements had little impact at this time. The nascent movement was strong mainly in the elite colleges and universities and on a few campuses located in large metropolitan areas, so most students were basically unaffected by these groups.

World War I and the ensuing period of the "roaring twenties" brought an end to the ISS and related groups, although glimmerings of political and social concern continued on campus, especially in the moderate and liberal religious campus organizations which were active at the time (Fass, 1977). The focus of these early student organizations was mainly on broader social, political and cultural questions, including foreign policy. Students had a considerable interest in cultural matters and followed the writings of such commentators as H. L. Mencken. Students sought cultural self-definition and separated themselves from what they perceived as a shallow popular culture of the period. In an effort to stimulate widespread support, student activists focused on intramural questions such as ROTC, the censorship of the campus press, and similar issues (Fass, 1977, pp. 339-43). Despite major efforts by the small minority of activists, the large majority of the student population was unaffected by either the political or cultural stirrings of the period. Without question, the twenties was a period of general campus apathy.

The decade of the 1930s was the period of the most intense student activism prior to the sixties. While the decade began with a feeling of social crisis, there was relatively little student activism until late in the decade. As the combined impact of the economic depression and a growing awareness of foreign policy issues such as the rise of fascism in Europe and the changing role of the United States in world affairs, students became increasingly involved in political activism. This period saw the emergence of large-scale ideologically-oriented organizations on the left. While communist and socialist student groups grew modestly during the early thirties, the major student organization of the decade was most active in the late 1930s. The American Student Union (ASU) was for most of its history a united front of socialists, communists and liberals (Wechsler, 1935).

The major motivating force for activism during the thirties was not the depression with its attendant economic dislocation, the rise of the labor movement, or the other dramatic changes in American domestic life, but rather it was foreign policy which most effectively mobilized students. This emphasis reflected the largely middle class nature of the student population. Peace demonstrations, including several annual national peace "strikes", constituted the main thrust of the movement. While politically conscious students were almost uniformly anti-fascist, there was a strong campus sentiment against American involvement in the war in Europe in the late 1930s. The Stalin-Hitler pact further confused liberals and radicals and damaged the student movement. Unlike Europe, there was no significant right-wing student movement during this period.

American entry into World War II brought student ac-

tivism to an abrupt end. For the most part, previously anti-
war students eagerly joined the war effort. Only a small minority of pacifists and socialists continued to oppose the conflict.

The immediate post-war period saw a revival of interest in politics on campus and the growth of considerable
idealism about the United Nations, the possibilities for world
peace and in general for the future of the post-war world.

There was a short-lived revival of the student movement in 1947 and 1948. Thousands rallied to groups like the
United World Federalists, and the presidential campaign of
Henry Wallace of the Progressive Party drew substantial student support. The bubble burst quickly. Wallace gathered
few votes in the 1948 election and the bright promise of world
government, the United Nations and Soviet-American cooperation ended even earlier. The Cold War, which probably began
in earnest with the Truman Doctrine in 1947, dealt a
serious blow to student activism, which did not resume to
any significant degree until the end of the 1950s. Most Americans were convinced that the Soviet Union constituted a real
menace and any social movement that was even peripherally
related to communism became deeply suspect, even on the
fairly liberal university campuses. The Korean conflict, while
never a popular war in the United States, focused clearly on
an external enemy and made campus activism increasingly
difficult. Outright repression during the 1950s also inhibited
political expression of any kind. Loyalty oaths were instituted
in many states. Communists and others were hounded from
jobs in universities and elsewhere while the campaigns of
Senator Joseph McCarthy, the House Committee on UnAmeri-
can Activities and other right-wing "communist hunters" were
in full force [3]. As a result of these pressures plus a notable careerism among students in the aftermath of World War
II, political activism virtually came to an end.

Student activism began slowly to revive in the late
1950s. McCarthy's repression was gradually discredited and
the expression of political opinion of an unpopular nature became less risky. The Sino-Soviet dispute and a growing political awareness in general made the "threat" of monolithic
communism less dramatic. America was in a relatively re-
laxed period of economic prosperity and peace. Yet, on the
campus, there was a growing unease. Triggered at first by
a fear of nuclear weapons and somewhat later by growing liberal sympathy for the emerging civil rights movement in the

South, student political awareness and activism grew in the late 1950s and early 1960s. The election of John F. Kennedy in 1960 was marked by a rhetoric of liberalism and involvement. America was in a mood for change, and the student community wanted to make sure that the rhetoric was translated into action. While it is not possible here to chronicle the early years of the revival of the student movement, it is clear that the combination of a liberalization in the society generally, economic prosperity and growth, a new understanding on campus of the problems of world peace, and the emergence of the civil rights movement as the "conscience" of many white liberals all combined to stimulate a revival of student activism (O'Brien, 1971, pp. 15-25; Altbach, 1974)

The Legacy of the Sixties

Like previous times of intense activism, the major motivating force of the sixties was foreign policy, specifically the Vietnam War [4]. Other elements added intensity to the activist thrust. The civil rights movement stimulated a new consciousness among blacks and an awareness of America's racial dilemma among some whites, especially on the campuses. Higher education, for a number of reasons, assumed an unprecedented position of importance in American society and this focused increased attention on the universities. An academic degree was seen as the key to professional status and a middle class life-style. Enrollment in post-secondary education also kept a student out of military service. Thus, enrollments grew rapidly, and unprecedented amounts of money were spent on higher education. At the same time students saw themselves as part of massive and bureaucratic universities at odds with the traditional spirit of American higher education.

Important changes were also taking place in American youth at the time which, at least temporarily, gave rise to notions of generational conflict and stimulated dissent. The growth of rock music coincided with the dissent of the sixties and in some ways reflected it. Rock music was an artifact of youth. The growing use of marijuana and other drugs at this period, on campus and off, was also a powerful symbol of youth dissent. Drugs became an accepted part of the youth subculture, although they were illegal and their use involved some risk. An unprecedented proportion of post-high school youth was going on to higher education, and the traditional middle-class consensus concerning the value and the norms of higher education was breaking down to some extent. While only a small minority of the students considered themselves radicals (5% in 1969 and 1.8% in 1978), this group was a numerically significant one on many campuses. Further, a much larger minority embraced elements of the "counter culture." Despite the minority status of radicalism, campus culture became identified, in the public mind, with dissent and cultural alienation.

The war in Vietnam was the key factor in stimulating what was the largest and most militant student movement in American history. However, the movement did not appear in a vacuum. The experience gained in the civil rights movement, the peace movement, and the willingness to engage in activism because of a more liberal political atmosphere in the nation all provided the background to the anti-war movement. But it was the war, and especially the draft, which directly touched the student community and stimulated massive activism. The war convinced many that the entire American political system did not work. Because students were unable to effect political change through peaceful means such as demonstrations, teach-ins, and other tactics, the movement increased in militancy through the sixties. Discontent with the educational system and a feeling among some students that the universities were an integral part of the dreaded "system" grew along with frustration. As a result, there was a willingness to attack the universities themselves as well as other societal targets. Unreasonable responses to activist demonstrations by university officials often further stimulated militancy and increased the numbers of students involved.

While the student movement was a major force on the campus in the sixties and had some impact on American politics, it was seen by many of its participants as a failure. Ideologically committed student leaders had as their goal major social change or revolution, and this did not occur. The rank and file participants in the movement were committed to ending the Vietnam War, and while it can be argued that student pressure was responsible, at least in part, for altering public opinion, students did not end the war.

The history of the Students for a Democratic Society (SDS), the major radical student organization of the sixties, dramatically indicates currents in the student movement. The SDS grew increasingly strident in its political and tactical approach, culminating its volatile history with organizational splits and an ideology which called for violent revolution. One element of the SDS, the "Weatherman," went underground and attempted to stimulate urban guerilla warfare. These tactics alienated the leadership of the movement from the large majority of students, and within a year greatly weakened its impact on campus and in society. Issues became complicated and in some cases the responses of the student movement unsatisfactory to most students. For example, the movement's increasingly strident anti-Zionism and sympathy for militant Arab radicals alienated many Jewish students, who had previously been sympathetic. The changing nature of the black movement and the response of the student movement to it also confused many white middle class students.

The student activism of the sixties marked the first time that university students became involved in militant, sometimes revolutionary and violent, political activism. And it was the first time that students turned on the universities as a target for attack because of academic complicity in an "evil" social system. For the first time, "university reform" was raised as one of the slogans of the student movement. Students proved during the 1960s that they could have an impact on national politics, that they could attract and to some extent use the mass media, and that thousands could be mobilized for demonstrations.

The Vietnam War did not come to an end as a result of student pressure (although one American president, Johnson, did not run for a second term in part because of student pressure), the black power movement emerged and rejected the support of white liberal and radical students, and the revolutionary rhetoric and militant tactics of the student movement did not, in the long run, attract much support off the campus and only a minority support even in those universities where the movement was strongest. In the end, the leaders of the movement despaired of inducing social change through campus activism in any case, and the student movement virtually came to an end by 1972. The legacy of this movement is, thus, one of ambiguity; there were successes and failures, but in the last analysis the movement left mainly a history on which future generations of activists might build at a later time.

The Current Student Scene

The seventies, with considerable justification, has been called a period of apathy on the American campus. Virtually all of the political organizations which flourished during the sixties have disappeared, and few new have taken their place. There have been relatively few activist demonstrations or campaigns, and student energies seem to flow in non-political directions. At least some of the "image" of apathy is a reflection of the lack of interest of the mass media in student affairs--especially in contrast to their hyperinterest during the late 1960s. I do not claim that activism is at a high level, but the campuses are not entirely devoid of political consciousness or organizations either. For example, in 1976, 18.6% of undergraduates indicated that they had engaged in some form of activism.

With the bifurcation and disappearance of the SDS as a campus-based movement, there was a general agreement among many radicals that organizational efforts should be based elsewhere, such as in the working class or the trade union movement. The campus, it was argued, had not proved to be an effective springboard to revolution. At least in terms of continuing ideologically committed radical student groups, the campus reverted to a political level not unlike the 1950s, prior to the emergence of a large-scale student movement. Even the traditionally most active campuses, such as the University of California at Berkeley, Harvard, and the University of Chicago, have only a few small, relatively inactive and usually weak student political organizations functioning. Most American universities had no functioning political organizations at all.

During the 1960s, a large number of student-oriented newspapers and journals contributed to political debate and consciousness. At present, relatively few of such journalistic efforts exist. Several serious publications which at one time were to some extent campus based have shifted their focus--and often their editorial offices--away from the universities. Socialist Revolution (which changed its name to Socialist Review), and Radical America are indicative of this trend. To help the emergence of a mass based radical movement, left journalists have placed many of their recent efforts in trying to start mass-circulation newspapers and magazines. Such publications as Seven Days, Mother Jones, and In These Times are in this category. The underground press, which was popular on campus during the 1960s and reflected alternative political and cultural perspectives, has virtually disappeared. Underground newspapers continue to exist in a few university locales, but in general these publications collapsed.

Thus, not only has the organizational base of the student movement declined seriously but the communications nexus which
helped to shape ideologies and communicate views has virtually ceased to exist.

While neither the numbers of demonstrations nor their
militancy can compare to the sixties, instances of sporadic
activism indicate that political consciousness on campus is
not entirely absent, and that dramatic issues can mobilize
students. Demonstrations in 1977 at Kent State University
protesting the proposed construction of a gymnasium at the
site of the 1972 shootings resulted in the arrest of almost
200 students. Students in California and in several other
parts of the United States have protested against American
policy in Southern Africa in general and against the investment policies of universities in particular. Although these
demonstrations resulted in several hundred arrests, they led
to no lasting movement and were confined to a small number
of campuses.

The news media has not paid much attention to local
student activism, and this has helped to limit its national impact. The issues have been diverse, the events sporadic and
somewhat unpredictable, and the scope of demonstrations and
other activities significantly smaller than was the case in the
sixties. The Kent State demonstrations were covered by national media but the South Africa protests received little attention despite arrests. And other demonstrations, such as
the substantial but ultimately unsuccessful efforts by students
at the City University of New York to retain free tuition in
the face of fiscal crisis, were hardly reported at all. The
internal communications networks of the student movement,
except for campus newspapers, had declined and the mass
media was no longer much interested in campus affairs.

In the traditional sense of leftist student activism and
organizational activities, the present period is a particularly
barren one. Some vestiges of the "old left" student groups
still exist and are active on campuses with a strong political
tradition, but these groups are very small and have a tiny
following. Students are occasionally aroused by a political
issue, although even in these cases demonstrations tend to be
small and no ongoing organizations or movement are created.

In part because of the lack of other student organizations, the established student government structures have assumed a greater role in campus affairs. Like the fifties,

when student governments were among the few organized forces on campus, these organizations again play a more important role, if only by default. The collapse of in loco parentis and a widespread recognition that students should have the major voice in determining their own extra-curricular life has given a greater role to student governments. In recent years, student governments have been given control over substantial sums of money allocated to extra-curricular activities and this has further increased their power. Further, one of the legacies of the sixties has been a grudging agreement by universities that students should have some role in governance and policy. Student governments are often the agencies which appoint students to academic committees and they have become involved in discussions of academic policies.

On relatively few campuses are student governments concerned primarily with political questions, but in some cases politics constitutes a part of the concern of governments. This too is part of the legacy of the sixties, when political issues intruded on the once placid student governments. Thus, while student governments have not become primarily political entities in the seventies, the political consciousness and the power of student governments has been enhanced. Although student government bodies are elected by students in open elections, they have not traditionally had much rank-and-file input. This trend continues--and both the elections and the other activities of student governments are not taken very seriously on campus.

At the state and national levels, student government organizations have been active. The U.S. National Student Association (NSA), which almost collapsed after its links to the CIA were exposed in 1967, managed to stay in existence and moved significantly to the left. It took a strong anti-war position in the late sixties, and continues to be well to the left of the general American student population. Its annual national congresses have consistently taken liberal or radical positions on civil rights, drug legalization, and on other topics. The NSA never had much impact on the local campus, and it remains virtually unknown to most students (Altbach, 1973, pp. 184-211).

Student governments have also engaged in lobbying efforts to protect student interests. These student lobbies have been active in state capitals and recently at the federal government level. Student lobbying organizations in New York and California have hired lawyers and professional staff, and

in general have brought student issues to the attention of legislators and government officials. The lobbies have been especially concerned with financial questions and issues of student rights and have kept away from ideological issues. As
in the case of the NSA, the student lobbies are generally little known on the campuses.

Very recently, the National Student Association and the
National Student Lobby, the main national group coordinating
lobbying efforts, have formally merged into one national organization. This new group has affiliations from about 360
colleges and universities--not a very impressive number since
there are more than 1, 000 such institutions in the United States.
But it is the first time in a number of years that there is a
nationally coordinated student organization.

Significantly, American conservative student movements
have never achieved the prominence of their European counterparts, where they have been powerful forces in the past (Steinberg, 1977), and as a consequence they have been largely ignored by analysts of student activism. During the 1950s, a
substantial conservative student movement was active in the
United States and threatened to take over the National Student
Association, normally a liberal bastion. Groups like the
Young Americans for Freedom attracted some media attention,
perhaps because campus conservatives were an oddity. There
is no active conservative movement on campus at the present
time, although the Intercollegiate Society of Individualists (ISI)
has a large "paper" membership and an active publications
program, including Modern Age, a respected conservative intellectual journal. It is not so much that American students
appear to have moved to the right, but rather that they have
ceased, at least for the present, acting on their political
views.

Campus attitudes do not seem to have dramatically
changed since the 1960s. As S. M. Lipset (1976, pp. xxxix)
has pointed out, students were radicalized during the sixties,
and their politics has remained somewhat to the left of the
American political spectrum. In 1977-8, for example, 27%
of college and university freshman reported that they considered themselves liberal or radical while only 16. 4% labelled
themselves conservative [5]. Liberals and radicals were even
more dominant in four-year institutions and in universities,
the prestige segments of the post-secondary educational system. When queried on specific social questions, such as the
use of marijuana, abortion, and similar issues, students were

even more dramatically to the left of the general population. Students have unquestionably remained liberal to radical on questions of life-style and culture. Politics, in general, have become a less important concern of American students during the seventies.

Several campus currents which are not directly related to activism deserve attention and can only be mentioned here. Religious groups have had a significant revival in recent years, and have had some impact on students (Judah, 1974). While the established Protestant, Catholic, and Jewish groups have seen only modest growth, "new" religious movements have been most successful. For a short time, varieties of Hinduism flourished on some campuses, especially those which had previously seen a great deal of political activism. Yoga, vegetarianism, and various schools of Eastern spiritual consciousness all have had some impact. While these groups have declined in influence, they still retain some impact on students and maintain a presence on many large campuses. Of wider significance is a modest revival of fundamentalist Christianity on smaller campuses. It is impossible to estimate the numbers of students involved in these religious movements, or to indicate whether they will become a permanent part of the campus scene. But for the present, they are an integral part of campus life. And if the well publicized "conversions" of former radicals like Rennie Davis and Eldredge Cleaver are any indication, the religious groups are attracting some support from students who might otherwise be attracted to radical politics. The fraternity and sorority movements have also regained some strength on campus in the seventies, after being severely threatened during the sixties. Although they have not reassumed their dominant role over the social and extra-curricular life of many campuses that they held prior to the sixties, they have increased their membership as students continue to look for a sense of community.

The religious revival, and especially interest in personalistic Eastern religions are part of a widespread concern evident on campus as well as in the middle class for psychological "self-improvement." The popularity of books like I'm OK, You're OK, the EST movement, transcendental meditation, and similar currents are all indicative of this significant strain in campus life. In a sense, the idealism which was focused on political and social concerns in the sixties has been directed toward the "inner life" in the seventies. Even the most popular campus social causes of the seventies, the environmental issue, is very much related to this current.

While the environmental emphasis and such related issues as the struggle over nuclear power, Earth Day, and so-
lar power has not succeeded in becoming a continuing movement, it has been one of the foci which has attracted student
attention. Campus newspapers are filled with environment-
related stories, and the sporadic movements related to the
environment attract substantial student support. There is a
heightened awareness of the issues involved, and considerable
interest in the technical aspects of environmental questions.
Most recently, the struggle against nuclear power facilities
has attracted student involvement. The small minority actively involved in the issue has related environmental questions
to broader social and political questions but most students do
not see the relationship. It is significant that the environment
is the issue which seems to have attracted the widest student
interest during the decade.

Some elements of the sixties retain their viability on
campuses in the United States. Perhaps in historical retro-
spect, the major contribution of the 1960s will be the women's
movement and the black student movement. During the 1960s
pressure from these movements created academic programs
in many colleges and universities, as well as political and
social organizations. These academic programs, although
under attack from conservative forces and threatened by efforts to cut university budgets, by and large continue and are
a focus for community. The organizational aspects of the
women's and black movements have survived better than have
the general political student movement although they are significantly weaker than they were during the 1960s. Although
the "counter culture" has disappeared from the headlines, it
also remains an important force on campus. If anything,
elements of the counter culture have been accepted by the
broader society. Recent steps in a number of states to le-
galize marijuana, the pervasiveness of rock music, and social concern about homosexuality and psychological well-being
all reflect concerns which were only a few years ago limited
to a small, largely campus-based minority.

The Causes for Decline

Since 1972, very little attention has been given to student activism. The spate of books and articles on the subject has
virtually come to an end. And since there are few demonstrations disrupting the campus or causing public concern,
neither academic administrators nor government officials ex-

press much interest in understanding the causes for the current decline of student activism in the United States. Yet, some of the factors which have contributed to the decline of student political concern and activism are clear.

The most dramatic change in the American political scene which has affected the campus is the decline of foreign policy as an issue of acrimony and of direct concern to large numbers. Specifically, the end of the Vietnam War and of the draft has taken much of the moral outrage from the student movement. The widespread involvement of large numbers of students--and the support of a significant section of the middle class ended when it became clear that the war was ending, although it should be recalled that it took several years for the conflict to actually end. This is not surprising, since American students have historically been motivated largely by foreign policy issues, and the Vietnam War, which directly affected the student population through the draft, was an especially dramatic instance. The war effectively combined a moral question with one of political expediency. Liberals, pacifists, radicals and many students who were just outraged by government lying could participate in the anti-war movement. While the movement's leadership tried hard to give a dominant political tone to the struggle, most students seem to have been "radicalized" only to the extent of opposing the war itself, and sometimes some of the institutions, like the universities which seemed to be supporting the war effort. Once the war issue was resolved, the movement, as a mass effort, was blunted.

Although the leadership of the student movement attempted to broaden the anti-war struggle to a multi-issue political movement, it had little success. Indeed, the frustration of the leadership either to directly influence American foreign policy or to "convert" rank and file activists to radical politics led to increasingly strident rhetoric and extreme tactics. These emphases alienated most students, and limited the effectiveness of the movement. The history of the SDS, mentioned earlier, is a good example of the effect of tactical militancy and ideological squabbles. Tactics moved from teach-ins and freedom rides to disruptive campus demonstrations which resulted in some violence (often precipitated by the police) to massive direct confrontation with the authorities such as at the Democratic Party convention in 1968 and the demonstrations in Washington, D.C. against the war in the following several years. The final tactical stage was underground urban guerilla warfare which included the bombing of

buildings. These fluctuating tactics, and an increasingly strident student rhetoric indicated to most students that the movement had lost its grasp of American political reality. While
large numbers of students rallied for specific anti-war demonstrations after 1968, they no longer took the ideological
leadership of organizations like SDS very seriously. There
is no question but that the tactics of the movement contributed
to its isolation and speeded its decline.

A basic fact of the 1970s is a massive demographic
shift which affects the university in many ways. The generation of the sixties was an "abnormal" one. It was quite large,
reflecting the post-war "baby-boom." The American population was, at that time, statistically "younger" than it had been
for some time, or will be in the foreseeable future. Thus,
numerically, youth was a force to be reckoned with. At present, the absolute size of the college-age generation is somewhat smaller, and the American population is "aging."

The sixties was the culmination of a period of tremendous growth in higher education. Enrollments had steadily
expanded, faculties were growing, and there was a sense of
optimism about the future of higher education. This growth
placed severe strains on the universities. Traditional norms,
such as in loco parentis, elements of the undergraduate curriculum, and others were under attack. A younger generation
of academics did not, in some respects, share the older values of the professoriate. Increased emphasis on research
and graduate education and newfound affluence in higher education all placed strains on the system which undergraduate
students felt. The academic scene of the seventies is very
different. Gone is the optimism in the face of the "steady
state," declining enrollments, and the loss of confidence by
public authorities in higher education. Fewer young people
are entering the universities, and there is a severe recession
in most academic fields at the level of graduate education.

The demographic crisis was accompanied by economic
recession. The sixties began with unprecedented economic
prosperity, with ample employment opportunities for college
graduates at all levels. The economic reality for college
graduates is by no means optimistic, particularly in the traditional liberal arts fields--the hotbeds of student activism in
previous years. There is a major unease among students
about future career prospects. Students have abandoned the
liberal arts for professional fields, where they assume that
career opportunities are better. The careerism of the sev-

enties is, in part, a reflection of the changing job market. Student interest in innovative courses in the social sciences and humanities has been replaced by demands for majors in accounting, business, pre-medicine and similar fields. Many of the liberties taken with the traditional grading system during the sixties have been eliminated as the "sorting" function of higher education has reemerged in a tight job market. The current trend toward general education in the undergraduate curriculum is in part a means of reestablishing control over collegiate life. The economic realities of the seventies have impinged not only on the curriculum but have also made students less willing to engage in political activism.

The role of the universities has also changed. No longer are the "best and the brightest" emerging from the Ivory Towers to save society. Public confidence in education in general and in higher education has declined to some extent, and the "taxpayers revolt" has directly affected allocations for higher education. Universities have lost much of their self-confidence as well, and without question they have moved from the center stage of society. Research funds have declined, and neither students nor faculty expect that higher education is the wave of the future.

Events in American politics generally have not been favorable to student activism. The movement of the sixties achieved some impressive victories and, in a sense, set the stage for other societal developments. Students were instrumental in bringing the war in Vietnam to public attention, in building an anti-war movement and in creating an atmosphere in which the public is much more skeptical of foreign policy initiatives by the executive branch of government. Students were especially crucial in the changing social mores of the period--a gradual public acceptance of the use of marijuana, the end of in loco parentis on campus, and the growth of rock music as a social force. But as was pointed out previously, the movement itself perceived failure in its action, and most students did not see the struggles of the sixties as victorious. Thus, in a sense, the legacy of the movement is one of success and failure, and it is therefore rather ambiguous.

There is no question but that the political realities of the seventies have been less favorable to student activism. The Nixon Administration proved especially unreceptive to both the substance and style of student demands, and the movement had no sympathetic ear in Washington. Indeed, administration leaders repeatedly attacked student activism and the academic community generally, and played a role in creating public opposition to the students. Without some sympathetic attention in the corridors of power and in the mass media, it is difficult for the student movement to become a national force. Even the Watergate affair provided few opportunities for student involvement. The opposition to Nixon was centered in the Congress and seemed to be functioning effectively. Thus, there was little need for intervention by the public, which remained on the sidelines as interested spectators. In general, when the "normal" political institutions are functioning effectively, there has been relatively little role for student activism. In Europe, for example, the massive student movements of the sixties developed mainly when many saw a need for an "extra-parliamentary opposition" to political systems which had no other viable opposition.

Student efforts at participation in the electoral process showed the combination of victory and defeat which disillusioned many participants. While students were credited with helping to force Lyndon Johnson to step down in 1968, they were unsuccessful in pressing for the presidential candidacy of Eugene McCarthy in that year, and strong support for George McGovern in 1972 did little to insulate him from massive defeat at the polls. Perhaps as a result of these unsuccessful efforts at participation in the electoral process, students did not take part in the 1976 presidential election. With the exception of electoral politics in a few local areas in which students are a significant part of the population, they have taken little interest in local politics. And even in places like Berkeley, California and Ann Arbor, Michigan, student political participation has in recent years been limited and mostly ineffectual.

The key mobilizer for student activism in the United States has been foreign policy, and there have been no foreign policy issues in the seventies which aroused much student interest. The Vietnam War was seen as a moral issue. In addition, it affected the student community quite directly through the draft. No current issue has this clear moral tone nor does any affect Americans directly. Small numbers of students have opposed America's policies in Africa, but even here Cuban involvement, international power politics, and very complicated socio-political questions blunt the moral force. And of course, American military forces were not involved. Other foreign policy issues seem too complicated; human rights is a laudable goal, but many see it as possibly damaging to detente, also a positive element. The oil crisis, balance of payments, and inflation are difficult to understand. No foreign policy issue touches a large number of students, and those questions which are important are seen as complicated. Significantly, the only issue to arouse even modest concern on campus is Southern Africa, which is the most clearly moral question in contemporary American foreign policy.

These are some of the reasons for the current lack of student activism on the American campus. Most liberals-- and the campus community generally--are not enthusiastic supporters of President Carter, but they do not actively oppose the Administration. There is substantial fear of a conservative current in the United States and concern about the impact of tax-revolts, recent Supreme Court decisions, and similar trends. Student movements have, in general, been most active and successful during periods of liberal power in Washington. The movement of the thirties contended with Roosevelt and the more recent period of activism began during the Kennedy Administration. Conservative administrations, and conservative trends in public opinion, have not in general been salutary for the growth of student activism. And the key moral issues which have aroused students in the recent past: race relations, Vietnam, and the like do not now exist. The direct problems of the student community: competition for grades in order to enter remunerative professional fields, unemployment of graduates in some of the liberal arts and widespread employment problems at the doctoral level, cutbacks in scholarship assistance, research funds, and in public assistance to higher education are all serious concerns for students, but have not led to student political unrest.

Despite the unlikelihood of the emergence of major student activism in the very near future, the sixties had an impact which is as yet incalculable on American students and on American culture and politics generally. The unprecedented amount of direct-action protest in a sense made such protest familiar to large numbers of Americans. Issues such as racism, imperialism, and some basic questioning of the direction of American society and policy were raised by the student movement and reported in the mass media. The environmental movement, for example, got its start on campus. The student movement and the largely campus-based underground press first raised questions about the life-style of Americans: rock music, the use of drugs, homosexuality, male-female roles, and other issues. These matters continued to be widely discussed.

There is, at present, no significant surge of student activism in the United States, although campus political life is not totally dead. And it seems unlikely that a major movement will emerge unless some external force, most likely a foreign policy issue, stimulates it. Yet, the impact of the most recent American student movement, that of the 1960s, continues to influence American life in indirect ways. If the campus has indeed moved from the revolution of the 1960s to the apathy of the 1970s, some of the intellectual residue of that revolution still has relevance. The causes for American student activism are complex, and the reasons for the decline of activism, as indicated in this analysis, are similarly complicated.

Acknowledgements

I am indebted to Arthur Levine, Arthur Liebman, Sheila Slaughter, Robby Cohen and Lionel S. Lewis for their comments.

Notes

1. This article provides further analysis and elaboration of research reported elsewhere (Altbach, 1974; Lipset and Altbach, 1969).
2. The press has in general ignored events on campus in recent years. For some recent analyses, see Fiske (1977); Nordheimer (1976) and Semas (1976). The Chronicle of Higher Education is probably the best source for following national campus trends.
3. While repression did reach the campus in the 1950s, it is probably the case that universities protected freedom of expression better than most other American institutions, although their record is far from spotless. See Caute (1978, pp. 403-86).
4. The sixties have been analyzed more closely than any other period. For a selection of references, see Philip G. Altbach and David Kelly (1973, pp. 211-260).
5. This data is from the American Council on Education's annual survey of American students, and included almost 200,000 in its sample. (Chronicle of Higher Education, January 23, 1978, pp. 12-13).

References

Altbach, P. G. (1973). "The NSA in the fifties: Flawed conscience of the silent generation," Youth and Society 5: 184-211.
Altbach, P. G. (1974). Student Politics in America. New York: McGraw-Hill.
Altbach, P. G., and Kelly, D. H. (1973). American Students: A Bibliography. Lexington, Mass.: Heath-Lexington.
Altbach, P. G. and Peterson, P. (1971). "Before Berkeley: Historical perspectives on the American student activism," Annals of the American Academy of Political and Social Science 395 (September): 1-14.
Caute, D. (1978). The Great Fear. New York: Simon and Schuster.
"The characteristics and attitudes of 1977-78 freshman" (1978). Chronicle of Higher Education (January 23), pp. 12-13.
Fass, P. (1977). The Damned and the Beautiful: American Youth in the Twenties. New York: Oxford University Press.
Fiske, E. (1977). "Campus mood: The focus is on grades," New York Times (December 23), p. 33.
Judah, J. S. (1974). Hare Krishna and the Counterculture. New York: Wiley-Interscience.
Lipset, S. M. (1976). Rebellion in the University. Chicago: University of Chicago Press.
Lipset, S. M. and Altbach, P. G. (eds.) (1969). Students in Revolt. Boston: Beacon.
Nordheimer, J. (1976). " '76 politics fail to disturb campus calm and cynicism," New York Times (October 17), p. 26.
Novak, S. (1977). The Rights of Youth: American Colleges and Student Revolt. Cambridge, Mass.: Harvard University Press.
O'Brien, J. (1971). "The origins of the new left," Annals of the American Academy of Political and Social Science 395 (May): 15-25.
Sale, K. (1973). SDS. New York: Random House.
Semas, P. (1976). "It's whatever you care to call it: Activism and apathy often exist side by side," Chronicle of Higher Education (April 26), p. 7.
Steinberg, M. S. (1977). Sabers and Brown Shirts: The German Students' Path to National Socialism, 1918-1935. Chicago: University of Chicago Press.
Wechsler, J. (1935). Revolt on the Campus. New York: Convici Friede.
Woodward, C. V. (1974). "What became of the 1960's?" New Republic (November 9), pp. 18-25.

STUDENT POLITICS IN AMERICA:
TRANSFORMATION NOT DECLINE*

by Arthur Levine and Keith R. Wilson

Introduction

As the 1960s drew to a close, student protest on American
campuses dominated center stage in the higher education community, and the American public believed it was the major
issue facing the nation (Gallup Political Index, 1970 p. 3).
There was considerable justification for that belief. The Assistant Secretary of the Treasury reported that between January, 1969 and April, 1970, over 400,000 bombings or threats
of bombings were recorded in the USA, and over 8,000 of
them were related to student protest and campus unrest.
During the week after President Nixon announced the invasion
of Cambodia in 1970, students began 200 new strikes each
day. After the Kent and Jackson State University killings in
May, there were 100 or more strikes each day and by May
10, 448 campuses were reported to be either on strike or
completely shut down (Chronicle of Higher Education, 1970).

All this seems to have vanished from American campuses in the 1970s. The aura of student revolution no longer
exists. The "Student Movement" of the 1960s is receding into
the pages of history and many activists have settled into their
own struggles with adult life: Sam Brown is now director of
ACTION in Washington, Gary Hart became a U.S. Senator,
Eldridge Cleaver found religion, Jerry Rubin announced he
was finally growing up at 37, and the last we heard, Mario
Savio was getting a Ph.D. in Los Angeles.

The 1960s was not the first time student protest erupted

*Reprinted by permission of the author and publisher from
Higher Education, 8:6 (November 1979), pp. 627-40. Copyright ©1979 by the Elsevier Scientific Publishing Co., Amsterdam.

on American campuses, and it probably will not be the last.
There have been three periods of relatively widespread student dissent in this century: in the decade or so before
World War I; during the social and economic upheavals of
the 1930s; and during the 1960s. Although the level of disruption and violence of student protest in the 1960s has no
counterpart in the history of American higher education, student activism in each period is identified and characterized
by what have become the familiar forms of student dissent:
demonstrations, strikes, boycotts, and the like. In each
episode, student activism seemed to end with surprising
abruptness. The early period came to a halt when President
Wilson and the Congress declared war in 1917; the widespread
student dissent of the 1930s similarly ended with the start of
World War II; the student movement of the 1960s collapsed
almost as quickly and unexpectedly as it had begun.

There is little evidence of 1960s-style student protest
on campus today. This is graphically demonstrated in a 1978
Carnegie Council on Policy Studies in Higher Education survey
of a representative sample of 870 colleges and universities.
Student personnel administrators (usually the dean of students
or vice-president for student affairs) were asked to compare
the occurrence of various forms of student protest on their
campus in 1977-1978 with 1969-1970. The results are dramatic and are given in Table I. They leave little doubt that
the forms of student protest so characteristic of the 1960s
have declined precipitously in the 1970s.

The survey also shows a decline in the more traditional student activist organizations. The number of campuses reporting chapters of Young Democrats has dropped
from 44% in 1969-1970 to 30% in 1977-1978. College Repub-
licans shows a similar decline: from representation on 43%
of the campuses in 1969-1970, they have fallen off to 28% today. Leftist political groups such as the Progressive Labor
Party, Young Peoples Socialist League, and the Communist
Party have gone from 9% in 1969-1970 to 8% in 1977-1978.
Rightist groups such as Young Americans for Freedom and
the John Birch Society have declined to an even greater extent from 10% in 1969-1970 to only 4% in 1977-1978. S. D. S.
(Students for a Democratic Society) is gone altogether. This
is shown in Table II.

The decline in 1960s-style activism is also reflected
in the scant attention such activity receives in the media, and
the almost total lack of serious research on student activism
in recent years.

TABLE I

Percentage of Institutions Experiencing Various Types of Student Activism, 1969-1970 and 1977-1978.

	Occurred in 1977-1978	Occurred in 1969-1970
Intentional destruction of property as a protest	1. 0%	11. 6%
Student takeover of building	0. 8	15. 4
Student threats of violence	2. 9	20. 3
Student strike	1. 0	13. 9
Student demonstrations (involving a number of undergraduates)	12. 8	39. 2
Organized student refusal to pay tuition	0. 2	0. 4
Other protest activities	27. 5	3. 5

Source: Carnegie Surveys, 1978.

TABLE II

Percentage of Institutions with Various Student Organizations in 1969-1970 and 1977-1978.

	Percent in 1977-1978	Percent in 1969-1970
Young Democrats	30%	44%
College Republicans	28	43
Leftist political groups	8	9
Rightist political groups	4	10
Students for a Democratic Society	0	16

Source: Carnegie Surveys, 1978.

Yet we are convinced that the turmoil of the 1960s has not simply vanished and been replaced by a political vacuum on campus, nor have today's students simply displaced the activism of their 1960s counterparts with political calm and apathy. For one thing, sporadic outbursts of student protest concerning a variety of issues continue to occur on campus. Moreover, some opinion polls have indicated that students today have as much interest in and commitment to political issues as their counterparts did in the 1960s. More important, however, is the fact that the 1970s have witnessed the evolution of a new mood in the nation and on its campuses.

A New Mood in America

In 1961 John Kennedy ushered in a new era when he summoned his fellow Americans to "ask not what your country can do for you, but what you can do for your country." Seventeen years later, Californian Howard Jarvis inaugurated another new era when he led a successful tax revolt premised on the notion that citizens were being asked to do too much for their country. Each was recognized as a "man on horseback" for his time.

The "man on horseback" is part leader and part follower. He or she is as much, if not more, a product of the public mood as the creator of that mood. Howard Jarvis began preaching his message of individual rights contemporaneously with John Kennedy's exhortation of individual responsibility to the community. For the Jarvis philosophy to eclipse the then popular Kennedy position has required a fundamental shift in the American world view--a basic change in our conception of the American community and our place in it.

The historical ideal of community is well depicted by Rosabeth Moss Kanter (1972, p. 1). She calls it "utopia."

> Utopia is the imaginary society in which human-kind's deepest yearnings, noblest dreams, and highest aspirations come to fulfillment, where all physical, social, and spiritual forces work together, in harmony, to permit the attainment of everything people find necessary and desirable. In the imagined utopia, people work and live together closely and cooperatively, in a social order that is self-created and self-chosen rather than externally imposed, yet one that also operates according to a higher order of natural and spiritual laws. Utopia is held together by commitment rather than coercion, for in utopia what people what to do is the same as what they have to do; the interests of the individuals are congruent with the interests of the group; and personal growth and freedom entail responsibility for others. Underlying the vision of

utopia is the assumption that harmony, cooperation,
and mutuality of interests are natural to human existence, rather than conflict, competition, and exploitation, which arise only in imperfect societies.
By providing material and psychological safety and
security, the utopian social order eliminates the
need for divisive competition, or self-serving actions which elevate some people to the disadvantage
of others; it ensures instead that flowering of mu-
tual responsibility and trust, to the advantage of all.

No known community or society has achieved this state,
but there are times when societies move in this direction--
periods of community ascendancy--and times when they move
in the opposite direction--periods of individual ascendancy.
The relationship between the individual and the community is
a continually changing one. At times when society is perceived to be moving toward the community ideal, individual
ties with the community are strengthened and community is
the dominant theme. At times when the society appears to
be moving in the opposite direction, individual ties with the
community are attenuated and the individual is dominant.

TABLE III

Changing American Attitudes from the Mid-1960s to 1977

	1964	1966	1977
What you think doesn't count much any more[a]		37%	61%
People running the country don't really care what happens to you[a]		26	60
Public leaders don't know what they are doing[b]	28%		52
Rich get richer and poor get poorer[a]		45	77
The government wastes lots of tax money[b]	48		76

[a]Based on surveys by Louis Harris and Associates.
[b]Based on surveys by Center for Political Studies of the Institute for Social Research, University of Michigan.
Source: Public Opinion, May/June 1978, p. 23; and Public
Opinion, March/April 1978, p. 23.

The years of the Kennedy administration are thought

of today as a period of community ascendancy and mythologized as "a brief and shining moment in Camelot. " The spirit of "Camelot" persisted through the early Johnson years, when the sense of voluntarism, mutuality of individual and community interest, and the individual's ability to profit from cooperation with the community began a precipitous slide, which has continued to the present. Since then, America has been in a state of individual ascendancy or declining community.

Recent surveys show that a majority of Americans now believe that what they think does not count for much; that the people running the country do not really care what happens to them; that public leaders do not know what they are doing; that the rich get richer and the poor get poorer; and that the government wastes a lot of money. The percentage of people reporting such attitudes shot up dramatically in the last decade and a half as shown in Table III.

Confidence in the leaders of major social institutions including medicine, higher education, organized religion, the U.S. Supreme Court, the military, major companies, the executive branch of government, the press, Congress, organized labor, and advertising agencies has declined from an average of 45% in 1966 to an average of 27% in 1977. This is shown in Table IV.

Moreover, a majority of the Americans surveyed in 1977 believed that the White House, state governments, the military, organized labor, the executive branch of the federal government, the U.S. Supreme Court, and Congress were out of touch with the people they are supposed to lead or help. This is shown in Table V.

The prognosis for the future is also gloomy. In March, 1978, 51% of the Americans surveyed believed it was likely the United States would be at war within the next three years. This is a 16 percentage point increase in seven months (Public Opinion, May/June 1978, p. 22). Among teenagers, 13 to 18 years of age, 58% of those surveyed believed in 1977 that the world will be a worse place to live in ten years hence (Public Opinion, May/June 1978, p. 29). More than 90% of the Americans polled believed if there is a tax cut it will benefit people unlike themselves (Public Opinion, May/June 1978, p. 25). Unhappiness increased and happiness decreased between 1973 and 1977. In 1973, 52% of the Americans surveyed reported themselves very happy and 3% described themselves as unhappy. By 1977, the percentage of very happy

TABLE IV

Proportion of Americans with a Great Deal of Confidence in
Leaders of Social Institutions--1966-1977

	1966	1977
Medicine	73%	55%
Higher education	61	41
Organized religion	41	34
U. S. Supreme Court	50	31
The military	62	31
Major companies	55	23
Executive branch of government	41	23
The press	29	19
Congress	42	15
Organized labor	22	15
Advertising agencies	21	11
Average	45	27

Source: "Confidence in Institutions, " The Harris Survey, Jan.
5, 1978.

TABLE V

Perceived Responsiveness of Leaders of Social Institutions,
1977

	Really know what people want	Mostly out of touch with people	Not sure
The White House	43%	44%	13%
State government	43	45	12
The military	40	43	17
Organized labor	40	47	13
The executive branch of the federal government	38	46	16
U. S. Supreme Court	38	47	15
Congress	31	58	11

Source: "Confidence in Institutions, " The Harris Survey, Jan.
5, 1978.

dropped ten points and the unhappy increased seven percentage points (Public Opinion, May/June 1978, p. 22). There has also been a nearly four-fold increase in the proportion of people who feel left out of the things around them. This attitude was reported by 9% of the Americans surveyed in 1966 versus 35% in 1977 (Public Opinion, May/June 1978, p. 23).

A refuge to which many Americans are turning to escape this horrible world is "me." "Meism" has been called "the third great awakening" by Tom Wolfe (1977), "the new narcissism" by Peter Marin (1975), and "psychic self help" by Christopher Lasch (1976). In 1979, Lasch went so far as to describe American society as the Culture of Narcissism. We see it today at bookstands where the shelves are lined with popular volumes such as Looking Out for Number One, Winning Through Intimidation, Getting Your Share, Pulling Your Own Strings, How You can Profit from a Monetary Crisis, and Your Check Is In the Mail--How to Stay Legally and Profitably in Debt. We view it today on television where NBC broadcasts a documentary about California's Marin County entitled "I Want It All Now." We witness it today in a burgeoning number of recently popular activities such as TM, EST, natural foods, Eastern religions, massage, rolfing, primal screaming, sex therapy, jogging, Esalen, and martial arts. And we hear it in our daily conversations.

This emphasis on "me" is what differentiates periods of individual ascendancy from periods of community ascendancy. The former are hedonistic, emphasizing the primacy of duty to one's self and the latter are more ascetic, stressing the primacy of duty to others. Individual ascendancy is concerned principally with rights and community ascendancy with responsibilities. There is a comparable dichotomy between taking and giving. The orientation of individual ascendancy is on the present while community ascendancy is targeted at the future.

"Meism" Goes to College

Though many would swear otherwise, the college student is a product of our larger society. In fact, as students have ballooned in number and grown more diverse in background, they have become increasingly representative of the society and reflective of its values.

When the Carnegie Council asked college and university student personnel administrators to choose from a list of fifty-two adjectives that described the majority of students on their individual campuses, only five, all characteristic of a period of individual ascendancy or "meism," were chosen by more than half--career oriented (84%), concerned with self (73%), concerned with material success (63%), well groomed (57%), and practical (55%). Students certainly appear to have brought more with them from home than their bags.

When asked to compare college students today with their counterparts of 1969-1970, the student personnel administrations reported shifts in the direction of increasing "meism." 1978 undergraduates were said to be more career oriented (at 71% of the campuses), more well groomed (at 57% of the campuses), more sexually liberal (at 55% of the campuses), more concerned with material success (at 54% of the campuses), more concerned with self (at 44% of the campuses), and more practical (at 40% of the campuses). They were also described as less radical (at 58% of the campuses) and less hostile (at 40% of the campuses). With this in mind, let us reconsider the issue of activism.

Student Activism in Age of "Meism"

Activism has at times served as a channel for mischievous or rebellious student impulses, but in this century it has more often been used as a vehicle for attaining desired student ends on campus or in the larger society. Students have changed dramatically since the late 1960s. The ends associated with "meism" or individual ascendancy are different from the issues associated with the protests of the late 1960s. And so too are the forms of activism that students are using to attain them. In recent years American colleges and universities have witnessed new forms of activism and the expansion of several types which were not previously considered part of the dominant motif of student protest.

New Tactics

Earlier in this paper (Table I), the use of familiar protest activities in 1969-1970 and 1977-1978 were compared. In almost every instance, 1969-1970 was the more active year, generally by a great deal. There was one exception, which

has not yet been discussed, and that is "other." Twenty-
eight percent of the institutions responding to the Carnegie
Council survey reported "other" types of protest activity in
1977-1978 versus 4% in 1969-1970. Included in this category
was much more frequent use of lobbying and litigation, activities which are geared to the current era--less dangerous,
more practical, more individual, and more accommodating to
causes lacking in popular support. Over one-third of the institutions (35%) responding to the survey reported increases
in the number of lawsuits threatened or initiated by students.
At the most visible institutions in the country--the Yales,
Harvards, Berkeleys, and Michigans--an increase was registered on 74% of the campuses. This is shown in Table VI.

TABLE VI

Percentages of Institutions Reporting Change in the Number of
Lawsuits Threatened or Initiated by Students by Carnegie Council Institutional Typology

	Type of change		
	Increased	Remained the same	Decreased
Research Universities I	74	19	6
Research Universities II	63	23	14
Doctorate-Granting University sities I	38	44	18
Doctorate-Granting University sities II	55	28	18
Comprehensive Universities and Colleges I	43	38	20
Comprehensive Universities and Colleges II	38	46	17
Liberal Arts Colleges I	34	63	4
Liberal Arts Colleges II	36	50	15
Two-Year Colleges	24	64	13
Total	35	51	14

Source: Carnegie Surveys, 1978.

New Political Groups

The 1970s have witnessed an enormous expansion in student
self-interest affinity groups. They are multiple issue asso-

ciations concerned with the rights of individuals and improving
the lot of a single group of people--women, minorities, gays,
Latins, native Americans, Bolivians, Iranians, or New York-
ers. The most familiar groups are the Black Student Union
and the Campus Woman's Caucus. In the past they were
thought of as extracurricular social groups. Today they epit-
omize the spirit of "meism, " serving as lobbies for their
constituencies on and off campus. They are growing like
wildfire, and, as with self-interest groups in national politics,
they are becoming an increasingly powerful force to reckon
with. Their growth is shown in Table VII. The proliferation
of such groups is indicative of a shift in student concerns
from one or two common issues, such as Vietnam and civil
rights, to multiple individual issues. These changes, along
with the local orientation and general use of nonviolent grievance procedures by self-interest groups, have caused the
news media to overlook them in their investigations of student
activism.

TABLE VII

Percentage of Institutions Having Selected Self-interest Groups
in 1977-1978 and 1969-1970.

	1969-1970	1977-1978
Black student groups	46	58
Women's groups	27	48
Latin or Chicano groups	13	22
Native American groups	6	13
Gay Groups	3	11

PIRGs and Lobbies

The new tactics of student activism and the self-interest emphasis have found a home in two organizations which made
their appearance or substantially enlarged their presence in
the mid 1970s--Public Interest Research Groups (PIRGs) and
student lobbies. PIRGs, an idea proposed by Ralph Nader in
1970, were by 1978 found at 11% of American colleges and
universities in 26 states (Carnegie Surveys, 1978). The theory of the PIRGs, which have more than 700, 000 undergraduates paying dues nationwide, is based on the notion that colleges and universities offer students theories of social change,

but provide no means for implementing them. PIRGs provide the structure and financial support through which students can step out of the classroom and work constructively at reform activities, while training themselves in areas of research, government, or simply good citizenship. Many of the skills are also potentially valuable for a job after college. The PIRG movement believes that as part of society, students are affected by the same social problems as everyone else, so why shouldn't they work to improve the conditions under which they live. This is a theme which should be very attractive to current students.

Student lobbies, which have more than doubled in number since 1969-1970, are found on 22% of the nation's campuses in 39 states and since 1971, a National Student Lobby has been active in Washington, D. C. (Carnegie Surveys, 1978). Student lobbies behave just like any other lobbying group--they fight for the legislation favorable to their constituents.

The activities of PIRGs and student lobbies can best be understood by examining their work in a single state, which is the level at which they operate. New York has a well-developed PIRG, called NYPIRG, and a very active student lobby consisting of several groups--the Student Association of the State University of New York (SASU), University Student Senate of the City University of New York, Community College Student Association, and the Independent Student Coalition. SASU is probably the best known of the lot.

Twenty of the 34 units of the State University of New York (SUNY) belong to SASU. Each school pays dues to SASU of 85 cents per full-time equivalent student (under certain circumstances the rates are lower). SASU is run by an executive board whose members are elected by the students at their home campuses. For their money and votes students get services such as block concert bookings, reduced-rate travel, and student shopping discounts; a voter registration drive in which 50,000 students were registered; litigation including a lawsuit over New York's definition of financial emancipation; testimony on pending legislation; and a legislative program. In 1976, for example, legislation included a coalition effort that successfully fought a tuition increase and a 10% reduction in state tuition grants and the passage of SASU-drafted bills mandating that all public bodies have open meetings, requiring student representation on the Higher Education Services Corporation which handles student loans and grants, lowering the drinking age from 21 to 18 under certain circumstances, and requiring SUNY trustees to hold four regional meetings each year. It is important to note, however, that most SASU-initiated bills were killed in committee.

SASU is able to accomplish much of what it does simply by providing information. According to SASU, New York does not have a professional legislature. As a consequence, SASU is often more knowledgeable about an issue than the legislators. In one instance, a piece of legislation would have resulted in an unintended cut in student aid. Simply by informing legislators of this, the bill was appropriately changed.

SASU is well thought of by New York state legislators for doing its homework and being professional. However, part of the clout of the organization is that it represents a sizeable block of voters. It has generated 5,000 signatures on petitions in a single day and promoted letter writing campaigns. More importantly it issues press releases which are printed, frequently unchanged, in campus and local papers around the state. SASU makes a point of publicizing the positions of political candidates on issues relevant to students. Although 18- to 24-year-olds vote in lower proportion than the general population, college students as a whole vote in equal proportion. And as noted earlier, SASU makes a point of registering them to vote. When all else has failed, SASU alone or in coalition with other groups has sponsored peaceful demonstrations with as many as 10,000 students in Albany and Washington, D.C.

The New York Public Interest Research Group is seven years old. It is well financed with an annual budget of over $400,000 derived largely from average dues of four dollars per student on member campuses. NYPIRG has more than 100,000 dues-paying members. (At its peak, SDS had only 6,000 dues-paying members and 30,000 locally affiliated members nationwide (Lipset, 1971, p. 75).) An additional portion of NYPIRG's budget comes from foundation, church, corporate, and federal government monies. Thirteen campuses throughout New York state are currently associated with the organization. There is periodic attrition but the number of campuses participating appears to be growing. Each campus has its own student-elected and -run PIRG board. There is, in addition, a statewide staff, hired by the local board, to research and investigate a variety of social and political issues of interest to students. In 1976-1977 this resulted in 27 publications including legislative profiles of all state senators and assemblymen; reports on nu-

clear energy, young people and jury selection, pollution of the
Hudson River, abortion, marijuana, and small claims court;
consumer guides on telephone service, sales tax, nuclear energy, property taxes, and medical malpractice; and much
more. In 1977-1978, NYPIRG added to its agenda research
and legislation on student financial aid and testing.

The consequences of the reports have been of three
types--drafting and lobbying for legislation, litigation, and
public education via media reports and community organizing.
The following are a small sample of NYPIRG's accomplishments.

--The New York legislature passed a marijuana reform act,
   which involved NYPIRG lobbying for decriminalization with
   the largest such campaign in New York State history.
--NYPIRG sued a New York legislator for illegal patronage
   payments to himself.
--NYPIRG uncovered widespread noncompliance with the Freedom of Information Law by state and local officials.
--NYPIRG drafted and lobbied into law, legislation affecting
   hearing aid sales, prescription drugs, unit pricing, and a
   host of other issues.
--NYPIRG established offices around the state to help people
   carry out small claims court judgments.
--NYPIRG sponsored and lobbied for several energy bills
   which the New York state legislature passed in 1977.
--NYPIRG documented a banking practice known as "redlin-
   ing" in Brooklyn and brought the issue to the media and
   local community.

Last year hundreds of students participated in NYPIRG
research projects. More than 300 received academic credit.
NYPIRG issues attract both liberal and conservative students.
For instance, the chief lobbyist for marijuana decriminalization was a conservative and member of Young Americans for
Freedom. Because NYPIRG is on the conservative and liberal side of different issues, because it has no axe to grind,
because it works in the open rather than behind closed doors,
and because it produces quality reports, Director Donald Ross
believes it is taken seriously. In fact, a study by the Community Service Society showed NYPIRG to be one of the most
active lobbies in Albany.

PIRGs and student lobbies differ from the familiar
activist organizations of the late 1960s in several respects.
First, they are tactically more eclectic, using a variety of

methods including lobbying, litigation, media, community organizing, and demonstrations. Second they are issue oriented
rather than ideological. The lack of a party line permits
them to build a wider base of support. Individuals can and
are marshaled solely for those issues they care about or are
affected by. Third, they are more pragmatic and probably
more effective. A former president of the City University
of New York Student Association pointed out that in the 1960s
students wanted "pie in the sky" and protested, to get even,
when they did not get what they wanted. Today students are
playing to win and will take whatever they can and push for
more.

Conclusion

PIRGs, lobbies, litigation, and self-interest groups are part
of the campus scene in the 1970s and represent a basic change
in the style, direction, and form of student activism since
the 1960s. They indicate that the present period is not as
politically barren and apathetic as it is widely thought to be.
They also show that current forms of student activism are
consistent with changes in the orientation and concerns of today's students.

Clearly, student activism is a complex, multiple-
determined phenomenon that cannot be reduced to a single
explanatory principle. Yet in view of the remarkable number
of studies of student activism, one could justifiably hope that
we would have arrived at a more comprehensive understanding of the nature of the phenomenon over time. As one writer has correctly observed, "... we have virtually no explanation for the changes in prevailing political trends in student
activism" (Pinner, 1971, p. 129). In hopes of advancing the
problem, this paper had tried to show that the political activity of today's student reflects a new mood on the campus
and in the nation. Thus, in addition to the various factors
traditionally offered as explanations of student activism (e. g.
the centrality of major events or conditions in the larger society, institutional characteristics, generational discountinu-
ity, etc.), this analysis suggests that as student character
and mood change, so do the forms of activism that students
employ.

It should also be pointed out that the research presented here calls for a different approach to the study of
student activism. As David Reisman has aptly observed,

most research on student activism has been "... firehouse research--the alarm bell rings, the researcher slides down the greased pole, rushes to the fire, and begins collecting data" (Keniston, 1973, p. xv). In part, this explains why the present period has received almost no attention from researchers in the past several years. Guided by the apparent calm on campuses today and the apparent political apathy of today's students, researchers previously concerned with student activism have turned their attention elsewhere. Our research indicates, however, that students today are not appreciably more apathetic than the students of the 1960s. To the contrary, there are important changes taking place in student political activity and the forms of activism they employ. This suggests first of all that in order to arrive at a more accurate and comprehensive understanding of the phenomenon of American student activism, the periods of apparent calm that seem to follow peak episodes of activism are important and deserve more serious attention than they have received in the past. Second, most research on the subject has focused almost exclusively on the "traditional" forms of student activism. The present research indicates that student activism is manifesting itself in a variety of forms, some of which have been developed primarily in the years following a high in the level and intensity of student protest activity. This suggests the possibility that previous periods classified as politically inactive may also have involved important student activism, but have gone unnoticed because researchers have tended to look only for the familiar, tried and true forms of protest activity.

References

Chronicle of Higher Education (1970). "The Scranton Report," Oct. 5:4.
Gallup Political Index (1970). "Student unrest seen as nation's top problem," 61 (July).
Kanter, R. M. (1972). Commitment and Community: Communes and Utopias in Sociological Perspective. Cambridge, Mass.: Harvard University Press.
Keniston, K. (1973). Radicals and Militants: An Annotated Bibliography of Empirical Research on Student Unrest. Washington, D. C.: Heath and Company.
Lasch, C. (1976). "The narcissist society," New York Review of Books: (Sept. 30): 5-13.
Lasch, C. (1979). Culture of Narcissism. New York: Norton Books.
Lipset, S. M. (1971). Rebellion in the University. Chicago: University of Chicago Press.

Marin, P. (1975). "The new narcissism," Harpers (October): 45-56.

Pinner, Frank A. (1971). "Students--a marginal elite in politics," The Annals of the American Academy of Political and Social Science (May).

Public Opinion (1978). 1 (1) March/April.

Public Opinion (1978). 1 (2) May/June.

Wolfe, T. (1977). "The Me Decade and the Third Great Awakening." Mauve Gloves and Madman, Clutter and Vine. New York: Bantam.

THE "OLD" NEW LEFT: A REASSESSMENT BY
FORMER PARTICIPANTS IN CANADA, THE
UNITED STATES AND WEST GERMANY

by Cyril Levitt*

The New Left was a phenomenon which belonged to the decade
of the sixties; it was born with it just as it died with it. It
was a movement of youth led by students from the universities
and colleges. It was a global phenomenon, even though international attention was drawn to the movements in the powerful industrial countries of the West and Far East. In spite
of its international ambience, however, the New Left was a
polycentric social movement, the various national leaderships
having had only sporadic and furtive contact with one another.
The impact of this new activism on the national political
scenes varied greatly from case to case just as the responses
of the various governments to the revolt of their youth varied.
But the New Left everywhere challenged the three major politically organized forces on the left: liberalism, social democracy, and Moscow-oriented communism. Paradoxically, the
New Left gained strength only when it espoused and acted on
the vision and values of liberalism, social democracy, and
abstractly, of communism. The rejection of the striving after the ideals of this tradition in favor of an attempt to establish an immediate, historically immanent revolutionary
movement, occurred along with the fragmentation and dissolution of the New Left.

The New Left died organizationally at the end of the
decade of the sixties, yet the general political and social
commitment of the New Left continued on in different forms.
The feminism, environmentalism, committed journalism, radicalism in the disciplines, etc., of the seventies owe their

*An earlier version of this paper appeared in Higher Educa-
tion, 8: 6 (November 1979), pp. 641-55. Copyright ©1979 by
the Elsevier Scientific Publishing Co., Amsterdam.

existence in part, but in no small measure, to the generation of the New Left. Yet the media have generally not emphasized the continuity between the movements of the seventies and the New Left of the sixties; certainly they have not investigated the specific character of that continuity. This is not to say that the New Left has not been fondly remembered.

Indeed, in the eulogies composed by the mass media in recent years the activities and accomplishments of the New Left of the sixties have been portrayed in a much more favorable light than those of the Old Left were, at any time. Former activists in the Federal Republic of Germany have referred to the post factum coverage of their movement by the media as a Nostalgiewelle--a wave of nostalgia--hearkening back to the time when the good fight was fought. In the United States and Canada the New Left is pictured in journals and newspapers, on film and television, on a continuum which runs from youthful indulgence to clairvoyant heroism, at least with respect to Vietnam, Watergate, and illegal police activities. The media have canonized the "good side" of the New Left in the public memory. But in spite of the media "hype," it does seem fitting to consider the New Left phenomenon from the vantage point of "ten years after" [1].

Recent studies (Fendrich, 1974, 1976, 1977; Fendrich and Tarleau, 1973; Krauss, 1974) of former New Left activists have shown that they have moved into very specific employment areas in society (teaching, social work, media, government and state bureaucracies, trade union organizing) and that they have generally maintained a basic social and political commitment which is continuous with their former New Leftism. In 1977 and 1978 the author conducted 64 focused interviews with former activists who were involved with the most prominent New Left groups in the sixties in Canada, the Federal Republic of Germany (FRG) and the United States [2]. Most of the individuals interviewed had served in some leadership capacity in New Left politics from 1965-1970 (although many had "dropped-out" organizationally after 1967-1968), and all but two (one Canadian and one American) did not join any of the vanguard parties which grew with the decline of the mass New Left organizations.

In all countries most of the former activists who were interviewed were found to be employed in areas which had been specified in earlier research (Fendrich, 1974, 1976, 1977). Most of them have maintained political and social views which are consonant with sixties activism, and many are currently involved in some form of low-key political work. The similarities of the three national groups are as striking in the late seventies as they had been throughout the decade of the sixties. The overwhelming majority of those interviewed expressed a commitment to socialism, even though there was little general agreement within each of or across the three countries about what it is, or how it is to be achieved. The interview questions were designed to elicit from the former New Leftists their present understanding and evaluation of their political activities in the sixties. The following analysis can thus be taken as self-analysis of the movement, or of a part of the movement. This line of questioning has been opened up partly in response to the one-sided treatment of sixties activism by the mass media, and partly as a contribution to the process of self-clarification of the student generation of the sixties.

The New Left as a Movement of Moral Criticism and Renewal

Most former activists explained the source of their radicalism in moralistic terms, as a response to the gap between the ideals of their society and the actual conditions which blatantly stood in contradiction to them. The themes arising out of the interview material will be developed in light of the changing social context of student activism and of the former activists.

The Germans expressed a deep concern with the disjunction between the ideal and real not within their own, but within American society. The generation of the New Left in Germany did not experience the war and the collapse of the Reich, but its members were intensely aware of the denazification and re-education programs sponsored by the American occupying forces in the late forties. The contradiction between the ideology of American democracy and the reality of American domestic and foreign policy was alluded to by many of the former student radicals in Germany as the source of their moral outrage [3]:

> After 1945 ... and this is what the politics of re-education in part naturally strove to accomplish--the image of American democracy offered, apparently offered, for the majority of bourgeois youth in Germany, an alternative to the history of its own class ... it is really surprising how strongly the ideals of the American revolution became the

ideals of bougeois youth after 1945. And the quarrel with the American war in Vietnam was also
centrally a quarrel with ideas of the American revolution and the reality of parliamentary, democratic
life like in the United States ... perhaps more intensely
than in any of the other countries, perhaps even
more intensely than in America itself.

This view is echoed by a former leader of the German SDS
in the following statement:

Totalitarianism means: concentration camps, killing people, aggression against nations, gassing Jews.
Democracy means: the guarantee against all this
happening. And Vietnam showed us that things
weren't that simple. A democratically constituted
society such as the American, had within itself ve-
hement racial conflicts and it threw itself into an
imperialist colonial war in S. E. Asia which equalled
the deeds of the German Reich under Hitler.

The Americans who were interviewed expressed a similar moral view of the opposition between the rhetoric of liberal democracy and social reality. The overriding issue in
this connection was discrimination against Black Americans,
but the bomb, the existence of poverty, and American foreign
policy (especially in relation to Cuba) were also frequently
mentioned. A former member of the American SDS describes
this shared moral disaffection when he says:

There was a grouping of children, or at least for
me and my friends, we come of age thinking ...
with the notion that America was the apex of society and that it was democratic, it was just, it was
a good society and the best that could be expected.
And at that time the beginnings of the Vietnam War
and the civil rights movement was a contradiction
with the mythology with which we had grown up,
and I think a lot of us entered the movement with
the notion of testing the ideas of democracy against
the reality that we found, pushing against the ideological fabric and seeing if America would deliver
the promises.

Another ex-SDS'er added to this same thought the notion that
at the time of her political engagement she felt she had the
power to really change things:

> I have a sense that from talking with other SDS peo-
> ple that my personal experience is shared a lot.
> For me it was growing up with middle-class parents,
> and with a whole bunch of liberal ideals about how
> the world ought to be, and that included people be-
> ing equal and not &!;%ing over people. And then
> I got out in the real world and after a number of
> years of just dealing with that clash, I started like,
> 'O.K., you ought to do something about it,' and I
> was also brought up with a real sense of my own
> power.

Interviews with other Americans also revealed not only a sense
of moral outrage at the discrepancy between ideals and reality
(indeed the student activists shared this quality with older
liberals and leftists), but a sense of power, a feeling that
one could and must personally effect changes in society on
the basis of society's own ideals.

The Canadians who were interviewed expressed views
similar to their German and American counterparts. The
civil rights movement in the United States had captured the
imagination of these Canadian students, although the CUCND
until 1963 was primarily concerned with questions of nuclear
war and disarmament. (The Student Union for Peace Action,
which rose out of the ashes of the CUCND after the so-called
'nuclear election' in Canada, became involved with community
organizing not unlike the SDS's (ERAP Economic Research
and Action Project).)

The role which American images played for Canadian
student radicals can be seen in this expression of emotion
concerning John F. Kennedy made by a former activist in
Ottawa:

> I just think if one is to understand the early part
> of that period, the early sixties ... you have to
> have some notion ... about the values that the so-
> ciety espoused. The most graphic demonstration
> of that I remember is a friend of mine who won-
> dered why, at one point in time he thought John
> Kennedy was a great man, and several years later,
> he wanted to jump on his grave in anger and indig-
> nation, about what the guy had actually done.

Other Canadian respondents named Kennedy, civil rights, and
American foreign policy (Cuba was most frequently mentioned)

as the central factors which gave rise to radicalism in the
early sixties; the war in Vietnam was cited by most as crucial in maintaining and extending the radical critique during
the latter half of the decade. Unlike the Germans and the
Americans, however, the Canadians very rarely made reference to domestic politics during the interviews, with the exception of the politics of the university. Canadians were more
concerned about the inequality of opportunity in higher education than either the Germans or Americans (although the Germans were also very concerned about this matter) and they
viewed this as a failure of the egalitarian ideal in the educational policy of the state. One former national radical leader
expresses the ideas of the others when he says:

> There was a rampant liberalism and I think most
> students--and the New Left was a student move-
> ment--most students felt that liberalism worked,
> that in particular ... [the] part of it having to do
> with the quality of educational opportunity ... worked
> for them. ... Though they were middle class, they
> got reinforced by success, felt that it was a fine
> system. But all of a sudden we came to learn that
> those of us in universities were a privileged few
> by class background; we didn't always call it class,
> but that's what it was.

Beyond the opposition of rhetoric and reality there
were two further components of the moral protest and they
were egoistic in character. First, the former activists felt
that promises had been made to them which had not been
kept. And when fundamental changes which would have realized the promises were not forthcoming (i. e., after the students "spoke truth to power"), the nature of the promises
themselves was called into question. Second, the members
of the New Left felt that they were called upon to act and
that they had the power to institute those changes which they
felt were necessary (either on the basis of the original promises, or on the basis of new abstractions culled from a foreign tradition).

One Canadian activist refers to the false promises in
this way:

> You know, the society promises this, that, and the
> other thing; by the time you're at university you're
> able to start to appreciate that, in fact, those
> promises were bankrupt and you get angry.

We must consider the nature of those unfulfilled promises which apparently had such a radicalizing effect upon the New Left generation. The promise which was made to the younger generation of the fifties was that of the realization of the promise of the great revolutions of the eighteenth century. But just as the liberal idealists confounded liberty as such with the liberty of business and trade, equality as such with the equality of exchange-value, freedom as form and content with purely formal freedom (Marx and Engels, 1972), so the New Left confounded these abstract universals with their concrete, historically specific contents, and viewed the latter as veritable incarnations of the former. The bourgeois, of course, locked in struggle with the remains of a feudal universe, had a practical interest in presenting the rights of the bourgeois individual as the rights of man as such. But where is the corresponding material interest of the generation of New Leftists? The answer to this important question is provided by the analysis of the egoistic roots of the movement which the former New Left activists themselves advanced during the course of the interviews.

The Egoistic Roots of the New Left

> Here we may reign secure, and in my choice.
> To reign is worth ambition, though in Hell:
> Better to reign in Hell, than serve in Heav'n.
> --John Milton

The New Left generation, the generation of the 'baby boom,' was nutured in the lap of relative luxury and its members did not have to take the ideals of society with a grain of salt as did the depression and war generations. They accepted the values of justice and equality as easily and as obviously as they expected and accepted the material comforts of life. The older generation was proud of its offspring, just as proud as it was of the GNP [4]. A student leader of the sixties in the province of Ontario emphasizes the high esteem in which the younger generation was held by society when he says: "We were valued, and the valedictorian classes were still the leaders of tomorrow... and that we were prized by parents, prized by society that we made it to university."

This "prized" generation which was literally promised "the world" began to move into the universities; but they quickly discovered that these institutions were losing their exclusivity, their "king-making" powers. A former national

radical leader now resident in Toronto evaluates the impact
of the changing character of the university on his cohort in
this lengthy but important statement:

> ... we went in there and got told we were going to
> be the captains of industry ... and you looked around
> the University of Waterloo, and you said, 'you know,
> there ain't gonna be no captains of industry come
> out of this place, they go to Harvard Business
> School, they don't come out of the University of
> Waterloo' ... we were going to be *** important,
> you know, we were going to be the leaders of the
> society, and we got to Waterloo and suddenly this
> didn't look like where the leaders got trained. It
> was more like where the privates got trained, this
> looked like boot camp; it didn't look like ... you
> know, it felt like boot camp cause it was boot camp,
> okay. And I mean, in retrospect this struck me as
> very important that we really thought we were shit
> hot, I mean we counted, okay, and what we thought
> and what we felt and what we did, was really im-
> portant to the future of the society ... if it was the
> shits, we were going to make something of it, okay.
> In retrospect, it really does seem somewhat naive
> and socially arrogant, and a kind of elitism that
> was built into it, but we really mattered and what
> we thought really mattered, and certainly when I
> look around at the students now in university, they
> don't think they matter, they don't think what they
> think matters, they don't think what they do mat-
> ters; they'll be happy to survive.

The sentiment expressed in this passage, that the student generation of the sixties was promised an education at
the university which would lead to the positions of social
dominance and that this promise was not fulfilled, was repeatedly made by those who were interviewed in all three
countries. Sociologically, this sentiment was the response
of the students to recent changes in higher education and in
the character of middle class social mobility, changes which
were in part occasioned by the post-war generation of youth
itself. During the fifties, the formal independence of the
middle class had been eroded, as the giant public and private bureaucracies spawned a middle class which had traded
autonomy for security and economic stability. Since World
War II, the economic life of that class of individuals who
own small businesses or who are self-employed but are not

required to hold a university degree to practice their profession or trade, has grown increasingly precarious. The university, which has always served as one possible means of social mobility for the middle class, became, during the fifties, the royal road to a secure middle-class existence. The credential society had emerged. Home, school, and state collaborated in canonizing the university, in singing its praises and promises to the younger generation. The so-called sputnik scare and the wants of the military and of industry for university-trained personnel (and for the results of scientific research) fueled the general euphoria. In addition to the qualitative change concerning the certifying function of higher education and the pattern of middle class social mobility, was the change occasioned by the demographic fact of the 'baby-boom children,' whose first shock troops began to arrive on campus in the early sixties.

This new generation, 'bred in at least modest comfort, housed now in the universities' was indeed looking uncomfortably to the world it was inheriting [5]. As our Canadian respondent said, the University of Waterloo was not the Harvard Business School; but the Harvard Business School of the mid-sixties was no longer the same Harvard Business School of the past. Students expecting (as they had been promised) a first class passage on a luxury liner discovered that they were in fact third class passengers on a tramp steamer. Exacerbating this already explosive situation was the spontaneous and uncontrolled growth of the universities, the so-called crisis of transition from an elite to a mass institution. Clark Kerr had the perspicacity to send up the storm warnings in 1962 in his collections of essays on The Uses of the University. But there was no constituency ready, willing, or able to take matters in hand.

The administrative bureaucracy was bounded by outmoded rules, regulations, and organizational forms, and the individuals working within these limits had no interest in defining new means and ends. Members of the faculty were enjoying their new-found importance in the public eye and had little incentive to lead a campaign to radically reform the university. The state did not intervene directly; its agencies defined the problem as economic and tried to solve it by giving the administration vast sums to spend. The students, finding themselves on a tramp steamer, with officers and crew who were acting as though they were in command of a luxury liner (or perhaps a battleship) set about making changes in line with their expectations based on the 'promise' made

to them. Ironically, it was the students who dragged the university kicking and screaming into the seventies.

If the students spoke of power and powerlessness, alienation and authenticity, domination and democracy, exploitation and freedom, it is incumbent upon us to interpret these
general references in terms of the specific conditions in which
they were employed. In this way, both the objective and sub-
jective factors are understood as different moments of the
historically specific reality. The sentiments of the students
are thus brought into line with changes in the university and
in middle class mobility which have already been presented.

A student leader in the Province of Ontario talks about
the disappointment of a generation in terms of the development of the 'education industry':

> You now have an incredible new industry that's been
> developed; it's a student industry, education indus-
> try. We saw ourselves as part of a mass, we
> weren't just a small miniscule element out there
> in the cold ... we were valued and the valedictori-
> and classes were still the leaders of tomorrow and
> that we were important and prized, prized by par-
> ents, prized by society that we made it to the uni-
> versity.

One response by students to the 'massification' of the university and the devaluation of the university degree was the as-
sertion of a political claim, not only within the university,
but globally. This is well-expressed in the following recol-
lection of a New Left student leader in Canada:

> It was probably at the CUS (Canadian Union of Stu-
> dents) seminar at London (Ontario) that represented
> the break when somebody actually got up and said,
> look, reforming the university isn't good enough;
> we have to reform the whole world.

The point concerning the students' acting as an agency
for change in the university is brought out by another national student leader in Canada:

> The universities were in terms of the technology
> and the developments in modern society, hopelessly
> out of date, hopelessly behind the times and God
> knows they needed, somebody had to point them in

the right direction and students in some sense, at
least in my mind, the student movement, democratization of certain institutions was inevitable at that
time.

The general theme of the broken promise and the frustration of the new middle class student generation is summarized by a former leading student editor:

> I think it was a matter of expectations that weren't
> being met that produced a lot of frustration in the
> middle-classes and lower-upper classes, and this
> to some extent, I guess, growing out of my own
> experiences, but it applies to many of the people
> who had gone through high school, gone through
> public school, growing up in their houses expecting
> that the lollipop of the world was going to be theirs
> and they so totally expected that.... The people
> who seemed to have control of both the bombs and
> the lollipops just were not listening, or weren't
> responding in any sort of concrete way.

These former student radicals are articulating the
feelings of that New Left generation concerning the changing
role of the universities and of the "massification" of the elite
in the sixties. The university remained a means of class
maintenance, and for some, of upward social mobility. But
the nature of the intellectual elite in society was changing;
in relative terms, the conditions of intellectual labor, of
mediate production [6], were deteriorating. As more and
more middle-class children attained university degrees, the
degree itself declined in importance. But the then-current
intellectual elite did not understand the changes which were
occurring; on account of their elite position in the old social
hierarchy, they understood the university as the ivory tower
and sought to shelter it from the storms of social struggle
which were threatening to engulf it. The student radicals
were more perceptive. Seeing that the social basis of the
ivory tower had in fact been eroded, they fought to bring the
university into line with its new content. The conflict between the old university-trained elite and the new "massified"
elite is expressed by one of the former radicals who was active in the early sixties in Canada:

> It just didn't feel to us like we, like why we were
> in school and what we were aiming for was holistic
> and had integrity and was going to fulfill its prom-

ise. I'd been told by people who were students in
the fifties that they still very much believed the
promises of the post-war years.... We certainly
didn't feel, the people I knew didn't feel the profound sense that we were part of the same country
that the powerful were part of.

These expressions of the perceptions of the social relations of the New Left are not isolated occurrences; they
represent a general theme which runs through the interviews.
One former SDS leader from Houston, Texas, who was exceptional among the Americans interviewed insofar as he was
associated with the Progressive Labor (PL) group within SDS,
contributes a complementary analysis:

What was happening to our class was that we were
being smashed. All of us were raised to be bosses,
to be creative people ... to direct things, innovate ...
and we get up to about college age and we find out
that the university is not ... the university was a
place where propertied people sent their sons and
daughters for social finishing, to have a good time,
and to get a smattering of liberal education. By
the time we got to university it was a dammed trade
school for the big corporations. That bothered us....
When I saw black people revolting and fighting back
... it struck a chord in me. I wanted to fight back
too, and I wasn't black, but I knew something was
wrong.

An activist from New York City offers a similar view:

I guess my own perspective on the student movement
was that it really had to do with certain contradictions that were developing in terms of college education and the economy; I went also through the realization that the dream which people had been
promised either at the beginning of college or else
by their parents, was not too much of a reality....
I guess I really interpret the student movement as
a middle-class movement as an expression of certain contradictions in the position of the middle-class.

The German students were equally clear in expressing
their thoughts on the decline of the new intellectual elite. A
former SDS activist, now a freelance journalist in Berlin, de-
cribes the situation facing the sixties cohort in the university
in the following words:

Where more children get the chance to go to the institutions the latter must necessarily change and they
lose much traditional middle-class (bürgerliche) room
for manuevering, e.g., that in an advanced seminar
of seven students meeting over tea with the professor at his home, all manner of things could be discussed. This could not occur in large seminars
where future prospects at the same time were called
into question (even if not in today's conscious manner). But their future there certainly did not hold
for them the matter-of-fact tradition of rulers, or
of attaining ruling positions which were formerly
open to intellectuals with certainty. And I believe
that this too was a problematic element of the student movement that really this promise to belong to
the ruling stratum, that that had been broken, was
supposed to be made good again through politics.

His thoughts are echoed by a music teacher in Frankfurt, who in the sixties was a representative on the student's
council for the SDS, when he says:

Abstract elite consciousness is mixed with the fear
of relative loss of class position (Deklassierung).
Along with an abstract elite consciousness went
student messianism. ... At the end of the restoration period of the FRG, a new want arose for a
modern kind of academic, in order to carry out
societal rationalization and bureaucratization. These
academics were supposed to be more numerous than
the previous academics ... and they were no longer
to have their former privileges, special status, per-
sonality and expectations.

If we take the extreme shifts of perspective within the
New Left, i.e., the shift from liberal moralism to neo-
Marxism, we arrive at the following characterization: the
shift was carried by a movement from the campus to society
and then from society back to campus, the latter now being
viewed in global perspective. One line of development, for
example, would then be characterized by: free speech on
campus--anti-war demonstrations--fight imperialist ideas in
the classroom.

However, the movement from campus to society could
not only be accomplished by turning the politics of the part
(the campus) into the politics of the whole (the society). Essentially, there were two ways in which this could have been

done. The first way was a gross exaggeration of the centrality
and importance of the campus in the political dynamic of society; the second was the complete denial of the campus and
the affirmation of a fantastic political agency in society. The
first is youth politics, or "youth-as-class" politics; the second, vanguard party politics. The youth politics and the vanguard parties of the late sixties both expressed the helplessness of the student population. The former made a virtue of
its helplessness, the latter a vice. The former puffed itself
up and substituted itself, a tiny part, for the much larger
whole; the latter denied itself in order to lead an imaginary
whole. The clearest expression of these two tendencies was
in the American SDS. The Revolutionary Youth Movement (I
and II) was the youth political inclination, and the Progressive
Labor-Student Worker Alliance represented the vanguardist
grouping. (The Weather Underground shared features with
both: it was the most ambivalent tendency--self-effacing and
self-inflating simultaneously; it was the expression of the
greatest impotence of abstract moralism in the form of egoism: terror [7].)

The New Left, The New Class and the State

The question concerning human emancipation or socialism was
raised by the New Left in the early sixties as an explicit
moralism with the framework of liberal ideals. Over the
course of the decade, the New Left moved from a moralist
critique to a "socialist" critique (although many early New
Leftists never abandoned their explicit moralism). We have
already seen that the student movement split over the questions of socialism--goals, strategy, tactics and, above all,
agency.

   The response of all students to the changes of the
university and in the character of the intellectual elite was
a political radicalism which quickly became anchored in their
home court: the university. A prominent Canadian student
leader of lofty class origin says more than he probably cares
to, in making the following statement:

> Education was to cure everything and yet they were
> a very select crew who were in the universities;
> lots of people whose parents were professionals or
> had made it in some way, and the equality of edu-
> cational opportunity wasn't working.

If we look beyond the moral-altruistic form of his condemnation to the egoistic impulse behind it, we see both a protest
against the existing state of affairs (i. e., the "massification"
of the elite institution) and an attempt to turn defeat into victory. If the privilege of the former elite had been partially
compromised by the opening of the university to the youth of
the broad middle strata, then why not become a leader of the
new masses? Moral-altruistic critique in political form could
be a potent weapon against the old intellectual elite which ran
the universities and set admissions policy. The criticism
that too many were being allowed into the hallowed halls of
academe became the criticism that not enough were able to
enter. At this point the stakes were raised and the critique
of the university became the critique of society. But the university was not "the real world" and the student movement
foundered because it could not by its very nature make the
transition from the one to the other except in fantastic forms.
The attempted movement from campus to city, the shift from
apparent altruism to apparent egoism, was expressed in the
cultivation of Marxist ideology in the New Left after 1966.

Robert Michels, who had an extremely important influence on the intellectual and political development of the thirties generation group of radicals (Lispet, 1962) was intensely
interested in the sociology of the intellectuals and especially
in their political identifications. In an important essay (Michels, 1931, 1932, 1979), he wrote about the commitments
of this grouping in the following way:

> One can distinguish two categories of intellectuals.
> The first succeeded in finding lucrative employment
> in state and society in a position appropriate to his
> class, while the second besieges the fortresses in
> vain, without penetrating them. The one group can
> be compared to mercenaries who defend with all
> means the bread-giving state out of a sense of duty
> or of concern over losing their positions, and other
> such egoism.... The others are the most sworn
> enemies of the state, restless elements who inflame
> every dissatisfaction, who put themselves at the
> disposal of every insurrection. To appease this
> second dangerous category of intellectuals the state
> sees itself from time to time forced to open the
> locks of its bureaucracy and thus to bring a line of
> malcontents and restless spirits over into the 'con-
> servative' camp.... It has need of this defence all
> the more urgently since the intellectuals are intel-

lectual warriors and, as a rule, when they are forced
to remain in the second category, they are inclined
to attack precisely that institution whose holding in-
tact the state sees as one of its central tasks: private property.

Although Michels' thesis rings true for his own period,
it is not an accurate portrayal of the historical development
of the sixties cohort. By and large the state opened its locks
to the new intellectuals; yet they did not generally go over to
the "conservative" camp; for the most part they remained
critics of the rights of private property (See Kristol, 1978,
pp. 175-177). The relationship between the radicals of the
sixties and the state has yet to be clarified. One important
SUPA leader explains it in this way:

> I basically now see the New Left as the activities
> of middle-class kids coming out of the liberal arts
> schools with fairly strong social consciences trying
> to remake the world and particularly the govern-
> ment, and I think this particularly involves the state.
> and 99.9% of what the New Left did involved the
> state. I mean, it was objecting to state policies,
> state institutions, state activities, criticizing gov-
> ernments in this way and that way ... it's not ir-
> relevant to point out that the initial movement was
> around military policy which is the absolute simple
> perogative of the state ... and I think what they
> were doing was creating the state in an image which
> would allow for themselves, occupationally, ideolog-
> ically, and my suspicion is one of the reasons it
> declined is by and large that effort was successful.

The impetus for New Left politics is portrayed in
light of the above understanding:

> The simple fact of the matter was that the number
> of university-trained people who were spilling out
> of the schools, could not possibly have been ab-
> sorbed in the economic structures that existed at
> that time.... There wasn't an acute perception of
> that; I wouldn't even say that people unconsciously
> knew that, but they simply did not find the social
> equivalence that the jobs, the institutions, etc.,
> that matched up with the ideology and the vocation-
> al training and the intellectual interests that these
> people had been given, and they were perfectly

right, they didn't exist. Social welfare was a relatively small thing; you had none of the sort of planning functions developed then to anywhere what they
are now, and these people really, they came out of
school with all the solutions in their heads to all
sorts of problems for which the social mechanism
was lacking; but what they were really doing was
going to the state and demanding that the state
create those social mechanisms, which I would say,
by and large, the state has done.

But this is only half the story. If this great transformation within the state has definitely occurred, then we
would expect to find an identification by members of the New
Left with the state. But all evidence points to the contrary.
We know of many cases of individuals who service the state
bureaucracy by day, and talk revolution at night. The plaus-
ible explanation then must begin with the hypothesis that this
battle within the state had not been definitively won, that the
outcome of the clash of social interests reflected in the struggle within the state has remained volatile and indecisive.

Furthermore, it is no accident of history that Marxism was seized upon by many elements of the New Left, especially toward the end of the sixties. Werner Sombart argued that socialists in general were individuals who had failed
in life's tasks and who were attracted to a revolutionary world
view (Michels, 1932). Karl Korsch, eschewing Sombart's
psychologism, on many occasions exposed the ideological interest of Marxism. He regarded it not as the "revolutionary
form of development of proletarian class consciousness and
class struggle, but rather as its fetters and limitation which
for the first time presented in bold strokes generally for all
to see the ideas and goals of the bourgeois class which were
revolutionary in a by-gone historical epoch" (Korsch, 1971).

The decade of the seventies has witnessed the fall of
the New Left and the rise of the feminist movements, ecological movements, and generally provincialist movements of
all sorts. In some sense they represent the phoenix which
has arisen out of the ashes of the student movement. Irving
Kristol (1978) has linked them to the rise of the "New Class"
[8] of intellectuals which is allied with the public sector and
locked in battle with private enterprise over matters of power and prestige. The feminist movement, perhaps the most
significant of them all, shares the same myopia with the New
Left. It has no historical perspective and cannot achieve

what its more radical exponents demand. The great historical
developments of the relations of exchange and social surplus
which have been recorded over the last five millennia at varying rates geographically, accomplished a world-historical
achievement several centuries ago--the capture of human labor capacity within their formal net (Krader, 1976, 1979).
It should come as no surprise to find that the relations between the sexes and between the generations have also fallen
under their sway. Feminism, as Norman Mailer (1971) vaguely understood, is the expression of the collapse of this for-
tress of historical privilege.

The "legacy" of the New Left is, in practical terms,
its own testament to itself. The battle of the "New Class,"
which we thought had been won at the end of the sixties, was
merely the first skirmish which established the legitimacy of
its right to exist. The "New Class" has thrown down the
gauntlet to the powers that be, but the latter (represented by
the "conservative" intellectuals) are calling their bluff. The
battle for the university is one part of the larger struggle.
The outcome is yet in doubt.

Conclusion

Former student activists interviewed in the three countries
specified have pointed to the disjunction of rhetoric and reality in their societies as the source of their respective movements. In addition, many of them sought to explain the
growth of political radicalism in terms of the material interest of egoism of youth and students. Although both explanations appear prominently in the interviews (the former somewhat more so than the latter), none of the former activists
interviewed indicated how these two apparently contradictory
sources of activism were related.

The activist movement of the sixties had tensions within it which were unresolved--and in my view may well be
unresolvable; the former activists regard the ambivalence
they perceive in the New Left as evidence of the persistence
of the tensions of the sixties. These tensions were the product of the relations of extremes, of altruism and egoism,
pacifism and terror, etc. Previous studies have taken note
of this ambivalence, this oscillation between extremes, but
they have generally failed to grasp it as the necessary expression of the character of the movement. The New Left
student movement was a movement of learners, trainees, re-

moved from the production process, from the motor of society. At the same time there was an anticipatory element in the politics of radicalism related to the changing relations of intellectual labor in the society of the sixties and to the concomitant changes in the role of the university related to them. The Old Left generation of the thirties raised the question of socialism in the context of the material want of the working class as a whole. The New Left raised the question of socialism in the context of the relative decline of the conditions of mediate production. The New Left was a one-sided movement which was propelled by its actual relations of non-production, and its potential relations of mediate production within the division of labor in society.

The former activists interviewed have followed paths of professional development which previous research has specified. As active members of the New Left Generation they have moved into teaching, social work, media, trade union activity, and government. Although they maintain a commitment to the concept of self-help of the oppressed and a basic opposition to bureaucracy, they have aligned themselves with the public sector. Intellectuals in civil society have generally been attracted to the state (as its ardent supporters or most feared detractors) and orthodox Leninism itself has emphasized the capture of the state in its revolutionary program (Korsch, 1941). With the "massification" of the intellectual elite (trained in the universities in the sixties) and the declining conditions of intellectual labor in the seventies, the former student activists concentrated on the campuses in the past, have become radical intellectuals diffused across the surface of society.

In recent years a neo-Marxism has filtered into intellectual life, especially at the universities and it has been carried in part by former student radicals. This new Marxism has become the ideology of the new intellectuals who are closely associated with the public sector and the state. It exists not as a potent social or political force (in fact it seems to be in retreat), but as a nuisance, "pour épater les bourgeois," or, as the Germans say, as Narrenschreck. De Gaulle was once reported to have said in response to a question concerning the free rein accorded J. P. Sartre by the French state: "on n'arrête pas Voltaire."

The student movement in theory and practice called attention to the nature and function of the state. Given the development of the social service industry in the sixties and

seventies (which the New Left helped to stimulate) which largely occurred under the aegis of the public sector, the New Left
was indirectly calling attention to itself. The theoretical expression of this within neo-Marxism intellectual circles has
been the elevation of the state in theory to a central active
factor within the motor of history. This is the illusion of
the apparent independence of the state (Krader, 1972; Levitt,
1978) and the expression of the Selbstwichtigtuerei (making
oneself important) of potential and actual "states-men. " The
eleventh thesis of Marx directed to his chapter on Feuerbach
in the German Ideology has been amended to read: The philosophers and statesmen have only interpreted the world in
various ways; the point, however, is for them to change it [9].

NOTES

1. Todd Gitlin (1977), president of the American SDS in
    1963-1964, has investigated the influence of the mass
    media (especially newspapers and television) on the
    growth of the SDS after 1965.

2. These three countries were chosen for the following rea-
    sons: Canada was selected on grounds of the author's
    familiarity with the history and development of the New
    Left organizations there. The movement in the U.S.
    was one of the largest and it served as an example
    and an inspiration for the New Left internationally.
    The Germans were the "theoreticians" of the New Left
    in the movement's international division of labor.
    Furthermore, the trajectory of the New Left in these
    three countries was remarkably similar. None of
    these movements had to contend with influential com-
    munist parties.
    In each country the author established contact with
    former leaders of prominent New Left groups, and
    in all cases they willingly provided the names and ad-
    dresses of former participants. The interviews were
    structured but open-ended and the questions were de-
    signed to elicit the present views of the sixties activ-
    ists concerning the growth and trajectory of the New
    Left. All but two of the interviews (one in Canada,
    one in Germany) were recorded on cassette tapes and
    later transcribed verbatim. Twenty-one Germans were
    interviewed during December 1978 and January 1979;
    23 Canadians were interviewed during February, March,
    and April 1979; 20 Americans were interviewed in June

1979. The former activists who were interviewed were
associated with the following groups:

Canada: Combined Universities Campaign for Nuclear
Disarmament (CUCND), Student Union for Peace
Action (SUPA), Canadian Union of Students (CUS).
In addition, many were heavily involved in local
campus groups bearing such names as the Radi-
cal Student Movement (RSM), Students for a Demo-
cratic University (SDU), etc.
FRG: Socialistischer Deutscher Studentenbund (SDS),
Sozialistischer Hochschulbund (SHB).
U.S.A.: Students for a Democratic Society (SDS). (A
further treatment of matters developed in this
paper will be found in Chapter III of Levitt [1980]).

3. All quotes are reproduced verbatim from the transcription
of the interviews.

4. The child-rearing practices of the parents of the New Left
generation were founded on the memory of want of the
depression years. The childhood experiences of the
New Left generation were founded on the security from
material want. These differences of generational experience were clearly brought to light in the cultural
expressions of the sixties.

5. A play on words from the Port Huron Statement of the
Students for a Democratic Society.

6. Mediate production is part of social production as a whole.
It encompasses all those producers who are not involved in the immediate process of production. In
civil society, the mediate producers are primarily
those who labor with their head in the social division
of labor (see Krader, 1979).

7. See the discussion in Hegel (1974) of absolute freedom
and terror.

8. The "New Class" is not a social class in the strict sense
of the word. It is part of the grouping of mediate
producers which, together with the immediate producers, constitute the class of social labor as a whole
(see Krader, 1979).

9. The original thesis reads: "Die Philosophen haben die

Welt nur verschieden interpretiert; es kommt darauf
an, sie zu verandern" (The philosophers have only interpreted the world in various ways; the point, however, is to change it).

References

Fendrich, J. (1974). "Activists ten years later: A test of
generational unit continuity," Journal of Social Issues
30: 95-118.

Fendrich, J. (1976). "Black and white activists ten years
later: Political socialization and adult left-wing politics," Youth and Society 8: 81-104.

Fendrich, J. (1977). "Keeping the faith or pursuing the good
life: A study of the consequences of participation in
the civil rights movement," American Sociological Review 42: 144-1547.

Fendrich, J. and Tarleau, A. (1973). "Marching to a different drummer: The occupational and political orientations of former student activists," Social Forces 52:
245-253.

Gitlin, Todd (1977). "The Whole World is Watching: Mass
Media and the New Left, 1965-70." Unpublished Ph.
D. Dissertation, University of California, Berkeley.

Hegel, G. W. F. (1974). Die Phanomenologie des Geistes.
Suhrkamp.

Korsch, K. (1941). "From liberalism to fascism," Living
Marxism, 5(4): 6-20.

Korsch, J. (1971). Die Materialistische Geschichtsauffassung.
Frankfurt am Main: Europäische Verlagsanstalt.

Krader, L. (1972). The Ethnological Notebooks of Karl Marx.
Assen: Van Gorcum.

Krader, L. (1976). The Dialectic of Civil Society. Assen:
Van Gorcum.

Krader, L. (1979). A Treatise of Social Labor. Assen:
Van Gorcum.

Krauss, E. (1974). Japanese Radicals Revisited. Berkeley:
University of California Press.

Kristol, I. (1978). Two Cheers for Capitalism. New York:
Basic Books.

Levitt, C. (1978). "Karl Marx on the law, the state and
collectivity," Catalyst 12: 12-21.

Levitt, C. (1980). University Rebellion. Assen: Van Gorcum (in press).

Lipset, S. M. (1962). "Introduction," in R. Michels, Political Parties. New York Free Press.

Mailer, N. (1971). The Prisoner of Sex. New York: Signet.
Marx, K. and Engels, F. (1972). "Das Manifest der kommunistischen Partei," in MEW 4. Berlin: Dietz.
Michels, R. (1931). "La psicologia sociale della boheme e il proletariato intellectuale," Atti Nazionale di Science Morali e Politiche, LIV, Naples.
Michels, R. (1932). "Zur Soziologie der Boheme und ihrer Zusammenhänge mit dem geistigen Proletariat," Jahrbuch fur Nationalökonomie und Statistik. 136: 801-816.
Michels, R. (1979, forthcoming). "On the sociology of bohemia and its connecting with the intellectual proletariat," C. Levitt transl.

The author wishes to thank the Canada Council and the Social Sciences and Humanities Research Council for generously supporting this research.

THE 1970s IN FRANCE: A PERIOD OF STUDENT RETREAT*

by Raymond Boudon

As in many other countries, the student turmoil of the sixties was followed in France by a period of retreat. With the exception of relatively minor episodes, no collective demonstration occurred which could be compared even remotely in intensity, creativity, mobilization and duration to the événements ("events") of 1968-1969. What was called earlier the student "movement" disappeared. In other words, the anabaptist flavor which characterized the movement of the late sixties was replaced by much more traditional types of conflicts, i. e., corporatist conflicts where students struggled to defend "their interests" as a body. The societal-universalistic cultural orientations of the 1968 movement gave way to a corporatist-particularistic-materialistic orientation.

This trend is obviously not unique to the French situation. As in other places, the decline of the student movement in the 1970s was partly due to its relative success at the universal-cultural level. Whether the 1968 events contributed to making the French university more effective remains debatable. But beyond doubt they were successful in sketching at an informal level new "rights, " or recalling older ones, including the right to question openly the legitimacy of authority, especially in its "traditional" form and the right to a really and not only formally equal treatment of all before the law (with regard to job security, educational opportunities, etc.). This "success" at the universalistic-cultural level is so undebatable that today no writer would dare picture the 1968 movement in a purely critical fashion: political parties have all to varying extents included in their programs some aspects of the 1968 cultural heritage.

*Reprinted by permission of the author and publisher from Higher Education, 8: 6 (November 1979), pp. 669-81. Copyright ©1979 by the Elsevier Scientific Publishing Co. , Amsterdam.

But success is not the only cause of the dissipation of the movement. Ten years ago, I proposed a tentative inter- pretation (Boudon, 1969, 1971) of the 1968 movement where I tried to show that criticism by students of university and so- ciety as well as the overall cultural orientation of the move- ment could only be made intelligible if the individual condi- tions of students were taken into account. I insisted that stu- dents from the lower middle class (whose proportion had in- creased tremendously in a relatively short period of time) were confronted with institutions whose structures and prac- tices were well adapted to an elitist upper-class student body but not to the new public of the universities. As a conse- quence of this "morphological" change, the functions of uni- versity had become multiple and unclear. Many students from all social classes viewed their condition as "absurd": getting a higher education degree was perceived as a social neces- sity (the greater the number of students, the more so); but the rules of the game which was to be played to get a degree appeared to many students to be culturally arbitrary.

My assumption in this article is that the "individual- istic" methodology which I used in this previous paper can help in understanding the new form of the students' collective behavior in the 1970s. I will try in other words to describe the consequences on the individual actors of the changes which have occurred since the early 1970s at the institutional and societal levels.

The Impact of 1968

Whether the effects of the 1968 movement on university itself was positive or not is debatable. One effect at least is clear. As a consequence of the Loi d'orientation de l'enseignement supérieur (1968) which followed the student turmoil and set up the main lines of the new organization of the university system, a hierarchy of councils and committees was built at the various levels (departments, individuals universities, uni- versities as a whole). All these councils and committees must legally include elected representatives of the various bodies of teachers and of students. As far as students are concerned the voters have to choose not individuals but lists. This form of the poll which was adopted mainly for technical reasons of feasibility had the consequence of making the uni- versity a field of activity for political parties. Most effective in this respect was and still is the Communist Party. The strongest student organization (since the Loi d'orientation be- gan), the Union Nationale des Etudiants de France (UNEF-

Renouveau) is close to the Communist Party. Over time, many other student organizations more loosely or not at all related to political organizations tended to disappear. As a result it often occurs that when the students of the Department ("Unité d'Enseignement et de Recherche") X of the University Y have to elect their representatives to the Department Council, they are often offered a very limited choice of "lists," but in most cases the UNEF list. This situation is one of the reasons why the vote turnout among students is small and steadily declining (Boussard, 1974). The other major reason is that, after 1968--as indeed before 1968--the French University never succeeded (apart from a few local exceptions) in arousing among students a feeling of community.

Through the electoral mechanisms it devised, the Loi d'orientation gave politics an official position in the university. This was a demand of a minority of students in 1968. This is still a demand of a minority. But this demand is now satisfied. Anyone interested in "making politics" or in political training not only can do so but is encouraged to do so. This statement does not apply only to students. At the teachers' level the electoral mechanisms have in many cases given rise to an informal transformation of a nominal into a list voting system. This circumstance in turn gave birth to surrogates of political parties within the university system.

The demand of a minority of students and teachers for opportunities of political activity within the university is thus met, formally or informally. Although it might appear at first view paradoxical, the (apparently unanticipated) introduction of politics in universities which resulted from the Loi d'orientation had the effect of making it less visible: university politics is being institutionalized and is the business of small, interested and organized minorities. Probably this minority is perceived by the "common" student as an oligarchy à la Michels to the effect of reinforcing his political retreatism.

Some data corroborate this analysis: a survey shows that rates of unionization among students are very low: (Le Monde de l'Education, 1977). a union close to the Socialist Party (COSEF) attracts less than one out of a thousand students. In 1977, a year when the total number of students in France was about 900,000, the number of students affiliated with the UNEF-Renouveau, a student union close to the Communist Party, did not reach sixteen thousand, i.e., less than 2%. The most important leftist (non-communist) union included about eight thousand students, while rightist unions attracted about five thousand students. These figures illustrate the political nature of student unions. As in political parties, the number of members is very small compared to the number of voters, even though the latter is itself small (Boussard, 1974).

As a consequence of this unintended application of Michels' iron law of oligarchy the university is no longer perceived by a large majority of students as a field where political aspirations can be expressed. The electoral mechanisms give a premium to the ideological trends which are able to express themselves at the organizational level (they must be able to hire and promote candidates and lists of candidates). These ideological trends are not necessarily the most popular. The survey to which I refer above shows for instance that the attraction of the Socialist Party among students is much stronger than the attraction of the Communist Party. While 12. 7% of the sampled students say they feel closer to the Communist Party, 24. 9% say they feel closer to the Socialist Party, 22. 1% to the Parti Socialiste Unifié and 15. 6% to leftist parties. On the whole, non-communist left parties attract the sympathy of five times more students than the Communist Party.

It is interesting to compare these figures with the figures dealing with the number of students not only feeling close to a party, but affiliated to a party: while 1. 7% of students are affiliated to the Communist Party, 0. 9% are affiliated to the Socialist Party, 0. 4% to the Parti Socialiste Unifié and 0. 7% with leftist parties. While among sympathisers, non-communists are five times more numerous than communists; among members non-communists are just a little more numerous than communists. These ratios, plus the effectiveness of communist organizations explain why about one half on the whole of the various elective positions created by the Loi d'orientation go to members of the union close to the Communist Party. The electoral mechanisms not only generate a Michels' oligarchy effect. They also ensure that the "ideologies" (I use the notion in a broad sense) most popular among students are also condemned to be underrepresented, if represented at all, by the political subsystem included in the university system.

We have just seen that 62. 7% of the students feel close to leftist non-communist organizations. Another 55. 9% (the question was of course of the multiple-choice type) say they

feel close to ecological movements; 15.1% say they feel close
to the Gaullist Party (RPR) or to organizations supporting
President Giscard d'Estaing's policy, while 4.8% are right or
extreme right. These distributions are to be contrasted with
the fact that a high proportion of elected students are close
to the Communist Party.

These data show why the proportion of non-voters is
extremely high in university elections. Because of the ideological distance between the candidates and themselves, many
students feel unconcerned.

Two additional points must be mentioned in this part
of the analysis. First these mechanisms of representation
had the further effect of increasing corporatism. In order
(among other reasons) to make their oligarchical position
more acceptable, the student organization and their delegates
(as well as some of the most influential teachers' organizations) played and still play a low profile role essentially oriented toward what they define as the "interests" of the various bodies they are concerned with.

Second, the demobilization effect produced by the electoral institutions created by the Loi d'orientation was to be
reinforced by factors external to the university system as
such. The rebirth and rise after the "Congrès d'Epinay"
(1972) of the Socialist Party created a pole of attraction for
a large number of students feeling distant both from the Communist Party and from the multiple leftist organizations. But
by contrast with the Communist Party, the Socialist Party
had at its disposal no organization implanted in the university
system. The same can be said, with still greater relevance,
of the various ecological movements. Although they have
great support among students, their activities are located
outside the university and developed without connection with
the university system and institutions.

A leftist motto says that institutionalization means
death. In one sense it is true that the unintended (?) but
official introduction of politics into the university system via
the election mechanisms to councils, committees, etc., had
the unintended effect of accelerating the "depoliticization" of
a majority of the student body and of confining the minority
willing to play or playing a "political" role in the new system into a corporatist role, the main aim of which is to defend particularistic interests.

Current Political Realities

In his essay Exit, Voice and Loyalty, Albert Hirschman (1970) claims that the restoration of quality in declining enterprises or institutions can be generated by two basic mechanisms: exit (customers leave a firm and go to one of its competitors provoking, if favorable circumstances are met, a restoration effect) or voice (customers exert a pressure on the firm, enterprise or institution to get a restoration of the quality of service or product they provide). Now, the apparition of exit or voice or of the two of them or eventually of none of them are unequally probable according to the structure of the situation. Other things being equal, exit is more probable than voice with non-durable goods. It is more likely if substitution goods are easily available. Voice is more probable than exit if goods are expensive and durable. It is more likely if no substitutes are easily available or if the producer is in a situation of monopoly, etc.

The situation of the French university in 1968 was such that it made on the whole voice more probable than exit. Firstly, the composition of the student body at that time (high proportion of students from lower middle classes) had the effect that a number of students did not find in the services offered by the university system a well adapted answer to their type of socialization, nor to their needs and wants. The higher class students on the other hand, began to understand that their social status was more threatened than ever in a society of "abundance" whose rate of growth had never been so high. Secondly, the university system at that time could be compared to what economists sometimes call a "lazy monopoly. " French universities were traditionally highly centralized. They were also relatively few in number. Thus, the choices available to students in choosing institutions, or for moving from one to another were limited.

Today, as a consequence of the Loi d'orientation, and of a number of subsequent political decisions, the French university system is more diversified. The University of Paris has been divided into several universities. Some of these universities are better than others. Some departments have a style of their own. It is recognizable and publicly known that the general orientation of, say, the department ("Unité d'Enseignement et de Recherche") of philosophy of University X is not the same as in University Y; that X has a strong department of social sciences while Y has a small and young one, etc. It is also known that philosophy is rather oriented toward positivism here and toward Marxism there. This differentiation has become more public and visible in recent years, since a number of magazines and publications for the use of students have started publishing information and ratings on universities and departments.

Not only the University of Paris but also many of the bigger universities in the provinces (Bordeaux, Lille, Strasbourg, etc.) have been split into a set of generally two or three smaller universities. Moreover, a number of new universities have been created. These new universities corresponded to a double purpose. In many cases, the objective was to bring universities closer to the potential population of students by creating institutions of higher education in middle size urban centers. In other cases, the purpose was to implant new types of disciplines or new types of research and new styles of teaching. Typical in this respect is the University of Dauphine (in Paris) whose main aim was to develop a program of teaching and research in fields such as management, private administration, etc. which were weakly represented in the older universities. Typical also is the University of Vincennes (in the suburbs of Paris) which has the peculiarity of admitting students without a high school degree and of developing new types of teaching and research. The "style" of Vincennes is deliberately "modern," "interdisciplinary," permissive, etc. In spite of some hostility from some parts of the public opinion against the sometimes called "Vincennes experiment" (l' "expérience" Vincennes) it has attracted a steadily increasing number of students.

An increase in the differentiation of teachers has also been evident since 1968. In Dauphine, for instance, a number of teachers are professionals (newsmen, former civil servants, etc.) appointed in general for a small number of years as associate professors. The number of types of curricula (and consequently of degrees) has been increased. For instance, besides the classical curricula and degrees, more professionally and vocationally defined curricula and degrees (such as the "maîtrise de sciences et techniques") have been created. Also, institutions of short-term higher education (two-year studies), such as the Instituts Universitaires de Technologie, have been incorporated into universities.

One of the key words of the Loi d'orientation is "autonomie." In contrast to the previous situation where all universities were directly dependent on the central govern-

ment, a greater number of decisions are now made at the
university level. But this "autonomie" is limited by a number of factors. First of all, the bulk of the resources are
provided by the government. Secondly, the salaries of the
teachers do not depend on the individual institutions. Thirdly,
a number of degrees are "national." That is, they have official state sanction. This implies that the universities who
want to deliver them have to follow a number of centrally defined constraints. The preparation for these "nationally defined" degrees absorbs a high proportion of the teaching resources of universities.

These features limit seriously the content and idea of
"autonomie." The autonomy is insufficient to give rise to
real competition. Also, this restricted autonomy keeps differentiation within narrow limits. Nothing remotely approach-
ing the American "academic market" is observable in France:
the rewards of all kinds the academic person receives depend
to a small extent on which institution he/she belongs to. This
feature, plus the fact that research is traditionally located
outside universities, at the Centre National de la Recherche
Scientifique (although many connections exist between CNRS
and universities), plus the fact that the best students go to
the highly selective Grandes Ecoles, plus the corporatist orientation of the representative bodies are all factors converging to the effect of making the present university system a
"lazy competition system."

Hirschman and others have shown that competition systems are not necessarily better than monopolies. Not only
the latter, but also the former can be "lazy" or strongly suboptimal. This is probably on the whole the case of the post-
1968 French University system, although some institutions
and some fields (such as medicine or humanities) have been
more successful than others in maintaining or reaching a
higher level (Boudon, 1977a; and b). Now, in the case of a
lazy monopoly, voice can be heard. In the case of a lazy
competition system, exit is more likely. In this case, however, exit will unfortunately not help to restore quality.

But what matters for our analysis is that the complex
differentiation process introduced as a consequence of the
1968 student movement by the Loi d'orientation and the measures which followed this law was sufficiently effective to give
the students real choices. This differentiation and the concomitant substitution of exit for voice mechanisms gives an
important clue to the sociological explanation of the progres-

sive substitution in the 1970s of an overall "retreat" from the part of students for the activism which had characterized the antecedent period.

Economic and Social Realities

The differentiation process generated by the Loi d'orientation was certainly not the only cause of the decline of the collective strategy (voice) and of the reinforcement of the individualistic strategy on the part of students. Many other factors acted in the same direction.

One of the causes is obvious and certainly not specific to France: the difficulty for a student to find a job was greater in the mid-seventies than in the mid- and late-sixties. Thus, among students with a "licence" degree ("normally" obtained after three years of higher education), 9.2% were unemployed in 1972 as against 13.1% in 1977. Among students with a degree from short-term higher education institutions (BTS = Brevet de technicien supérieur, DUT = Diplôme universitaire de technologie) 8.1% were unemployed in 1972 as against 16.1% in 1977.

Unemployment among students was greater in 1977 than in 1972. But, and this is an essential complementary aspect of the situation, unemployment is also much lower among those who have just achieved a higher education degree than among those who have just obtained a high school degree, at the intermediate or terminal level. Among those with a terminal high school degree (baccalauréat), 9% were unemployed in 1972 as against 20.7% in 1977. Among those with an intermediate high school degree (Brevet d'Etudes du Premier Cycle), 10.8% appeared in the statistics as unemployed in 1972 as against 23.1% in 1977. Thus, a higher education degree is a more effective protection against unemployment than lower level degrees.

Statistics on level of employment display similar effects as figures on unemployment. The higher the degree, the higher the social expectations. Taking 1972 and 1977 as comparison points, the social expectations of all were smaller in 1977 than in 1972. But the relative protection against overall dwindling of social expectations tends to be greater, the higher the degree. Thus, among students entering the job market with a terminal high school degree (baccalauréat) in 1972, 13.6% got a lower class position (workers, service), 74.4% a lower middle class position (clerks, salesman, civil servants/lower category, etc.) and 6.1% a higher class position (professionals, managers, civil servants/higher category, etc.). In 1977, the equivalent percentages are respectively 15.8%, 72.2% and 3.2%. Among students entering the job market with a "licence" degree the corresponding percentages were 1.2%, 26.8% and 71.2% in 1972 and 6.5%, 26.5% and 64.4% in 1977. In 1972, students with a higher education degree were twelve times more likely to get a higher class position than students with a high school degree. In 1977, they were not twelve but twenty times better off in this respect. Their relative protection against lower class jobs had, however, diminished.

In summary, these statistics indicate that:

(1) Trying to get a higher education degree is for any student a good strategy: it provides high differential returns.

(2) It provides high differential returns in terms both of protection against unemployment and level of employment.

(3) Protection against unemployment does not decrease when overall unemployment increases.

(4) Differential advantage with regard to level of employment does not decrease when (essentially as a consequence of the increase in the total number entering the educational competition, (Boudon, 1974)) overall social expectations decrease for any given level of education.

In other words, the overall change in the economic and educational contexts from the early seventies to the late seventies had the consequence of making the absolute returns of education smaller (for all levels of education), while the differential returns of higher education degrees relatively to lower degrees remained at worst constant when it did not become greater. These trends have likely favored individualistic orientations and strategies.

An assumption which can be made is the following: because of the persistence of high differential returns, trying to get a higher education degree remains for any student a valuable strategy. Because of the decrease of absolute returns however, it is "rational" or at least advisable for a student to try to get the degree at lowest cost. Since all students are in the same situation, all are likely to make the same calculation, so that none are likely to suffer individually from the fact that he will try to get the degree at lower cost.

Some data provide an indirect and tentative corroboration of this assumption. Levy-Garboua (1976) has shown using a cross-sectional survey on the time budgets of a sample of students, that students tend to take the time they spend earning money on part-time jobs from the time they would otherwise spend on academic work. More precisely, assume students' time budgets include three basic items: time spent on part-time jobs to get money, time spent in lectures, seminars, reading and working for degrees, and leisure time. The survey shows that the proportion of time devoted to leisure is constant except when time spent working for money is proportionally very high. In other words, all students (with the exception of the minority who are employed for more time than the average) try to take the time they spend working for money, not from their leisure time, but from the time they spend on academic work.

This statement must be supplemented by an observation drawn from overtime data: on the whole, the time spent by students working for money tends to increase. In 1963-64, 31.4% of all students earned money on part-time jobs. In 1973-74, the overall proportion has changed very little: 30.2%, but on average, students work a longer time on part-time jobs. In 1963-64 among the 31.4% working on part-time jobs, 21.7% had a half-time job or a job taking more than half-time (i.e., twenty hours a week or more). In 1973-74, among the 30.2% working in part-time jobs, 29.5% which is a much higher percentage than in the previous decade, work twenty hours a week or more.

In summary:
(1) On the whole, students spend a higher proportion of their time working for money;
(2) They tend to take the additional time they spend working for money from the time they would have spent working on academic topics rather than from leisure time.

Hence time spent on academic work tends to decrease. As a consequence, for an increasing number of students, academic work and academic life are more and more part-time activities.

Among students from lower class origin, the proportion of students working for money has increased only slightly when it has not decreased in the decade. Thus, among students from working class families 37.8% have at least a half-time job (twenty hours or more) in 1963-64, as against

31. 6% in 1973-74; among clerks the corresponding percentages
are 22. 5% (1963-64) and 22. 3% (1973-74). The trend goes in
the opposite direction for students from the higher classes:
in 1963-64, among students from higher class families (professionals, executives, etc.) 7. 8% have more than half-time
jobs. In 1973-74, the percentage is as high as 27. 6%.

This trend is probably mainly due to the effectiveness
of the public subvention policy which has succeeded in reducing the cost of education for lower class families and students.

These data imply two interesting consequences. Firstly, they indicate that the differences between classes, more
exactly the differences in the condition of students from the
various social classes, are much smaller in 1973-74 than
they were in 1963-64. Secondly, that the ideal-typical student characteristic of the pre-war university and of the university of the fifties is on the way to disappearing. This
ideal-typical student, who was often from higher class origin,
went directly to the university after having completed high
school. Economically dependent on his or her family, he/she
divided the time available between leisure and academic work.
After completion of a higher degree ("licence" for example),
he or she looked for a job. Now, the ideal-typical student
is lower middle class and combines academic work with employment.

Thus, for students of the late seventies, academic life
represents in comparison with their elders a smaller part of
their total life in terms both of time and probably of personal commitment. Getting a degree is socially and economically rewarding. It is possible to get a degree without reducing
too much the proportion of time spent on leisure. It is possible to work for a degree and at the same time to have a
part-time job to get money. Moreover, working for money
has the advantage of providing the student with useful information concerning the job market and of preparing for the world
of occupations. Finally, the increased diversity of the French
University in the post-1968 era had the effect of making it
easier for the student to find an institutional environment, a
combination of fields, a style of teaching, eventually an ideological orientation more adapted to individual tasks, needs or
desires.

These circumstances explain or at least contribute to
explaining why in a survey two thirds of the sampled students
say that they have chosen the right type of field and curricu-

lum. Among these two-thirds, about half are satisfied by
their educational choice because it is a good preparation to
their desired occupation, while the other half underline the
intrinsic interest of their studies. On the whole, this survey
gives the unexpected impression that students are relatively
satisfied with their condition. This is unexpected seen from
the viewpoint of teachers. Many of these display an acute
consciousness of the defects of the present university system:
the corporatist effects resulting from the increased weight of
unions in the government of universities and departments or
the multifunctionality of the higher education institutions for
instance. The traditional function of universities, producing
and transmitting knowledge and culture, could be dominant at
a time when the universities devoted chiefly to humanities or
science had the essential function of training future teachers
or researchers. Today the demand for teachers and researchers is dwindling, while the proportion of students choosing
humanities is ever increasing. As a result, science-oriented
universities and to a still greater extent humanities-oriented
universities have to provide multiple services to a body of
student characterized by very heterogeneous occupational expectations. Hence, the role of the teacher tends to become
increasingly ambiguous, while the values he or she tends
traditionally to place higher (production of knowledge) are often perceived by students as secondary.

But what is often perceived by the teachers as ambiguity is perceived by the students as diversity. The multifunctionality of university is negatively valued by many teachers
while it is positively valued by many students.

Conclusion

I have tried in this article to describe the structural changes
which occurred in the roles of the actors implied in the university system since 1968. These changes were generated
both by the institutional changes that followed the 1968 turmoil and by the economic and morphological changes which
occurred since that time.

During the seventies, student protest resulted in street
demonstrations on only a few occasions. The most noticeable
street demonstrations took place in 1976. They were provoked by a technical reform of the "second cycle" (i. e. , the
part of the curriculum leading to the "licence" and "maîtrise"
degrees). This conflict, like the others which occurred in

the seventies, was of a classical type: particularistic, corporatist and materialistic, as I have said above. Briefly, a conflict in the style of the strongly institutionalized social conflicts and, as such, contrasting strongly with the universalistic-cultural character of the 1968 movement.

I hope that this analysis provides useful hints to a better understanding of the overall mood of retreat and passivity which characterized the collective behavior of students in the seventies. To summarize, our core assumption suggests that converging effects of the above mentioned changes have produced a system of orienting students toward individualistic strategies. Those interested in political activism can try to get one of the numerous elective positions offered by the post-1968 institutions. Those interested in getting a degree at low cost in an easy field can find their way. Moreover, the university system, even though it appears as strongly suboptimal from the viewpoint of knowledge production and transmission, is a very effective machinery in one respect: it is able to produce sizeable differential economic and social rewards. It offers the students a really diversified range of choices.

But this is only one part of the story. We have already mentioned a study which shows that, though few students are members of political parties and unions, only a small minority feel close to the political parties composing the governmental majority, while among the others a majority feel closer to movements weakly represented if at all at the level of political institutions than to the main opposition parties (Socialist and Communist Parties) (Le Monde de l'Education, 1977). Such data express unmistakably a significant level of dissatisfaction with society as well as with political institutions. This dissatisfaction has a hard time finding an ideological expression, however. And this circumstance might be an additional cause of the apparent political passivity of French students. The neo-Marxist intellectual "stars" and half-stars (philosophers, sociologists, etc.) who dominated French intellectual life of the late sixties and early seventies have lost much of their prestige in the past few years and have not been replaced. Why is that? How long is the present climate of ideological pluralism going to last? These are difficult questions in the theory of ideologies which are evidently located beyond the scope of this article.

References

Boussard, I. (1974). "La participation des étudiants aux élections universitaires en France, 1970-73," Revue Française de Science Politique 24: 940-65.

Boudon, R. (1969). "La crise universitaire française: essai de diagnostic," Annales 24: 738-64.

Boudon, R. (1971). "Sources of student protest in France," Annals of the American Academy of Political and Social Science 395: 139-149.

Boudon, R. (1974). Education, Opportunity and Social Inequality. New York: Wiley.

Boudon, R. (1977a). Effets pervers et ordre social. Paris: Presses Universitaires de France.

Boudon, R. (1977b). "The French university since 1968," Comparative Politics 10: 89-119.

Hirschman, A. (1970). Exit, Voice and Loyalty. Cambridge, Mass.: Harvard University Press.

Levy-Garboua, L. (1976). "Les demandes de l'étudiant et les contradictions de l'Université de masse," Revue Française de Sociologie 17: 53-80.

Le Monde de l'Education (1977). October: 5-18.

STUDENT POLITICS IN ITALY:
FROM UTOPIA TO TERRORISM*

by Gianni Statera

Introduction

The Italian student movement has recently experienced a revival, and it has been compared to the dramatic events of
1968. This most recent manifestation of student activism
has been stimulated largely by the despair and growing rage
of marginal youth, including many in the universities, over
the continuing crisis of Italian society. Many social scientists predicted a "continuity" of the current movement with
the protests of 1968, and this has not happened. Today's
movement stems from somewhat different roots and has taken
a different tactical and political road. In Italy, it is possible
to see at least two contradictory trends; some students have
turned to increasingly militant tactics and ideologies while
others have given up ideological politics and have taken shelter in "private" life. Our major concern is to understand
the societal causes for the current wave of student activism
and to describe some of the movements. Sociologists have
repeatedly warned of the consequences of the economic crisis,
the unemployment of graduates, the declining standards and
worsening conditions in the universities and of bureaucratic
inefficiency. They indicated that this situation would have inevitable results in terms of instability of democratic institutions and weakening the underpinnings of the state.

More than one million young people attend universities,
and these individuals have been increasingly alienated from
the major social structures. They have been unable to find

*Reprinted by permission of the author and publisher from
Higher Education, 8:6 (November 1979), pp. 657-67. Copyright ©1979 by the Elsevier Scientific Publishing Co., Amsterdam.

suitable positions and the universities have not provided them
with the professional skills needed to successfully enter the
job market.   Thus, students have increasingly identified with
the "excluded," those segments of the society who feel marginal and without power or status.   High school and vocational school students along with migrants from southern Italy
who form a kind of metropolitan lumpenproletariat in the
northern cities have joined with university students in a social movement whose impact is still uncertain and difficult
to assess.   What is clear is that the Italian "crisis" continues to have a major impact on the society and that the newly
revived student movement has a major role in reflecting that
crisis.

The Rebellion of 1977

In February, 1977 between 30, 000 and 40, 000 students in
Rome demonstrated against the Minister of Education.   Demonstrations also took place in other Italian cities, often with
violent results.   At the same time the terroristic Red Brigades (Brigate Rosse) have carried out assaults against judges,
lawyers, civil servants, businessmen and others.   A segment
of the student movement supports the Red Brigades and in a
sense the universities have become a kind of center for activist opposition to the general current of Italian society.   In
March, mass demonstrations, led to some extent by students,
occurred in Rome.   Attacks on public buildings by armed
groups were part of these demonstrations, including the tactics of urban guerillas.   For the first time, several policemen were seriously wounded, setting off shockwaves among
the population.   The demonstrations split the New Left.   The
militants, led by the "Autonomia Operaia" supported the use
of violence and of weapons in social struggle.   The majority
of leftist groups, however, opposed violence but did not openly attack the "Autonomi."   The powerful Communist Party
began a campaign against the New Left, accusing it of irra-
tionality and latent fascism, further confusing the political
situation.

        The role of the Italian Communist Party (PCI) in sup-
porting the "Historical Compromise" which included accomo-
dation with the Socialists and the ruling Christian Democrats
is of critical importance in understanding left politics.   The
PCI's impact on the working class, the intellectuals and to
some extent on the middle class is considerable.   The Communists could not tolerate the emergence of a revolutionary

force on their left, which has the possibility of undermining
their traditional support. Hence, the Communist leadership
has taken a very harsh view toward the New Left in general
and toward the terrorists in particular. According to PCI
Secretary General Berlinguer "Criminal actions are carried
out by fascist-like squads, but they are justified and even
supported by leftist student groups. "

     While important elements in the student movement have
supported terrorism, the movement is far from being pro-ter-
rorist as a whole. The movement is a kind of "melting pot"
of divergent ideological currents, including "hippies, " anarchists, and many others. Most oppose the communists (usually from the left) and are disillusioned with parliamentary
and most other state institutions. Unlike the 1968 student
movement, however, the protests of 1977 lacked a mobilizing
utopian vision. The movement is not attempting to win public opinion, and its alienation from the "system" is clear.
An indication of the alienation of the movement is the attack
on Luciano Lama, the leader of the powerful CGIL labor federation, who came to the University of Rome to speak on
February 17, 1977. Lama was brought to the campus by the
Communist Party, which arranged to protect him. When he
spoke, however, New Left students disrupted the proceedings
and attacked the podium. Violence between the "Autonomi"
and the communists ensued and resulted in injuries and in a
war between the communists and segments of the New Left.
Struggles of a similar kind in Bologna (long under communist
municipal control) and other cities also broke out, led by the
"Autonomi. " Several deaths and many injuries resulted from
this violence.

     The spring of 1977 on the Italian campuses turned out
to be violent, and the movement spread beyond the universities. In the large cities, urban guerilla warfare became
commonplace, and the Red Brigades increased their attacks
on individuals.

1978 as a Turning Point

The Red Brigades, founded by the sociology graduate Renato
Curcio, claimed to be the purest form of Marxist-Leninism.
They attacked the communists for being reformist, and pre-
sented terrorism as a means of destroying state institutions.
By using the logic of the 1968 student movement, the Bri-
gades argued that violent pressure was necessary to dislodge

the established system and produce social change and revolution. They aimed at developing insecurity, diffused fear, and
wanted the State to impose increasingly repressive tactics that
would eventually alienate the populace. The Brigades tried
especially hard, in 1974, to disrupt the debate on divorce and
to make it impossible for non-violent political debate to occur
in Italy. Similarly, the Red Brigades attempted to disrupt the
1975 and 1976 elections, and were especially opposed to the
formal participation of the communists in the government.
While none of these efforts effectively disrupted the society,
the established political system was clearly affected by the
terrorism.

After the 1976 elections, many social scientists pointed
out the risks of the communist strategy of the "historical
compromise, " by indicating that by leaving the left and right
out of the legitimate political structure, large numbers of
people would be alienated from the system. Many on the left
would see the PCI as the "betrayer" of the revolution, and
young people, slum dwellers, and others with special social
problems would be especially alienated. The government's
performance played into this analysis. Policies aimed at improving employment prospects and implementing social reforms were ineffective. The Italian crisis continued unabated,
and the PCI now had some responsibility for it. Without a
legitimate political opposition, the sociologists predicted, the
alienated youth and students would turn increasingly to extreme politics. The continued growth of the Red Brigades
supported this analysis and culminated in the kidnapping of
Aldo Moro on May 16, 1978. Moro's kidnapping shocked
Italy, and the ineffectiveness of the authorities in solving the
crime further weakened the government.

The political result of the kidnapping was, however,
the opposite of that expected by the extreme left. A new
government of national unity was formed, and popular opinion
turned more strongly against the extreme left. While the Red
Brigades continued to circulate manifestos and ultimatums,
they gained little political advantage.

Within the student movement, most groups seek a new
perspective, and there is some impetus toward unity among
the various organizations. However, different orientations
toward terrorism continue to divide the movement. Some
groups maintain that the Red Brigades are simply "comrades
who are wrong" but they feel that revolution in Italy is very
close. Others oppose terrorism, but just as strongly oppose

the violence shown by the State. These groups, currently strongest in the student movement, have the slogan, "Neither with the State nor with the Red Brigades. " And some groups accept the idea of "proletarian violence" but differentiate them- selves from the Red Brigades by claiming that terrorism is not acceptable "mass violence. " Among these groups is the Autonomia Operaia.

During this period, a basic complementarity has devel- oped between the Red Brigades and some other extreme left groups such as the Autonomia Operaia, all of which accept the idea of violence as a means of social change. These groups are composed mostly of students, ex-prisoners, and migrants. The autonomi are organized loosely into neighbor- hood or factory groups. They oppose the clandestine violence of the Brigades, but are in favor of "mass proletarian vio- lence. " They participate in robberies of stores, and often carry arms. Members of the autonomi often go "underground" to work with the Red Brigades and become "fighting commu- nists" (Acquaviva, 1979). The Autonomia Operaia groups in Padova, Genoa, Reggio Emilia and Rome constitute a kind of "reserve force" for the Red Brigades. Despite their activi- ties in terrorist groups, the autonomi continue to function in the student movement, thus calling into question the effective- ness of police actions in recent years.

The universities remained relatively quiet during the period of Moro's imprisonment, but the extreme alienation of many students and others on the fringes of Italian society re- mains, thus leaving the possibility for further violence. The failure of the Moro affair to improve the chances for the rad- icals stimulated a new debate on the issue of terrorism. Be- ginning in the autumn of 1978, there is further fragmentation of the New Left and of the student movement. Groups such as Lotta Continua and Democrazia Proletaria split among those who favor mass violence (but oppose the Brigades) and those who condemn violence completely.

The Collapse of the New Left

Between November 1978 and February 1979, there was an of- ten violent struggle between those who oppose the violence of the Brigades and of the Autonomia and those who favor "mass struggle. " The Autonomia accused their enemies of being "accomplices of bourgeois justice. " The newspaper Lotta Continua denounced the murder of a young left extremist by

the autonomi. Apparently, the activist was killed by the radicals because he knew too much about an armed robbery. The
murder was previously blamed on fascists. This event shocked
segments of the radical community. The Autonomia Operaia,
for their part, countered these attacks by radical opponents
by criticizing their opponents and turning to ever more radical tactics. Their aim is to overturn all social norms and
values. Personal dignity needs to be broken down, they
claim, to speed a revolutionary situation. In the schools,
the autonomi attack liberal and democratic teachers, and in
the factories it assails political and union representatives.
The contradictions of society must be forcefully articulated,
according to the views of the autonomi and all ameliorative
efforts opposed.

From 1978, the Autonomia Operaia spread a spirit of
warfare between the "outcasts" of society against all those
with a stake in the established order. This extreme radicalism forced many students to turn to privatism rather than
identify politically with an extreme group like the autonomi.
The threat of insecurity in the schools and universities convinced many of the best teachers and students to leave the
institutions or to carefully avoid any activism at all. Utopian
leftists have simply been drowned out by the strident radicalism of the Autonomia Operaia.

The social isolation which has been so avidly stressed
by the extreme left in Italy had its origin earlier and has had
a role in New Left ideologies since as early as 1958. Early
manifestos of such Third World leaders as Mao Tse-tung and
Sukarno stressed the marginality and alienation of Third World
peoples. Fanon's writings stress similar themes. In the
mid-1960s, Marcuse's writings criticized the integration of
the working class in advanced capitalist societies and pointed
to the "outcasts" of Western society (students, racial minorities, migrants and the lumpenproletariat) as the major revolutionary force in Western nations. These ideological currents provided a powerful impetus to the 1968 student movements in Western nations. In Italy, where social contradictions are particularly dramatic for an industrialized society,
these ideologies had a particular appeal to large numbers of
students. The participation of the socialists in the center-
left government and the later tacit cooperation of the Communist Party in the Italian political establishment provided further fuel.

The hopes of many people for the center-left govern-

ment declined during the 1970s, and further increased political
alienation. The economic boom of the 1950s dissipated, the
cost of labor increased, and Italy found itself at a disadvantage in international trade. The differences between the north
and the south grew, and northern prosperity did not reach the
south. The demand for education grew at a time when the
government did not have the fiscal means to meet the demand.
Further, the educational system was still structured to meet
the needs of a pre-industrial society.

The "educational crisis" of the 1960s and 1970s had,
of course, a major impact on development of a student movement and on the ideological and tactical orientations of the
movement. Universities, because of their outmoded organizational structures and archaic curriculum, represented authoritarianism, cultural obsolescence and inefficiency. The sons
and daughters of the bourgeoisie experienced this outmoded
educational system at first-hand and called for educational
reform. Students saw the universities as symbols of the basic problems of industrial societies, and linked university issues to societal questions such as the Vietnam war. They
attacked the structure and hierarchy of the university as a
symbol for the power structures of the broader society. Italian students also tended after 1968 to oppose the dominant
culture of the society, and criticized the universities for being representative of this culture. The student movement
which emerged in 1968 represented these various strands of
protest and opposition to establish authority. The basic movement was anti-authoritarian and opposed to the bureaucratic
structures of society. In general, the movement was "left"
in its orientation, but there was no clear ideological perspective which emerged at that time (Statera, 1975).

The defeat of the various European student movements
after 1968 had an impact in Italy. The end of the Paris
movement, the downfall of the Prague Spring and the decline
of the German movement all had an impact. The student
movement searched for a more firm ideological base, and
found only the identification with the proletarian class. The
industrial working class, which had previously been accused
of "selling out" to capitalism were again seen as the major
thrust of revolution. The movement of the 1960s, which
could be characterized as utopian, became more ideological
in its orientation. At this point, what had been a loosely
unified movement split into numerous small groups, many of
which were in conflict with each other. Marxist-Leninists,
Trotskyists, Maoists and others all were represented among

the groups which made up the Italian student movement and New Left. Groups, such as the Potere Operaio, were oriented to political violence. In 1969, extreme leftist students were able to link with workers in a struggle to renew the National Labor Contracts. This struggle increased the support for the extreme left on campus. Despite this effort, however, the isolation of the New Left from the working class grew following 1971.

At this period, the social crisis in Italy grew steadily more serious. Two million were unemployed in 1976 and industrial production was at a low level. Foreign capital was necessary to keep the economy going. The government, at this time, did not seem to be able to initiate any innovative policies. Alienation, on and off the campus, spread and political terrorism grew rapidly. The universities, which had expanded rapidly because of their commitment to provide admission to anyone with a high school diploma, became a kind of ghetto for young people without job prospects. Pushed by the economy toward higher education targets, the universities became "parking places" for the unemployed middle classes.

TABLE I

Enrolled Students in Four Western European Countries (Approximate Figures)

	1958-59	1966-67	1968-69	1977-78
France	248, 000	504, 000	630, 000	900, 000
Italy	246, 000	476, 000	604, 000	1, 080, 000
West Germany	300, 000	447, 000	560, 000	800, 000
United Kingdom	257, 000	478, 000	480, 000	500, 000

The problems engendered by overcrowded universities, growing unemployment, and the general economic crisis all contributed to a growing disillusionment, alienation, and radicalization of the student community. Students from middle class or upper working class backgrounds became sympathetic to political terrorism. These are the roots of the 1977 student unrest, which turned from cultural revolution to violent revolt with strong anti-intellectual currents.

Intellectual Unemployment

Graduate unemployment has been an endemic characteristic of

Italian society since 1870. As Ernesto Nathan said in 1906, "We are at the same time too ignorant and too learned; a people afflicted by illiteracy on the one hand, and by a university culture on the other. " In 1880, 48.9% of Italians were illiterate, while in 1901 32.6% remained illiterate (Barbagli, 1974). Despite this illiteracy rate, the universities were at that time producing more graduates than the economic system could absorb. In the 1870s, for example, Italy had a higher proportion of lawyers and physicians than such economically more advanced societies as Germany. More students were in universities, as a proportion of the population, than in France, Germany, or Holland. These figures remain accurate for the recent past, and indicate that Italy is first among European nations in the proportion of the 18-25 age group enrolled in universities. From the 1960s especially, Italian graduates of universities have been too numerous for the economy to absorb.

Large university enrollments are a structural feature of Italian society, dating back a century. Enrollment statistics are not linked with economic growth--they are high during periods of boom as well as in recessions. Indeed, the enrollment situation in Italy is an indication of economic underdevelopment. Enrollments tend to be highest when the possibilities of remunerative employment in the labor market are lowest. Indeed, the proportion of university graduates is highest in southern Italy, where the economic situation is worst. These statistics support the notion, developed by several scholars, that the universities serve as a "parking place" for the unemployed labor force. The more access and attendence to higher education is made easier, the more the institution is able to fulfill its role as a means of absorbing excess labor power. In addition, especially in the humanities faculties, the amount of work expected from students is minimal.

In the economic context of recent years, the Italian university is no longer a "parking place. " It is more like a "tunnel without exit. " It has become a ghetto which isolates the students from the society. The Italian universities have always performed functions which are not common to other European countries. They have legitimated the new ruling classes by providing degrees for them. This was an especially important function in the years following Italian national unity. Thus, the Italian university was quite different than the German model, pioneered in the 19th century by Wilhelm von Humboldt.

The fact that the complaints about the nature of Italian higher education date back more than a century is an indication of the ingrained traditional functions of the university system. The complaint that university graduates, particularly lawyers and teachers, were the "true plague of the South" is commonly heard. The University, particularly in the South, has helped to develop the myth of upward mobility by holding out possibilities of government and professional jobs for graduates. The fact that the children of the lower middle class tend to congregate in the law, humanities and education faculties is a further indication of this situation. This stratum, linked as it is to government employment through the bureaucracy or in the school system, has generally supported Italy's colonial ventures and also supported fascism. Its reward is that of receiving a secure and permanent position in the lower reaches of the power structure, and through the expansion of the bureaucracy.

Hidden for a period during the "economic miracle" of the 1950s, the lower middle class has proved to be an unproductive tertiary sector of the economy, defined by Robert Michels as being "the social class of the intellectual proletariat." This growing group has become an increasingly volatile force in the economic downturn of the seventies. Today, the economy is saturated by university graduates; the excess supply is estimated to amount to no less than 246,000 individuals. The largest surplus is in the humanities, but surpluses are also found in physics, chemistry, mathematics and medicine (Statera, 1978). Data from a recent survey at the University of Rome--the largest university in Europe with an enrollment of more than 150,000--reveal the dramatic reality.

TABLE II

Occupational Status of University Graduates--University of Rome (In Percentages)

	M	F	M and F
Employed	71.9	38.2	55.0
Previously employed	19.3	39.9	29.6
Unemployed	8.8	21.9	15.4

Source: G. Statera, (1977).

Those graduates who have found a stable job after three years as a graduate are only 55% of the total, and the

rate of employment for females is only 40%. In addition to
the fact that 15. 4% of the graduates are unemployed, it is
worth emphasizing that one-third of the employed group hold
marginal jobs. This fact emphasizes the alienation and anger
of this mass of semi-employed intellectuals. Another important fact emerges from this survey: students from relatively
lower socio-economic backgrounds are more likely to regularly attend classes than their colleagues from more affluent
backgrounds. Further, these students tend to graduate with
higher grades. Yet, their career prospects are not as good
as more affluent graduates. Thus, the university no longer
provides much upward mobility for the lower middle classes--
rather, it perpetuates the class order (Statera, 1977).

It is not surprising that political radicalization occurs
in the universities particularly among the students from lower
middle class background. Humanities students are also prone
to radicalism, in part because their prospects for jobs are so
very limited. The lower middle classes wish to use the university as a path to non-manual employment and higher social
status. But higher education no longer serves this function
very adequately. It becomes increasingly apparent that professional jobs will not emerge from university degrees, and
that the degrees themselves have become somewhat debased
as standards in some fields have declined. At this level, the
university no longer serves as a "parking place" but is more
analogous to a parking lot to which one is confined permanently. Graduates in such fields as humanities, law, economics,
business, political science, especially in central and southern
Italy are confined to this "parking lot. "

It is not surprising, given this situation, that many
young people have been attracted to militant radicalism and
to political violence. It is not illogical to try to destroy a
society which seems to offer nothing.

Terroristic Delirium

Italian youth live in a situation of devastating psychological
isolation and marginality. Resentment is caused by a variety
of frustrations related to politics and to the economic situation. Personal goals do not seem practical within the political system, and none of the radical movements offers a satisfactory alternative. Urban isolation increases this outlook
and drugs, violence, crime and a lack of social and political
commitment are part of normal life for many. The social

realities of the cities and the general marginality of the student community lead many to identify with the outcasts and migrants. They have developed theoretical analyses which justify terrorism and urge the destruction of the established social fabric. This terrorist delirium reached a highpoint in March of 1979 when students, common criminals, marginal workers and others engaged in a rash of violence. A group of armed radicals claimed credit for the assassination of a prominent jeweler, who resisted a previous robbery and killed one of his attackers. They justified his killing by linking it with the struggle for revolution, and claimed to have taken their guidance from the Red Brigades. They went on to justify "small crimes" as a means of inducing instability and permitting the workers to avoid work, and urge petty crime on the working class.

This political current is the lowest point in the recent history of the Italian left. Thousands of Italian youth and students are at present supportive of political violence as stressed by the Autonomia Operaia. The universities have, in a way, become gymnasiums for practicing intimidation, overpowering brute force and ignorance. Violence is thriving on social discrimination and desperation. These issues, such as the unemployment of intellectuals, will help to decide the future of Italian democracy. No social system, particularly a democratic one, can permit the marginality of so large and socially important part of its population.

References

Acquaviva, S. (1979). Guerriglia e guerra rivoluzionaria in Italia. Milan: Rizzoli.

Barbagli, M. (1974). Disoccupazione intellettuale e sistema scolastico in Italia. Bologna: Il Mulino.

Statera, G. (1975). Death of a Utopia: The Development and Decline of Student Movements in Europe. New York: Oxford University Press.

Statera, G., ed. (1977). Il destino sociale dei laureati dell'Università di massa. Naples: Liguori.

Statera, G., ed. (1978). Il diploma di disoccupato. Chapter 4. Rome: Lerici.

THE SIXTIES AND THE SEVENTIES:
ASPECTS OF STUDENT ACTIVISM IN WEST GERMANY*

by Wolfe-Dietrich Webler

Introduction

The first twenty years after World War II were called the
"period of reconstruction" in the Federal Republic of Germany.
In this era economic growth was the main force causing social change. In 1966/67 the first recession took place and
one of its political consequences was the formation of the so-
called Grand Coalition of Christian Democrats (C. D. U.) and
Social Democrats (S. P. D.), leaving only the small Liberal
Party (F. D. P.) as a weak parliamentary opposition. This
situation lasted until 1969. Students together with other intellectuals organized an extra-parliamentary opposition which
arose from an anti-nuclear-war movement. At the same
time, the first large demonstration and protests took place
against the Vietnam War, imperialism in Africa and the political system in Greece. When the authorities over-reacted,
more and more students joined the student movement and a
mass movement began.

     The student protest movement in West Germany, like
similar movements in the U. S. A. , France and Italy, took
the form of major demonstrations at universities and in the
cities, mobilizing on some occasions many thousands of people. The situation is different today: some maintain that the
student movement died in 1970 when the Sozialistischer Deutscher Studentenbund (S. D. S.), the most influential organization, dissolved itself. What are the basic aims of the student movement today? Are the aims, organization and forms

*Reprinted by permission of the author and publisher from
Higher Education, 9:1 (March 1980), pp. 155-68. Copyright
©1980 by the Elsevier Scientific Publishing Co. , Amsterdam.

of action different from what they were in the sixties? Did
the underlying critique, demands and programs of the earlier
period produce any lasting changes in society or in the university? Are West German universities in a "continuing academic crisis" (Mason, 1978) as an effect of the student movement? Or is the time between 1968 and 1978 to be called a
decade of change, in contrast with the years from 1948 to
1968 which have been described (Robinsohn and Kuhlmann,
1967) as "Two decades of non-reform in West German education"?

To answer these questions we must first look at the
background to the events of the sixties. Then we shall illustrate some of the reasons for changes in student activities.
Finally, it will be necessary to analyse how differing social
circumstances may have affected student responses: the shift
from activism to privatism, and for some, the further move
to terrorism may help us to understand the changes which
have occurred.

The Student Movement as a Political Impetus for Academic Change

The main concern of the strategies of the West German student movement, which had its peak between 1967 and 1969,
was to analyse and criticise society and to support--partly by
revolutionary means--social change (Bergmann et al., 1968).
But this was only one phase of the student movement. From
the very beginning students were seeking social theories about
the position and task of the university within modern society
and about the structure of society itself (Sozialistischer Deutscher Studentenbund 1965; Nitsch et al., 1965). In addition
to this students experimented with new forms of living together, new ways of socialization, the development of anti-authoritarian types of education and new forms of partnership not
only to seek to change the existing patterns of society but
also to provide solutions to their own personal problems
(Bauss, 1977; Mosler, 1977).

In the student movement it is possible to distinguish
three stages: first, a phase of criticism of common political
problems; then a phase in which students focussed on university problems, and finally, a phase of founding and developing
explicitly political organizations and parties on the basis of
political ideologies. At that time many students found that
in the existing society it was impossible to practice science

without supporting the capitalist system through "Herrschafts-wissen" (governing knowledge). Many active students refused to continue to work in the universities, and shifted their attention to establishing political parties and other forms of social activism (Klüver and Wolf, 1973). Nevertheless the ideas and demands of the student movement were partly adopted by other groups like the "academic assistants" and have had a deep influence on university reforms in West Germany.

In the seventies, the political organizations, competing to win student support, ranged from right wing national democrats (at only a few universities) to some small groups of traditional student "corps," to young Christian Democrats (conservative), various liberal groups, to "Young Socialists," left socialists, traditional Marxists and some Maoist groups. The result of university elections show--with some local exceptions--in general a left/liberal majority. In the sixties, this was different: the S. D. S. was the largest of all German student organizations at that time, and had the most influence on the student movement. In its political development and gradual dissolution it illustrates the main steps of theoretical development and differentiation of the student movement, because new ideas, analyses and programs for change then came only from the left.

The S. D. S. was founded in 1949 as the student branch of the S. P. D. In 1961, when this party adopted a new non-Marxist program, the S. D. S. did not approve and hence it was excluded from the S. P. D. In May 1967, in the first split in S. D. S. , a well-known group of anarchist members was excluded. In September 1968, some members of the "traditionalists' wing" were excluded; in January 1969 these people founded the "Spartakus" group which favoured a Moscow-type of communism. In September 1968 at a conference of the S. D. S. , the Maoist-tendency of some S. D. S. groups, such as those from Berlin and Heidelberg, became obvious and the ideological differences within the S. D. S. paralyzed further activities. The anti-authoritarian movement with the S. D. S. at its centre thus split into many short-term organizations, out of which five main groups can be recognized: (1) the Spartakus-group; (2) the Maoist Communist group (Marxist-Leninist) and its sister organization, the "Kommunistischer Bund Westdeutschland" (K. B. W.); (3) the socialist "basic groups" acting as typical heirs of the anti-authoritarian movement; (4) the so-called spontaneous groups, directed by "spontaneous needs of the masses, " hostile to any steady organization, acting for, and instead of, the workers; (5) small local groups of socialists, since 1969 supported by the "Socialist Bureau" at Offenbach. In March 1970, the S. D. S. federal executive committee declared its formal dissolution, and the last existing group at Heidelberg was outlawed after a battle with the police after an anti-imperialist demonstration in June 1970. The student movement in the traditional sense had come to an end, but all the different groups continued their policies in different directions under new conditions. For many of them higher education became less important than political work in the industrial sector, inner-city problems, and the trade unions.

The S. D. S. was the theoretical brains, the avant garde of the student movement. How did it succeed? To show the change in social conditions, which formed student policies in the seventies, we can look back at the sixties. In an international comparison, Halliday (1969, p. 315) started his answer with two questions: "How did the extraordinary transformation of West German politics by the S. D. S. take place? Why, in particular, did it achieve such a rapid and deep radicalization of the student body?" He found two main reasons, the theoretical preparedness and the structure of studies in Germany: "In the first place, the Germans were theoretically and ideologically prepared for taking the revolutionary road. The examples of the American student movement, of the Persians and of the Dutch Provos had been studied. The West German students were also much more receptive to political theory than, say, the British. " In his opinion the influence of the Frankfurt School of sociologists, Adorno, Benjamin, Marcuse, Habermas and others, had meant that students were conversant with Marxism. "Concepts such as exploitation, repression, manipulation and liberation were understood and accepted. Subsequently the influence of Mao, Guevara and Debray became important. " Moreover, Halliday pointed out, this general ideological preparedness had been of crucial importance in shaping the student movement once it had started.

As a second material factor Halliday pointed out that the length and conditions of university study in West Germany at that time facilitated the growth of the student movement. "Students have always been free to move from one university to another, accumulating the necessary amount of study. They are free to choose when to take their examinations, and can start their theses before taking them, provided they have attended a small number of seminars. " Because of these conditions he resumes, "students can take time off to organize and be politically active in a way that would be impossible with a shorter course and more frequent examinations. There is also more time for students to become politically formed, more time for them to think, read and struggle before they are re-absorbed into capitalist society." Despite some over-generalization, Halliday's analysis is correct. It points to some of the quite different conditions currently existing in the German universities. Mobilization was caused by the following factors: structural (rigid, idealistic norm-orientation of students, marginality of the student role, absence of influential conservative milieu), situational (availability of the S. D. S., of Dutschke as a charismatic leader) and finally common political factors (Vietnam, Cold War policy, Grand Coalition, emergency law) (Kaase, 1971, p. 166). Because of the idealistic orientation, concepts of high morality (justice, equality, freedom against oppression, imperialism, etc.) found support among students quite easily. The contradictions between strong idealism and the realities of German society produced militant activism.

Student Activism Since 1970

The student activity of 1966/70 led to various ways of coping with the political frustration caused by the impossibility of social change: (1) very few students took the path to terrorism; (2) many retreated from political activity into different kinds of isolation and privacy; (3) others turned away from university politics and moved into civil politics; (4) the greater part of active students tried to continue the student movement in a way adapted to the new conditions.

On the radical left, there was a group of people very sensitive to the injustice of the capitalist system and with a sense of guilt due to worldwide imperialism. This group despaired of political change "within the system," and argued that revolutionary violence against the system would be justified (Eckert, 1978; Fetscher, 1978). In April 1968, two department stores in Frankfurt were bombed and the perpetrators, when finally sentenced, told the court that they destroyed property as a protest against the indifference of the society toward the war in Vietnam. These individuals were Baader, Ensslin, Söhnlein and Proll. In May 1970, Baader was freed from prison by three women, one of whom was Ulrike Meinhof (Schwind, 1978, pp. 26-31). These were the beginnings of the Baader-Meinhof terrorist movement. The first generation of this movement consisted largely of students and while the later terrorist activities of the Red Army Faction had little to do with the student movement, the roots are clearly in the campus struggles of the sixties. Terrorism is, of course, only one of a number of different ways of reacting to the same social structures. The "Bundesjugendkuratorium, " a board of scientists counselling the German Federal Government in questions of youth-policy, has recently made this point.

Another type of retreat from an unaccepted society is to escape into youth sects, into privacy, self-experience-groups or total individualization by alcohol, drugs, suicide or psychiatric sickness. A growing number of students went in these directions and the university authorities showed little interest in assisting them.

A third way of responding to political conditions was to turn away from university politics and move into civil politics. This was done because of the realization that university problems were marginal in terms of the "class-struggle" and the attraction of cooperating with workers and of joining existing or even founding new left wing parties.

The fourth way--the most favored--was to continue in the student movement as it had been modified to meet the new circumstances of the seventies. The student organizations themselves have changed but so too have the forms of action even though the problems being tackled are still the ones familiar in the 1960s.

Eight factors seem to have influenced the development of contemporary student activism most; these factors are discussed below.
1.   an improved theoretical analysis of state policy and its relation to the economy;
2.   the new social democratic-liberal coalition of 1969 and the Federal Government's promised reforms;
3.   the newly established student participation in academic decision-making;
4.   changes in the student population;
5.   the numerus-clausus-problem;
6.   labour-market and employment problems;
7.   growing tendency for state authorities to limit student political aims;
8.   the decree against radicals in public services, the so-called "Berufsverbot" of 1972.

First of all, there was the experience of the sixties.

Social theory had a considerably strong influence on the student movement. The "critical theory" of the Frankfurt school of sociology was followed by a new perception of Marxist theory and its applications to "modern industrial" or "late capitalist" society. A new chapter of sociological analysis and the development of new theories about the state and the relationship between the economy and government policy developed. Using these theories, people worked out explanatory models for social change and failure. The borders between factions of the New Left were marked by different theoretical positions.

One of the effects of these new models was the acquisition of long term political perspectives. Hitherto, students had tended to a very short term view of problems in their politics. Students had previously measured success and failure in the time span of the student career, and this had led, naturally, to considerable frustration and even a tendency toward violence when social change in three or four years proved to be an impossible goal. The new more sophisticated approach permitted students to measure political movements in a longer time frame; the better integrated student groups were politically more realistic. As students recognized the transitory nature of the student experience, they prepared themselves for longer term political involvement, and many shifted away from the confrontation tactics of the sixties.

While the Grand Coalition had much influence on mobilization and radicalization of students, the new Federal Government resulting from the elections in 1969, consisting of Social Democrats and Liberals with Willy Brandt as Chancellor had a demobilizing effect. This government raised many hopes in the students by promising large scale social reform. Observing the failure of the greater part of this program, students learned much about the structure of West German society. They also got an idea of the time which is necessary for social change.

Another demobilizing, integrating effect came with the introduction of student participation in academic decision-making. According to the new university laws of many of the "Lander" (federal states) from 1968 onwards, student representatives were elected to academic bodies and commissions, with on average about 25% of the seats. The groups supporting the idea of representation developed an institutional strategy and having achieved a measure of success became convinced of the correctness of this policy. The greater their success the more likely were they to maintain a policy of moderation.

TABLE I

Changed Population in Higher Education in West Germany
(Numbers in Brackets Indicate Students at Universities)

	1966	1976
Working Class youth in higher education	10. 3%	19. 2%
	(6. 5%)	(16. 0%)
Students with professional experience	3. 7%	6. 2%
Delayed students because of numerus-clausus		36. 0%

Source: Der Bundesminister für Bildung and Wissenschaft
(1978).

Changes in the student population meant that the new generation of students had different experience, feelings and aims.

The number of children from working-class people increased in higher education in West Germany from 10. 3% in 1966 to 19. 2% in 1976.   The number of students with professional experience increased from 3. 7% to 6. 2% at the same time (Table I).   Students who had to wait several years for university admission were nearly unknown in 1966 (Der Bundesminister für Bildung and Wissenschaft, 1978).   Because they were getting professional experience during this time, these students behaved in a way different from former students with only school experience the majority of whom were of middle class origin.

The numerus-clausus-problem has been a further factor against activism.   In West Germany people become eligible for university by passing the final school examination after 13 years of school.   Since 1965, the number of people who wanted to study increased much faster than the expanding universities could cope with, and the numerus clausus device was used to set a maximum number of university admissions. The average of all the marks in the final school examination was introduced as a criterion for university admission.   Increased competition for better marks caused an uncritical adaptation to the norms of the teacher, and children learned these norms and met them, in the hope of improving their chances. Recent university policy has led to studies being organized more stringently than before. This was introduced to give students more "orientation," in contrast with the traditional German pattern of academic studies which left the student very free. These new students had to take part in more and increasingly crowded seminars and lectures and to complete more assignments than before. Having little time left for reflection, this new generation of students did not want to ask too many questions, but preferred to get on with their training.

Change was also caused by growing labour-market and employment problems, particularly for teachers. While the generation of the sixties had good opportunities to find the work of their choice, their followers felt personal anxiety concerning employment. As a result, more people tried to get good marks (in certain parts of West Germany students were accepted as teachers only if they had good grades) or to get an additional qualification. In such circumstances conspicuous political behavior might well be considered undesirable.

There was also an increasing tendency for state authorities to seek to limit student political ambitions. Authorities were particularly opposed to the anti-Establishment resolutions of student organizations in many German universities. These organizations were representative of all students, since membership was mandatory. One of the first steps, beginning in West Berlin, was to abolish these student organizations as part of new university legislation. In addition, legislation was passed to discipline students. In some places conservative students went to the courts to prevent the expenditure of student funds for political causes. There was a widespread attempt to root out student activism through legal and legislative means.

These were effective means to paralyze student politicians, but an even better one seemed to be the so-called Radikalen-Erlass or Berufsverbot, a decree promulgated in 1972, declaring that everybody who wants to enter the public service has to guarantee to defend the constitution. This, taken alone was not very alarming, but the bureaucratic system established to seek out "constitutional enemies" turned out to be not unlike "McCarthyism." Prospective teachers, who had passed exams and wanted to start teaching at school, were often confronted with pamphlets or petitions they had signed during their university studies, with photos of demonstrations they had participated in, and were told there was too much doubt about their attitude towards the constitution to accept them as teachers. It is not surprising that in consequence students often hesitated to choose a socially critical theme for their written examination, fearing indirect punishment by the authorities. Lately, the growing protests against this unjust process succeeded in obtaining rulings against certain severe cases and even caused politicians to speak out against the decree. Nevertheless, there is still deep suspicion about the decree and this affects the students' policy.

Unlike the sixties, the student strategy of the seventies has no longer been based on mass demonstrations and protest. This change is based on the altered situation both in the universities and in society at large. The following section will seek to explain the reasons for this change in strategy. Further, we shall relate the student movement to some basic data on current student attitudes and opinions at the University of Bielefeld (Holtmann, 1980). Although this survey may not be fully representative of all German students, it is nevertheless regarded as being indicative.

In 1968-69 Allerbeck (1971, p. 192) explained the intensity of protest and attractiveness of the student movement to the mass of students by the extent to which the students identified themselves with their roles as students in society. One of the indicators he used, was the students' opinion concerning whether or not studies are primarily regarded as having an instrumental function i.e., aimed at preparing for a career. In the seventies the majority of the students had a different conception of their roles from those held by the students of 1968. This led to an increasing conflict between role-expectation and role-conception. It is true that students still consider their roles as marginal, but for these students identification with the "traditional" university role-expectations (usually involving non-conformity and political activism) seems to have decreased dramatically. Studies are regarded not as an end in themselves but rather as a phase of transition before getting a job. Therefore, studies assume something of an instrumental character for two different groups of students. For the less politically minded who aim at rapid professional preparation, and for students who are oriented towards socialist theories, who consider their studies partly as a theoretical preparation for their later political involvement within their jobs. Towards these ends, both groups are not interested in staying at university for too long. The number of students who tend to take studies as a phase to be passed quickly can be illustrated by the Holtmann survey: 51% of the students wanted to finish quickly.

Only a minority of students who mainly have concentrated on their own private or student problems still have a high role-identification. This type of student does not make plans for a longer period than a few terms, partly because of a lack of reflection and partly because of presumably poor expectations with regard to professional opportunities. These people regard their studies as an end in themselves.

Current student attitudes, as described in the Holtmann survey, can provide some insights into the status of the student movement:
16% of the students had not yet developed a professional aim. Most of these students were followers of a liberal group (Sozialliberaler Hochschulbund, S. I. H.).

In assessing their professional chances, 25% expected them to be good, and 27% expected them to be bad. The political distribution of the latter were basic groups first, left socialists (Sozialistischer Hochschulbund, S. H. B.) second, and the Spartakus third; all more "moderate" groups were on the more hopeful side.

Answering the question as to whether or not they could reckon on obtaining a position after finishing their studies, 31% answered "no" and 51% of these belonged to basic groups.

Asked if they intended to study over a longer period of time or if they wanted to finish as soon as possible, 49% wanted to take time--with 77% of that number belonging to basic groups. These results indicate that these students consider their studies primarily as non-instrumental. This indicator is part of the variable "role-identification. " Allerbeck has proved the correlation of this indicator with role-identification and student radicalism (1971, p. 192). Moreover, the data illustrate that this group of students with high role-identification consists to a great extent of followers of the leftist basic groups. It is out of these that students can be mobilized for political activism. These leftist groups are relatively small at individual universities and their numbers would become significant only in a national demonstration. According to the survey at Bielefeld, basic groups were regarded by the students to be in fifth place on a popularity scale of groups after the Young Socialists, liberals and two groups of left socialists (S. B. /S. H. B.).

More and more students are affected by a norm-system imposed on them from outside the university, by anticipated norms of their future jobs because of a high degree of unemployment for academics, or by political repression as an effect of the decree against radicals in the public services. In so far as students accept Marxist theories they adopt the norms and values, including behavioral norms, which come from the workers' world. At the end of the sixties, among politically left students, the conviction of marginality grew after long debates over the possible role of students and intellectuals in the class struggle. In addition, they learned by experience that students can never be the avant garde of the proletariat, and that mass movements of students cannot replace masses of workers. This kind of orientation is influential in groups like the Maoist groups, the spontaneous groups, the Spartakus groups, the left socialists and the Young Socialists; in other words nearly the whole political basis formerly bearing or supporting the student movement of the sixties now has a very different motivation.

This adoption of leftist norms drawn from outside the university indicates two trends: the tendency to seek potential partners for alliances in large external political organizations, such as trade unions and political parties and the wish to establish solidarity with the unorganized workers, especially foreign and unskilled assembly-line workers i. e. , the real mass-workers. These so-called Sponti-groups and the Socialist Bureau often feel a deep hostility against large organizations, particularly trade unions, or at least against their present politics.

Both of these orientations delay identification with the "traditional" student role in different ways. The political orientation towards large organizations by the first group forces some conformity with the contents and the forms of struggle of these parent organizations. Deviations will be punished by the withdrawal of support, financial and political, from the student groups or by total exclusion as the S. P. D. did twice with its student organizations. Students have few opportunities to influence these large organizations, and they tend to lose their identification as students in this context. To answer the question of how many students are affected by this influence, of course, first of all one has to distinguish active members from mere followers of these organizations. The Bielefeld survey shows:

• that 10% of the students were members of a union,

• a further 45% could "imagine easily" being members,
• and an additional 28% thought this would be "thinkable. "

This shows how large the group of potential members
could be. In the survey there was no item concerning party
membership. Nevertheless, Holtmann found that the Young
Socialists and the liberals (who stay close to the S. P. D. and
F. D. P.) got most popularity votes, and the Young Socialists
are normally members of the federal party. In the general
political party popularity question, the "green list" (Ecological Party) was in front followed by the S. P. D. Earlier in
the seventies, this was still a little bit different. In a nationwide survey in 1973-74 (when green lists did not yet exist)
students voted on a popularity scale for political parties. They
voted 46% in favour of the Social Democrats, 17% in favour
of the Free Democrats (F. D. P. , the liberal party), 13% for
the Christian Democrats (C. D. U. /C. S. U.), 5% for the Communists (D. K. P.) and 15% voted for none of these parties of
the parliamentary system (no answer: 4%). In the social
sciences there was a remarkably high percentage of followers
of the D. K. P. (16%) and of students who did not vote for any
of these parties (28%), (Infratest, 1974).

From these results we can gather that large political
organizations have a deep influence over the aims and forms
of student policy today, despite the extra freedoms achieved
by the student organizations. All these findings indicate a
very radical element in the university. Basic groups and
spontaneous groups do not concentrate on their own personal
problems as students or on their interests in the university,
but focus instead upon political work at factories, in inner-
city areas, etc. Their behavioral norms are influenced by
the practical and ideological considerations which derive from
their political intentions. Because of their militancy and their
impulsiveness (Kuckuck, 1974) one can speak of radicalisms;
but these groups face difficulties in recruiting members in
the university because they are hardly able to communicate
with students who are not very much politicised. Thus, their
influence on students had declined, as the fifth place in the
popularity rating scale among students shows.

Although the number of working class youth at university has doubled, radicalism has not been strengthened. On
the contrary, it has decreased considerably. There is some
doubt about Allerbeck's statement that politically minded working class children as students tend to be radical. One would
expect this group to be successful in entering university by

means of adaption or to be characterized at least by a critical, leftist, nevertheless pragmatic attitude. This view is
supported by Holtmann's results: working class students prefer a liberal group most (S. I. H.) and the left socialists'
(S. H. B.) are next. Even if you take the low income and
educational standard of the students' fathers as variables,
most of these students are followers of the Young Socialists,
liberals (S. I. H.) and left socialists. The trend among lower-
income students is toward the Social Democrats, and a more
leftist radicalism is not evident.

In contrast, middle and upper class children find their
way around the university more easily than working class
children. They seem to be more mobile and have more personal independence. For them, any certain social order does
not have the relevance of a "law," but rather, there is a
variety of orders to choose from. That is why they are
ready to criticize, to question things, to protest against any
grievance, to think of alternatives. Feeling financially secure they are less uncertain about their future. Holtmann
found that the children of professionals and of highly educated
fathers were most numerous among the followers of the far-
left basic groups. Second in popularity among this strata was
the liberal student group (L. H. V.) or the student group of
the conservative Christian Democratic Party. Students with
fathers who have high incomes show a different political tendency; the Liberals were in first place, but the far-left basic
groups were in second.

The increasing number of students who either obtained
their university admission via night school or started their
studies with a delay due to the numerus clausus seemed to
be critical, but also realistic and goal-oriented. In this
group, an instrumental conception of study prevails. They
are older, having gathered professional experience in the
meantime. Therefore, they tend less towards radicalism
than freshmen coming directly from high school. According
to the Holtmann survey this group is not politcally homogeneous. It tends to prefer (in order) the Spartakus, Young
Socialists and the R. C. D. S.

Conclusion

We can see that out of the four variables for determining
whether students are "backing the student movement" (role-
identification, extent of the perceived contrast between norms

and attitudes of students and of the rest of society, political attitudes of parents, and the political climate of the different disciplines) which were interpreted by Allerbeck, at least the first two have lost importance. The potential for radical protest which supported the activists in the sixties has almost disappeared in the seventies. Explaining this phenomenon we have to keep in mind many different reasons which together have affected this development. The situation depends as much on the state's policy as on the different theoretical backgrounds or on the influence of large political organizations and finally, on changes within the student population.

In the seventies the students' strategies are marked by cooperation with other social groups whereas in the sixties actions were with few exceptions merely student protest. Inside the university, student policy is much less spectacular. Only the central strategy of the sixties, namely to explore the "true structure of the capitalistic system" by provoking confrontations with the authorities has been abandoned. Spectacular actions have been replaced by less perceivable but continuously effective means like personal negotiations with professors and heads of departments, resolutions of the student body, attending of proceedings of the departmental governing body or pushing through the students' demand by using the powers of student representatives in academic government.

References

Allerbeck, K. (1971). "Eine sozialstrukturelle Erklärung von Studentenbewegungen in hochentwickelten Industriegesellschaften," pp. 179-201 in K. Allerbeck and L. Rosenmayr, ed., Aufstand der Jugend? München: Juventa.
Bauss, G. (1977). Die Studentenbewegung der sechziger Jahre. Köln: Pahl-Rugenstein.
Bergmann, U., Dutschke, R., Lefèvre, W. and Rabehl, B. (1968). Rebellion der Studenten oder die neue Opposition. Reinbek: Rowohlt.
Der Bundesminister für Bildung und Wissenschaft (BMBW), ed., (1978). Grund- und Struk-turdaten 1978. München: Gersbach.
Eckert, R. (1978). "Terrorismus als Karriere," pp. 109-132 in H. Geissler, ed., Der Weg in die Gewalt. München: Olzog.
Fetscher, I. (1978). "Ausweg aus einer Verzweiflung--über die gesellschaftlich-politischen Ursachen des Terrorismus," Das Parlament 3: 8.

Halliday, F. (1969). "Students of the World Unite," in A. Cockburn and R. Blackburn, eds., Student Power. Harmondsworth: Penguin.

Holtmann, D. (1980). Gesellschaftliche Lage und BewuBtsein von Studenten. (Unpublished survey, to be published Autumn, 1980). Bielefeld.

Infratest Sozialforschung, eds., (1974). Hochschulbarometer. Befragung von Studierenden. Wintersemester 1973/74. Zusammenfassung wichtiger Ergebnisse. München: Infratest.

Kaase, M. (1971). "Die politische Mobilisierung von Studenten in der BRD," pp. 155-178 in K. Allerbeck and L. Rosenmayr, eds., Aufstand der Jugend? München: Juventa.

Klüver, J. and Wolf, F. O. (1973). Wissenschaftskritik und sozialistische Praxis. Konsequenzen aus der Studentenbewegung. Frankfurt/Main: Fischer.

Kuckuck, M. (1974). Student und Klassenkampf. Studentenbewegung in der BRD seit 1967. Hamburg: Association.

Mason, H. L. (1978). "The continuing academic crisis in West Germany: Perceptions and imponderables," A. A. U. P. Bulletin March: pp. 12-15.

Mosler, P. (1977). Was wir wollten, was wir wurden. Reinbek: Rowohlt.

Nitsch, W., Gerhardt, U., Offe, C. and PreuB, U. K. (1965). Hochschule in der Demokratie. Neuwied-Berlin: Luchterhand.

Robinsohn, S. B. and Kuhlmann, J. C. (1967). "Two decades of non-reform in West German Education," Comparative Education Review, 11: 311-330.

Schwind, H. -D. (1978). "Zur Entwicklung des Terrorismus in der Bundesrepublik Deutschland," pp. 25-44 in H. -D. Schwind, ed., Ursachen des Terrorismus, Berlin-New York: De Gruyter.

Sozialistischer Deutscher Studentenbund (S. D. S.), ed., (1965). Hochschule in der Demokratie. Denkschrift des SDS zur Hochschulreform. Frankfurt/Main: Neue Kritik.

JAPANESE STUDENT ACTIVISM IN THE 1970s*

Michiya Shimbori
in association with
T. Ban, K. Kono, H. Yamazaki, Y. Kano,
M. Murakami and T. Murakami

Before 1960 all Japanese student activism was instigated by the national federation of student governments (Zengakuren). In 1960, however, the Zengakuren was split by antagonism arising from different strategies of opposition proposed by various sects against the U.S. -Japan Security Treaty. Throughout the latter half of the 1960s, during a period of student unrest and anti-war movements, the organization of Zengakuren became more and more chaotic. Three distinct stages in Japanese student activism since around 1965 can be identified (Shimbori, 1963; 1964).

The first stage (1965/1970) was a period of mixed cooperation and struggle between ever-diversifying sects. The New Left continued to split into more organizations, while they cooperated in campus revolts with each other and with general student bodies as well as with non-sect radicals (unorganized radicals). The second stage (1971/1975) was a period of violent and bloody struggles for hegemony among these sects, usually called uchi-geba (uchi means within, inner, or inter, and geba comes from the German word, Gewalt, i.e., violence). Sects attacked each other to destroy forcibly those with different ideologies and tactics. Table I shows the number of students killed by this kind of violence. The third stage (1976 onwards) has seen increasing terrorism by an anarchist group which has become disillusioned with the New Left sects. This group, whose radicalism has recently attracted a wide concern owing to its escalating anti-

---

*Reprinted by permission of the author and publisher from Higher Education, 9:1 (March 1980), pp. 139-59. Copyright ©1980 by the Elsevier Scientific Publishing Co., Amsterdam.

TABLE I

Number of Students Killed in Uchi-geba.

1969	1970	1971	1972	1973	1974	1975	1976	1977
2	2	5	2	2	11	19	3	10

Source: Daigaku-sekai, March, 1979.

social activities, supports the ideology held by Ryu Ota that
the center of world revolution should move from the proletariat of the advanced industrial countries to the deprived proletariat such as the Ainu aborigines in Japan. They have directly attacked enterprises and organizations such as Mitsu-
bishi and Keidanren (Japan Federation of Economic Organizations), which they consider to be discriminatory and exploit-
ive, by killing their leaders and destroying their buildings.
Ten such attacks occurred in 1977, five times as many as
in 1976. However, while radicalism and violence on the part
of a small number of professional activists has been escalating, the majority of students have increasingly retreated from
activism, as is shown in Table II.

TABLE II

Estimated Number of Student Members of the New Left (in
1,000's)

1972	1973	1974	1975	1976	1977	1978
44	37	30	20	18	15	13

Source: Yearbook of Education (Tokyo: Gyosei, 1977) and
Asahi Journal, June 23, 1978.

Needless to say, there was much overlap in each of
these three periods. There is still frequent uchi-geba against
the opening of the new international airport in Narita, the
sects sometimes cooperate with each other. Their primary
interest is now in social issues and most of their activism
is conducted off-campus (Shimbori, 1968).

Campus Calm

This trend is the result of both domestic and world situations.
The new campus calm is due partly to the new Law for Re-

covering Order in Universities but also to a decreased global prosperity which is reflected in rising unemployment and more pragmatic attitudes amongst most students. This change can be summarized as follows, under the headings world, domestic and educational situations.

World Situation

When the U. S. began to bomb North Vietnam in 1965, protest against the war became a common rallying point for student movements all over the world. The general worldwide sense of discontentment among students was heightened by anachronistic systems of higher education and various other problems in many countries. Despite superficial differences, there was a common pattern in the student movements in most countries. For example, the American SDS (Students for a Democratic Society), had as its original goal the emancipation of blacks and abolition of racial discrimination, but it grew into a large organization which included Marxists, anarchists and liberals, and focused much of its protest against the Vietnam War. A similar pattern was followed by the Japanese Zenkyoto (National Union of the Militant Students). Toward the end of the 1960s two groups, Peace for Viet-Nam! and Citizens Union (Be-hei-ren) led by Makoto Oda and the Committee of Anti-War Youth (Hansen Seinen Iinkai) acted as spearheads of activity for various other groups. On October 10, 1969 Be-hei-ren was able to mobilize some 32, 000 New Left students for national unified movements against the war.

Thus the world situation, especially the Vietnam War, was an instrumental factor in student movements in many western nations. The end of the war in January 1973 dissolved this common target for New Left radicals and student movements became calmer. The general student populations withdrew from activism and the small numbers of professionalized radicals looked for new targets. In America and Germany, although there was no uchi-geba radical sect, militant groups such as the SLA and the Baader-Meinhof group spearheaded a number of terrorist attacks using bombs and guns in the same way as the Japanese Red Army (Nihon Sekigun) (Shimbori, 1971).

Aside from such internal targets, the increasing tension in the Middle East provided an international focus for radical groups. For example, the Fourth Middle East War in October 1973 provoked the Palestinian guerrillas into a new militancy. The Japanese Red Army which recruited its leaders from among ex-student radicals, has always claimed solidarity with the Palestinian Arabs and been active in its declared war against world capitalism. In May 1972, Kozo Okamoto, a Red Army sniper, killed 27 people at the Tel-Aviv International Airport. In July 1973 the Red Army hijacked a Japan Airlines jumbo jet. In January 1974 it attacked the Shell Oil Base at Singapore. In September 1974 it occupied the French Embassy at the Hague, and in September 1974 it hijacked another JAI plane.

Domestic Situation

The Middle East situation was a focus for Red Army terrorism but more serious was the effect of the worldwide energy crisis in October 1973. Upon the outbreak of the Fourth Middle East War, OPEC declared a decrease in oil exports and raised its prices fourfold. This resulted in world inflation, especially in Japan where the industrial sector depends heavily upon imported oil. Economic order in Japan was partially restored by 1974. Simultaneously, cars and electronic equipment were so heavily exported that the country's balance of international trade showed constant improvement which was reflected in an ever-increasing rate for the yen and accompanying international approbation.

The decreased productivity of the Japanese industrial sector has been followed by a sharply reduced job market which has made it difficult in recent years for university graduates to find suitable jobs. As is seen in Table III, only 70.7% of all graduates in 1976 found jobs, the lowest ratio since 1950 when the number was 63.8%. In 1978, more than 40,000 university graduates did not find employment.

TABLE III

Ratios of Employed and Unemployed University Graduates

	1969	1970	1971	1972	1973	1974	1975	1976	1977	1978
Employed	79.0	78.0	78.0	75.7	75.3	76.8	74.3	70.7	72.0	71.9
Unemployed	8.0	8.2	8.0	9.3	8.6	7.6	9.8	11.6	11.0	11.2

Source: Survey Reports of School Statistics. Ministry of Education.

In this difficult job market, most Japanese students

have become more conservative, realistic and apolitical, putting greater emphasis on good grades and making favorable impressions on prospective employers. This new attitude is reflected in Table IV.

In contrast to the period of campus unrest, Japanese students today attend classes regularly, tend to be passive and obedient, and make a clear distinction between their private lives and their academic work.

TABLE IV

Attitudes of Youth (%)

	1972	1977
Question: Are you satisfied with your school life?		
1. Satisfied	17. 2	24. 2
2. More or less satisfied	37. 5	39. 2
3. More or less dissatisfied	27. 7	22. 6
4. Dissatisfied	17. 5	9. 9
Question: If you were dissatisfied with society, what steps would you take?		
1. I would use my voting rights but nothing more.	54. 5	39. 3
2. I would actively resort to a variety of means permitted by law.	36. 6	26. 0
3. I would resort to violence and/or other illegal means if necessary.	3. 6	3. 2
4. I would retreat from society.	4. 8	13. 4

Source: The Prime Minister's Office, Report of the International Survey of the Attitude of Youth in Several Countries, 1978.

Education Situation

The country's quieter campuses were due not only to the international and economic situations but also to the Law for Recovering Order in Universities which had been passed in 1969 and was to be in effect for five years. This law provided university presidents with considerable power to settle campus conflicts and gave the Minister of Education the right to close troubled campuses and, in cases where unrest continued for longer than nine months, to suspend faculty. In

effect, it meant that by the end of 1970 when the law was en-
acted, most of the universities with student unrest had resorted
to the intervention of armed police to dismiss students who
were occupying buildings and to restore order by force.   Before the passage of the law, such an action would have caused
outrage amongst students and faculty as a threat to academic
freedom.   The law proved to be quite effective.   While 147
higher institutions were barricaded by student radicals in
1967, only 31 were barricaded in 1970.

In addition to this immediate remedy, the government
tried to structure the new universities in a more effective
manner.   The governing Liberal Democrat Party in June 1969
established a Round Table on New Universities and published
a master plan for new universities in August 1969.   Initial
plans called for an investment of a thousand billion yen over
20 years to establish 15 or 20 new universities.   In actual
fact only the University of Tsukuba was opened in 1973.   However, other non-university institutions of higher learning were
developed on the new model, including independent medical
colleges, graduate schools of teacher education, and graduate
schools of technology.   A new Open University based on the
British model will soon begin operation.   The initial idea
of an open university won support partly because such an
institution would be immune from concentrated student attacks.

The administrative infrastructure of the new model was
found to be particularly effective.   It is characterized by a
centralization of power in contrast to the traditional and prevailing system of decentralized departmentalism and autonomy
of individual faculties.   Further, non-academic persons can
be elected to the board of trustees.   Although this is a common practice in American universities, it is often regarded
as antithetical to faculty autonomy in Japan.

Simultaneous with this governmental effort to design
more efficient and powerful administrations, many Japanese
universities attempted to reform their own administrative systems.   83% of all the universities published reform plans in
1971, and 54% tried to improve their administrations in 1973
(see Table V).   A major thrust of this reform has been to
give a stronger voice to junior faculty in the election of university authorities, such as presidents or deans, and to allow
them full membership in faculty associations.

Effect of Student Movements

The effects of student movements upon the Japanese universities can be seen from two perspectives: firstly, how the universities reacted to the problems raised by the dissenting students (i. e. , institutional reform to remove the direct causes of student unrest); and secondly, what natural or inherent changes the movements carried.

In 1969 a vast number of reform plans were proposed by both the universities and the government. They were concerned mostly with education and research, administration, ideals and principles, student problems and so on. Table VI documents some of these plans. Unfortunately, few of them

TABLE VI

Proposed Plans of Reform (1968/1970)

Subject of proposal (number)	Number of proposed plans				
	1968	1969	1970	1967 or 1971	Total
I. Outer bodies					
(1) Government Councils (11)	0	10	5	1	16
(2) Japanese Congress of Science (1)	2	3	4	0	9
(3) University Associations (4)	3	7	14	1	25
(4) Political Parties (4)	5	14	2	0	21
(5) Other Organizations (7)	3	7	2	0	12
Total (27)	13	41	27	2	83
II. Universities					
(1) National Universities (52)	9	136	97	7	249
(2) Municipal Universities (8)	2	12	1	0	15
(3) Private Universities (9)	10	30	22	7	69
Total (79)	21	178	120	14	333
Grand Total (106)	34	219	147	16	416

Source: K. Kitamura, "Preliminary survey of the trend of university reform, " Reference (June, 1971): 92.

were actually put into practice so that the contradictions and dilemmas which the student movement disclosed cannot be said to have been fundamentally resolved. The fact that campuses are now calmer despite these unresolved issues, shows that the student movements were not primarily aimed at resolving internal problems but were more focussed on political issues.

Although large scale and fundamental reform was not realized, a number of minor changes have been instituted on a piecemeal basis. This is particularly true of the level of general education offered by the universities. Undoubtedly the mass of students were dissatisfied with the type of general education that they were being offered and were in agreement with much of the criticism made by the student movement. There was much dissatisfaction with the style of general education being offered to freshmen and sophomores. Generally speaking, it was viewed as inferior to the education given in the professional faculties. General education faculties had larger numbers of students, poorer equipment, and smaller budgets than professional courses in the physical sciences, technology, medicine, etc. Further, general education curricula were often similar to high school courses. Therefore substantial reform was necessary to upgrade the level of general education and to integrate general and professional education courses. Initially this reform was curricular, not institutional. In 1971 and 1972, the criteria for university accreditation were reformed in accordance with the request of the Association of National Universities. As a result, most universities curtailed the requirement for a minimum number of units in general education, began to offer integrated or comprehensive general education courses, and designed "vertical" curricula, i. e. , general education courses were offered to juniors and seniors and professional education courses were offered to freshmen and sophomores. Table VII shows the pattern of changes in general education in national universities from 1968 to 1973.

The reform of general education was not limited only to curriculum reform but also has included faculty reform. At Hiroshima University, the third largest national university, the faculty of general education was abolished after more than four years' deliberation, and replaced with the faculty of integrated sciences. This was one of the few universities which successfully implemented comprehensive reform. The success of the Hiroshima University reform had some effect on other universities in that they too tried to introduce faculties of integrated sciences. Further, universities like Osaka and Na-

TABLE VII

Numbers of Reformed General Education Courses in National
Universities

Content of Reform	1968	1969	1970	1971	1972	1973	Total
Opening comprehensive classes	0	3	3	10	5	9	30
Opening seminars of general education	0	2	5	5	2	1	15
Opening new general education classes	0	2	4	8	1	0	15
Emphasizing basic of professional education	0	1	8	28	9	10	56
Extending and appreciating electives	0	1	12	25	10	5	55
Changing the grades for attendance to a class	0	10	23	15	9	7	64
Changing the number of required units	0	4	9	21	6	8	48
Others	2	4	9	3	4	1	23

Source: M. Seki, "Essay on general education movement, "
Daigaku Ronshu, vol. 3, Hiroshima University, 1975.

goya made partial reforms in foreign language and physical
education programs. At the present time approximately one
third to one half of all the national universities are reviewing their general education programs. However, the basic
problems of overcrowded classes at the undergraduate level
cannot be solved with such reform and the general dissatisfaction of students in the general education programs will
continue to be greater than that of students in the professional education programs.

The private universities, in contrast, are less concerned with problems of general education, and more with
the difficulty of securing financial support from the government. Until the late 1960s, Japan's private universities,
which are supported neither by donations from industry and
alumni as in America, nor by government as in England, had
to depend entirely upon the fees of students. Consequently,
tuition fees were much higher than at the national universities, maximum numbers of students were accepted, and minimum numbers of teachers employed in order to balance the
university budgets. Constant fee increases and large classes
were the inevitable result of this situation and caused much

student dissatisfaction which frequently erupted into open revolt. Partly in an effort to contain student unrest, the Ministry of Education began to give financial aid to private universities in 1970. Initially, support was in the amount of 130 billion yen annually, but this figure has been steadily increased and in 1978 more than 2,000 billion yen was allocated to the private universities. Government subsidy now accounts for one-third of their overall incomes. As a result, tuition increases have been brought under control, enrollments have been kept at more manageable sizes, and faculty are better paid.

Another focus for the Japanese student movement was the democratization of university and faculty administrations, especially, for example, in medical schools, which were regarded as authoritarian and hierarchical. While the government recommended a centralized administration, as already mentioned, younger faculty tended to favor decentralized administration. The administrative reform in the national universities can be summarized as follows.

Administrative systems were greatly expanded, as a result of the division of power between more faculty members and the establishment of many new committees. Faculty meetings which were formerly attended only by full professors have now been opened to younger staff such as assistant professors, lecturers, and teaching assistants. This group of younger faculty is beginning to take an active part in university administration. At about half the national universities, even teaching assistants are now entitled to vote in presidential elections. Generally speaking there has been a remarkable increase in the allotment of administrative duties to all faculty members.

Despite such formal democratization, however, full professors remain most powerful in fundamental matters such as personnel administration and institutional decision making. This causes continuing discontent among younger staff. Moreover, students are still not permitted to participate in administrative decision making. Attempts were made at the Universities of Tokyo and Kyoto to recognize a student right to recall the president but this proposal was not passed. Similarly, at Kyushu University the election of deans by students, staff and faculty, was not officially approved by the Minister of Education.

Effects upon Research

Needless to say, during the period of campus unrest, the bar-
ricading of offices and laboratories, the endless and fruitless
"collective bargaining" (mass negotiation) with dissenting students, and the long and inconclusive faculty meetings and the
like prevented professors from continuing with their research
activities. There is no hard data to prove objectively this
observation, but we have measured the scientific productivity
of professors of education around the period of the severest
student unrest in the late 1960s. In 1970, a year after 1969
when nationwide campus revolt was highlighted by the Battle
of the Yasuda Auditorium at the University of Tokyo, the average productivity of professors of education at all the major
universities decreased by one-half in comparison with the previous years. Since papers tend to be published a year or 18
months after initial submission this is clear proof of the negative impact of the student movement upon faculty research
activity. As a possible reaction, the productivity curve in
1971 was twice as high as in 1970 (Shimbori, 1979).

Stimulated by the problems raised by the students,
many faculty members developed an interest in the interac-
tion of society and the university. University problems also
became favorite themes for journalists. Magazines and journals published frequent special issues on university problems
and newspapers and television provided day-by-day coverage
of student revolts. In our literature search for articles about
university problems appearing in all the Japanese general and
scientific journals from 1963 through 1977, we found that the
average annual number of such articles was less than 500 in
the middle 1960s, and that this grew dramatically throughout
the 60s as campus unrest became widespread, reaching a total of 1,344 in 1969. Although as campuses grew calmer,
the number of articles decreased, there was still a much
higher proportion of articles on university problems in the
1970s than in the early 1960s. This is partly because journalists became fond of writing about the relationship between
society and the universities and partly because scholars focussed on these subjects in their thinking and research. Thus
the student movement had considerable effect on research productivity and direction.

At the same time a few scholars who were critical or
skeptical of the social role of the traditional university have
left the universities and become active as journalists or as
spokespeople for social movements, attacking the university

and society. Others remained on the campus to attack the
universities from within. They criticize the universities as
they are now organized, the prevailing science and technology,
and the various types of pollution which result from economic
growth. In some cases they have established their own classes apart from those offered by the universities.

During the period of student unrest, university teachers
were forced to state their political or ideological attitudes,
namely whether they were for or against the established regime. Consequently ideological opposition appeared in the administrative sector as well as in research orientation. Professors were divided into two camps: those who clung to political neutrality and objective academism and those who committed themselves to social action, were politically minded,
and in some cases belonged to political parties. Faculty unity
was thus lost. Added to this was a tendency towards research
rather than teaching among faculty (which was a further cause
for student protest) and a growing disinclincation to speak openly lest the student body be antagonised.

Trends of Student Unrest

Professional Activists

As has already been discussed, contemporary student movements have become less active since the Vietnam War. A
series of Japanese student movements continued throughout
1965-70 under a unique umbrella organization called Zenkyoto
(Union of Militant Students), which developed from the initial,
spontaneous stage participated in by masses of general students, through the middle stage led by organized New Left
sects, to the final stage run by the non-sect radical groups.
The movements during these years purportedly developed under Zenkyoto, but in reality they differed to a great extent
from year to year. Because they had little coherent political
ideology and tactics they could not maintain consistent and cooperative struggles. The later decline in the 1970s could be
anticipated by this confused early style of Zenkyoto. The organizational weakness which was already apparent at the end
of the 1960s resulted in the ultimate alienation of the mass
of general students after the passage of the Law Recovering
Order in Universities and the introduction of police forces
on the campuses. The movements eventually were composed
of only hard core radicals because they offered little relevant
focus for most students.

Because of their decreasing memberships, the movements were forced to strengthen their partisan antagonisms. Underground struggles for hegemony grew more violent, especially among sects of the New Left, and escalated into the so-called uchi-geba which characterized the student movements in the 1970s.

The underground guerilla activities were not merely inter-sect struggles, but were also directed against the establishment. The Japanese Red Army exemplifies this style of armed movement. Predictably, those anarchist groups who do not belong to any established political party or to any New Left sect have been the most militant activists against the establishment. They are usually called Forces of Black Helmets. It is reported that there were 320 groups of this sort in 1978, most of them composed of several members. Membership constantly changes so it is difficult to get a clear picture of these groups. Ideologically they are not necessarily Marxists like the New Left, but sometimes nationalists. On the other hand, the Communist Party-affiliated activist group is so coherently organized that its influence cannot be ignored, although because of the poor public image of socialist countries, its membership has not increased.

In recent years all of the minority sects except the Communist group have recognized the limitations of tactics like throwing stones and organizing street demonstrations and have felt a need to improve their weapons. Inspired by the Red Army, they have made ready use of more powerful weapons such as secretly made bombs, and robot-controlled cars and trucks full of gasoline. These tactics were used widely in 1978 in the struggle against the opening of the Narita International Airport.

It is of interest that students have become less and less predominant among the New Left radicals [1]. While 165 universities were racked by campus unrest in 1969, only 18 suffer such problems today. In 1978 only 13,000 of the estimated 35,000 New Left radicals were students. What does this mean? While the campuses have been calmer, the social and labor movements led by the ex-student radicals are growing more violent. The leaders who had been trained as students in violent campus movements are now leading violent movements in the streets and offices. The radical violence which is present in teacher union movements in secondary and elementary schools, for example, owes much to the direction of teachers who earlier were leaders in the student movement. At the same time, there are fewer radicals on the campuses and those who do exist are powerless in the universities and isolated from the general mass of students. They are active away from campuses and often cooperate with non-student radicals. Japanese student activists of the early 1970s, who were characterized by more radicalization and professionalization, have gradually ceased to be the leaders of student movements.

Solidarity with the Deprived

Although student movements in the strict sense have grown powerless, social movements run by the wider strata including ordinary citizens, as well as students, has persisted in the 1970s. The relatively greater proportion of students to laborers became predominant in the struggle against the U. S. - Japan Security Treaty in 1970. Since then, the leadership of these movements has gradually been assumed by the generation of ex-students who were active in the Zenkyoto, and the arena of the movement has moved from the campuses to the urban centers.

New focusses have appeared in these social movements, which are characterized by diversity of aims and by solidarity with the weak or deprived. Thus the activism in the 1970s has occurred spasmodically and separately: the struggles against the Narita International Airport and against the atomic power plants, and the fights for the liberation of the "invisible caste, " for the independence of the Ainu community, for the liberation of women, for the liberation of the handicapped, etc. Clearly such targets are not unique to the interests of the students, but have much wider social implications. Tactics too have varied from radical violence in some cases to orderly protest through legal means. Nonetheless there has been increasing indifference to such activism among general students and a continued decline of on-campus movements.

Orientation to Orderliness

The frequency of bloody inter-sect struggles (uchi-geba) and the inflexibility of ideological positions have fostered apathy to activism among most students. The number of university students is three times higher now than in 1970 when the greatest struggle in the history of Japanese student activism took place against the US-Japan Security Treaty, Ampo Toso. Nonetheless, most of the present leaders of leftist student movements receive little ideological support from the mass of students. In fact, the prevailing political attitudes on campuses for the past few years has been somewhat conservative with a slogan of "normal Campus." Today's students are said to be the generation of uchi-geba-phobia or Zenkyoto-complex.

This new conservatism is characterized by an orientation towards orderliness, which is demonstrated by the fact that today university authorities do not hesitate to call police to the campus as soon as there is an outbreak of student protest and students usually quietly accept the consequences of such action. In earlier times university authorities were reluctant to call for police intervention since they regarded this as a decay of institutional autonomy. Under this overriding desire for order and normality, the National Federation of Universities for the Study of Basic Principles (Zenkoku Daigaku Genri Kenkyu-kai), a rightist organization, is becoming increasingly influential among students. This organization, which has close ties with the International Union of Anti-Communism, has already won control of student governments in a few universities. Minsei, the Democratic Youth Union, led by the Communist Party, is also trying to expand its influence in this conservative climate by capitalizing on the decline of the New Left movements. However, there is much hostility between the Genri and the Minsei, despite their similar orientations.

Other conservative student groups such as the Union of Pure Students and Youths (Gakusei Seinen Junsei Domei), and the National Liaison Committee of Student Governments (Zenkoku Gakusei Jichikai Renraku Kyogikai), which were organized around 1970, have a nationalistic basis which is quite distinct from the emphasis of the established rightest organizations. While they were most active in 1970 in opposition to the New Left movements against the US-Japan Security Treaty, they have again become popular in recent years among the growing numbers of conservative students.

Prospect

The above description suggests that Japanese student movements have been changing gradually both quantitatively and qualitatively in the 1970s. Judging from the trend in this decade, some predictions could be made for the future development of the movement.

There is a popular "ten years" cycle theory of student movements, according to which the Japanese universities mark peaks of student unrest every ten years (Table VIII).

These major world events which occurred at ten-year intervals stimulated student activism since they offered the opportunity to fuse Marxism, internationalism, and revolutionalism with peace, democracy, and nationalism. Each peak has followed a similar pattern with the leftists first gaining supremacy followed by a brief upsurge of rightist power. It is doubtful however, in view of the recent calmer campuses, whether another peak will be reached in 1980, especially in view of the current economic situation.

TABLE VIII

Year	Societal event	Target of struggle	Initiative
1950	Korean war	Against Red Purge	Communist Party
1960	Revision of US-Japan Security Treaty	Against the Revision	Bund (Kyosan-Do, Union of Communists)
1970	Prolongation of US-Japan Security Treaty	Against the Prolongation	New Left (Zenkyoto)

Most Japanese youth consider college attendance as a sort of initiation ceremony. It is important for them that they find a good job after graduation. Aside from a few professional activists, most students participate in the movement only when they are sure it will not jeopardize their chances of finding employment. Around 1960, during the struggle against the Security Treaty, the Japanese economy had begun to develop so remarkably that students had no employment problems, especially since they constituted, at the time, only 8.2% of the college-age population. By 1970, when the rate of college attendance had gone up to 17.1%, the labor market was even more favorable for the graduates as Japan was undergoing a period of rapid economic growth. Today, however, since the oil crisis of October 1973, and the sudden economic recess, the labor market has been completely reversed. The attendance rate at the institutes of higher education, however, has continued to grow, to a high of about 40% for males in 1977. In view of these circumstances it is hardly surprising that students have shown reluctance to become involved with radical movements.

It follows that there will be little psychological incentive for an increase in student radicalism as long as the present low level of economic growth continues. Recently, the numbers of students going on to higher education have also remained static and this too will be a negative factor against a new upsurge of student activism.

It can be argued that the student movements in 1960 differed from those of 1970 in terms of style and quality. The 1960 movements were supported by most students in defense of democracy, with only a few indifferent non-participants, while in 1970 the university was characterized as a knowledge factory by a minority of radicals and the majority of students viewed the movement as a kind of game. Perhaps the generational factor was partly responsible for this difference. L. S. Feuer says, "The distinctive character of student movements arises from the union in them of motives of youthful love, on the one hand, and those springing from the conflict of generations on the other" (Feuer, 1969: 3). Feuer interprets the student movement only as the conflict between younger and older generations and seems to overlook the change in the nature of the conflict. In 1970, students in a system of mass higher education were trying to find their own identities by casting doubt on a system of knowledge established and accepted by the older generation. Rapid social change gives rise to multiple strata of generations, so that different sorts of student movements will occur. Apathetic young students may form a movement which is entirely different from previous ones and which the older generation would not view as a student movement.

Accordingly it is difficult to predict the future of student movements in Japan. For one thing, it is certain that postwar Japanese student movements have been greatly influenced by world disputes on socialism and communism. For instance, the New Left, the leader of the most recent student movement, was born from the disturbance and confusion of socialism doctrine, stimulated by the criticisms of the Soviet Communist Party of its Japanese counterpart in 1950, of Stalinism, and of the invasion of Hungary. In the 1970s, the

continuous hostilities between the Soviets and the Chinese had
a profound effect upon the disputes over socialism and communism in Japan and elsewhere. These seemingly endless
disputes, added to the disillusionment of citizens of many socialist countries, have contributed to the loss of appeal of
socialism and communism for many students. If the myth of
socialism and communism completely disappears from among
students, there will be little probability of large-scale student
movements of a confrontation type in the near future.

Notes

1. For example, there were only 200 students among the
    1, 600 Chukaku-sect activists who participated in the
    protest against the Emperor's visit to America in
    September, 1975. Students, including high school
    students, composed about one-fourth of those arrested
    on charges of destroying the Operations Center of Na-
    rita Airport on March 26, 1978.

References

Feuer, L. S. (1969). The Conflict of Generations. New
    York: Basic Books.
Shimbori, M. (1963). "Comparison between pre- and postwar
    student movements in Japan, " Sociology of Education
    37(1) 59-70.
Shimbori, M. (1964). "Zengakuren: A Japanese case study
    of student political movement, " Sociology of Education
    37(3) 229-253.
Shimbori, M. (1968). "The sociology of a student movement:
    A Japanese case study, " Daedalus 97 204-228.
Shimbori, M. (1971). "Student radicals in Japan, " Annals of
    the American Academy of Political and Social Science
    395 150-158.
Shimbori, M. (1980). Gakusha no Sekai (Scholar's Commu-
    nity). Tokyo: Fukumura.

CONTRARY IMAGINATIONS: STUDENT ACTIVISM AND BELIEFS IN ENGLAND IN THE MID-1970s

by Pamela J. Yettram

While the 1970s has seen a reduction of student protest in England, activism has continued in a number of universities and polytechnics. Some of these protests have been over limited and often instrumental demands, but a number have continued to be concerned with participative democracy and with aspects of equality, two of the major issues of protest in the 1960s. Co-existing with this continuity has been an important discontinuity. Where, in the 1960s, these goals were seen to be attainable only in the context of new forms of life, in the 1970s, participative democracy and equality have been pursued in practical ways, less linked to a search for a counterculture and non-Capitalist social arrangements.

Two case studies, in 1974 and 1977, found that this change occurred to the least extent among revolutionary socialists and among activists deeply involved in protest. It occurred to the greatest extent among activists who did not hold leftwing beliefs and among those who were comparatively less involved in activism. This suggests that the socialist ideology of the former acts as a barrier against the full effect of changed social conditions in the 1970s, while the absence of a sophisticated socialist ideology amongst the latter facilitates the full impact of changed conditions. It also suggests that socialist ideology has the capacity to generate, as well as to prevent, particular responses and patterns of action.

Two versions of activist socialist ideology were examined. It is suggested that the total ideology--focussed through one of its central values--structured perception, evaluated events, specified goals and selected means at the level of student political action. In other words it initiated responses and patterns of action. In addition, the ideologies defined problems and solutions at the level of national politics. Advocates of the ideologies perceived these national events and problems as having important interconnections with protest within the university.

During the period from the Second World War to the early 1960s, student grievances were expressed predominantly through peaceful means. This changed during the mid to late 1960s, when student protest took the form of occupying buildings, disrupting meetings and other kinds of "direct" or non-peaceful action. Though there had been early signs of student discontent in 1965, it was not until the academic year 1966/67 that, as Crouch points out, the first outbreak of activism occurred at the London School of Economics [1]. By the end of the 1967/68 academic year, it was estimated that seventeen universities and approximately six polytechnics, or colleges under Local Education Authority control, had experienced some form of protest [2]. Among the institutions affected, the London School of Economics (L. S. E.) and Essex University were two of the universities undergoing the most prolonged and extensive confrontations. They have remained important centers of activism and symbols of student protest in the minds of students, press and public.

Otto Klineberg [3] argues that these outbreaks of activism did not constitute a student movement because only a minority of students were involved and because activists were more oriented towards cultural, rather than political, changes. This agrees with the view of Frisk, President of the National Union of Students during the late 1960s and a supporter of the reformist left. Frisk argues that "only a small minority possessed any detailed knowledge or acceptance of" New Left thinking. Similarly, Blackburn stresses the lack of a "truly political perspective," arguing that 1960s activists did not have access to revolutionary concepts and analyses due to the lack of a strong Marxist tradition in Britain.

In view of these comments, one must concede that the level of political consciousness among the rank and file student body was, perhaps, not high and certainly far less extensive and developed than among the leading activists. However, though a number of protestors might have had strongly political goals and though the protests themselves might not have constituted a movement in the sense that this existed in other European countries, nonetheless, the leadership did, as Crouch points out, "belong in that fragmented group known as the New Left" and did share and apply the beliefs and analyses of the New Left. The following discussion of issues which precipitated protest during the 1960s will provide evidence of this. In addition, though only a minority of British students became activists, at those institutions where prolonged direct action occurred, a substantial proportion of the students supported the confrontations. Moreover, the impact of the protests in the consciousness of students, press and public gained an importance that belies the small number of institutions involved.

Crouch identifies in the first outbreak of protest a "confusion of issues" which he argues were later adopted "sometimes in isolation, by a number of other institutions. " He writes that "behind these different focuses stand three major and related areas of concern. " One might see these areas of concern as related to New Left commitment to an extreme equality and to highly decentralized rank-and-file political control. The areas identified by Crouch show a concern over questions of authority, over questions of community and over the relationship between the university and the outside world. Crouch argues that the concern with authority was reflected in sit-ins and occupations pressing demands that students should participate in all the decisions that affected them and in a new questioning, revealed by these demands, of the legitimacy of university authority. Students felt that rules and practices constraining them were an illegitimate exercise of power, unless they had themselves participated in decisions instituting such measures. This view was echoed in their commitment to a radical participative democracy outside, as well as within, the university. They stressed that all members of all groups and collectivities, not only students, should participate in decisions which affected them. One might describe this extensive form of participative democracy as a commitment to a "collectivist autonomy, " in which personal autonomy is to be gained through, and together with, the whole collectivity. Crouch sees this concern with student participation rights and the legitimacy of authority behind what was the second most frequent form of protest.

Concern with the relationship between the university and the wider society provided the issues for what Crouch sees as the most frequent form of protest: the disruption of meetings of unpopular speakers. From 1968 to the end of the decade such disruptions were numerous and frequent. Officials who were connected with Defence, with the government's immigration policy, with strong rightwing views and a commitment to capitalism, visiting members of a Government Select Committee investigating student protest, and scientists working on government programs of germ and chemical warfare--all had to abandon speeches at universities following disruptions by activists. Students claimed the right to deny freedom of speech to those advocating what they saw as immoral policies. Ministers were criticized for immigration rules that were perceived as racist and for advocating repressive defense policies, including immoral programs such as work on chemical and germ warfare. Indeed, any visiting Minister drew criticism because students felt the Labour government had betrayed socialist principles for the sake of making capitalism more technologically effective at home, while tacitly approving of oppression overseas; for example, and among other things, by allowing British investment in countries such as South Africa.

One might argue that behind this range of issues connected with the university's relationship to the wider society, is an underlying commitment to various aspects of equality and a condemnation of what students defined as exploitation, repression, hierarchy. In other words, linking the unpopularity of the various speakers whose meetings had been disrupted, was an underlying commitment to racial, international, and class equality, accompanied by a disapproval of capitalism and all forms of oppression.

The third area of concern identified by Crouch is that of community. He argues that when students demanded participation, this was not only as an "instrumental" means of arriving at just decisions, but also as a form of "meaningful personal involvement." Allied to this commitment to participation as a process of self-development, was a commitment to a structureless, roleless form of counterculture social relationships. These desired social arrangements were to be characterized by lack of hierarchies, inequality, and all distinctions. This form of structureless community was seen, particularly by the more cultural wing of the student activists, to constitute the only context in which to realize a radical, roleless form of self-development.

Crouch points out that this strand of the protest was linked to other developments in the realms of music and art, and had its roots in earlier developments in the decade. A similar argument is advanced by Klineberg who sees the roots of this strand of British protest inhering in the peace marches of the early 1960s and the "esthetic and artistic revolution" revealed by the miniskirt styles and the pop music of the Beatles and the Rolling Stones.

Among the major configurations of the 1960s activists, one might, therefore, identify a cultural wing with a primary

commitment to counterculture values and goals: structureless community and roleless self development through the
heightened experiences of drugs and sex, and maybe violence
(though there was little violence during the 1960s protest in
Britain). In contrast, one might also identify a political
wing, predominantly committed to notions of class equality
and "true" rank-and-file control. It is important, however,
to remember that the two sets of values were not as divorced
from each other as the above comments imply. As Crouch
points out, the two political values were seen as the counterpart, the form of political authority, that corresponded to the
social relationships specified by the counterculture form of
community. In other words, each "wing" was committed to
all four values, though primarily concerned with either the
cultural set or the political set.

The major groups constituting the 1960s political wing
included the Socialist Society at the L. S. E. , committed to a
Marxist revolutionary socialism and formed some time before
the outbreak of the first protest. At the national level were
other revolutionary socialist groups, such as the Radical Student Alliance and the Revolutionary Socialist Student Federation, the latter not formed until 1968. This "revolutionary"
subsection of the political faction accepted the need for violence in the transformation to an equal society. Another
sub-section of the political faction was comprised of more
moderate socialists who believed in radical but gradual
change. They were supported by the National Union of Students, a national representative body of all students in Britain. The N. U. S. tended to lag behind the revolutionary socialist leaders, adopting positions, for example on participative democracy, some time after these had been abandoned
by the revolutionary socialist leaders. For instance, the
revolutionary socialists [4] had already decided that participation within university structures was of minor importance in
the drive to eliminate capitalism by the time N. U. S. got
around to urging student unions to seek more participation.
However, the N. U. S. role was important since its adoption
of such issues led to student unions outside London staging
their own protests. This advanced the spread of activism
to other British universities. As has been hinted above, the
moderate and revolutionary factions of the political wing at
times became more interested in the clash between them than
in what might be seen as "common enemies. "

Student Protests in the 70s: Continuities and Discontinuities

These three areas of concern described by Crouch are felt
by Hoggart to give to protests in the 1960s an idealistic and
leftist orientation [5].   One might feel that, in contrast, protest in the 1970s has been less leftist and far more oriented
towards practical, limited, and sometimes instrumental goals.
For example, Ian Bradley notes a rightward turn among students in the 1970s.   Hoggart agrees that "the energy left the
student movement all over the world as the 1970s advanced"
and suggests that in Britain this was the result of a "very
much bleaker climate ... when jobs are at a premium. "
He argues that such conditions mean that "it is harder to
persuade any large number of other students to risk a revolutionary act. "   In addition, he feels the end of the Vietnam
war and what he describes as "the well-known and inescap-
able British inertia" and refusal to be rushed into action,
also contributed to a reduction of student activism.   Despite
this, however, he stresses that "the number of active radical students may be not at all or only a little smaller. "
In other words, it might be that we should look for an explanation of the reduced level of activism in the effect of
changed conditions on the general student body, rather than
in any lessening of leftwing commitment among activist
leaders.

        In this connection, it is interesting to note Blackburn's
view that student protests in the 1960s left an "enduring legacy" of "a radical, anti-capitalist current of thought" that
constitutes what one might almost describe as an "Anglo-
Marxism. "   This suggests that socialist activists in the
1970s might have been better equipped theoretically and ideologically than they were seen to have been by Blackburn in
the 1960s.   This would further imply that the student left
leadership might still have had the potential to express the
idealistic criticisms referred to by Hoggart above, had the
leaders been able to mobilize sufficient rank-and-file support
for such initiatives.   Indeed, it will shortly be argued that
there were in fact a number of protests during the 1970s
which shared some of the typical concerns of 1960s protests
and that student activism had not ceased to occur.   The existence of continuing activism is demonstrated in the following
Table [6].

        As can be seen from Table I, it is clear that acti-
vism has not disappeared in the 1970s.   In this connection
it is interesting to note that the first disruption at L. S. E.

TABLE I

Numbers of Institutions of Higher Education Experiencing
Protest Over Issues Revealing Similarities and Discontinuities
on Key Issues

Year	Rents, Accommodation	Other "Instrumental" Demands	Overseas Student Fees, Quotas, Defined as Racist and Inequality-Promoting	Other Economic and Class Equality Issues	Participative Democracy, Legitimacy of College Authority Issues
1973/74	5	0	0	0	0
1974/75	36	3	0	2	4
1975/76	22	3	7	3	1
1976/77	0	5	10	0	4
1977/78	0	1	4	3	1
1978/80	0	2	69	0	0
	63	14	90	8	10

There are 38 universities, 44 polytechnics in England [7].

in 1967 lasted eight days and the Union meetings held to decide the progress of the confrontations drew attendance of
800 and, on one occasion, 1,200. The 1977 occupation of
the administrative offices, described below, lasted sixteen
days while the almost daily Union meetings attracted 800,
though never as many as 1,200. [8]

Table I supports the argument that there has been in
the 1970s a much greater concern among activists with material demands. For example, particularly up to the end of
1975, there was a large number of protests over such matters as rents charged by universities for student accommodation that were felt to be too high, grants that were felt to be
too low, library and other facilities that were felt to be in-
adequate. There were few protests in the 1960s over such
matters. For instance, Crouch lists only one, at Manchester
University, over library facilities.

It is important to note, however, that this discontinuity with earlier protest masks a related continuity. A number of protests in the 1970s, in response to N.U.S. policy,
begun over rents and grants but escalated after stern disciplinary measures were taken by the university authorities.
At this point the protests became transformed and the pri-

mary concern altered to demands for more student participation and to rejections of the legitimacy of university authority. University staff were condemned for disciplining individual students for actions voted on and participated in by many of the student collectivity. Activists described this action as a "violation of student union autonomy" and demanded the right of representatives to be regarded as delegates mandated by the student collectivity. This recalls the 1960s commitment to collectivist autonomy. This pattern of escalation occurred during the first half of the decade at Essex, Keele, Warwick, and Lancaster universities and also at a number of local education colleges. It repeats the pattern identified by Crouch which began over some issue that, argues Crouch, "gave tangible organizational form" to high student expectations and then escalated into a rejection of the legitimacy of university authority. One might argue, therefore, that this pattern, plus a continuing concern with student participation and with the legitimacy of university authority represent underlying continuities with 1960s protest.

During the second half of the decade these continuities became even more marked, following the appearance of widespread confrontations over racial equality. Indeed, as can be seen from Table I, where, up until 1975, protests concerned with instrumental demands outweighed the number of protests concerned with participative democracy, legitimacy of authority, and aspects of equality, the position was reversed after 1975. The appearance of numerous sit-ins, occupations, picketing and demonstrations over an increase in fees to overseas students, defined as racist, resulted in a greater number of protests showing some continuity with 1960s protests. This number outweighed protests over instrumental demands [9].

The fees increases had been brought about by public expenditure cuts beginning in 1975 that reduced funds to the universities. Public expenditure cuts were imposed by the Labour government. Although fees were increased all round, overseas students were charged at a higher rate. Further reductions followed the change to the Thatcher government in 1979. Overseas student fees were increased again and the question of quotas, restricting the intake of foreign students, was raised. A further wave of protests, attacking the fees increases as racist, broke out and continued into the summer term, 1980. It is interesting to note that, following such protests, some institutions rejected plans to restrict the intake of foreign students to fixed quotas. In addition, in one case where accommodation charges to overseas

students were at higher rates, student protest led to the reduction of charges to rates paid by home students.

Overseas students had in fact been charged higher
fees than home students since 1966. However, though there
was some protest in 1974, it was not until the two sharp
fees increases that major confrontations occurred. Overseas
students, and home self-financing students who were also affected, participated in these protests and thus can be described as pursuing, among other possible aims, practical,
instrumental goals. However, the majority who initiated and
participated in the confrontations were undergraduate British
students who were not personally affected as their local education authorities paid all tuition fees. Therefore, one can
argue that the majority were not protesting over instrumental
issues but were supporting overseas students due to a commitment to racial equality. The fees increases were defined
as racist due to the large proportion of overseas students
who come to Britain from ex-colonies in the Third World.

The fees issue united activists from a number of factions. For example, important initiators of protest included
overseas students, many, though not all, advocating Marxist
and revolutionary socialist beliefs. The N. U. S. played an
important part that was similar to its role during the 1960s.
For example, its condemnation of the fees increases led to
student unions staging confrontations. Two other important
leadership groups in the 1970s, the Far Left and the Broad
Left, were represented on the Executive over the decade,
with perhaps rather more Far Left involvement up until
1977/78.

The Broad Left was founded during the early part of
the 1970s. This faction includes student members of the
Communist party, sympathisers with the leftwing of the Labour party, i. e. , the Tribune group, and some non-aligned
socialists committed to Parliamentary, gradual, and peaceful rather than revolutionary change. One might describe
the Broad Left as the descendants of the 1960s moderate but
radical-reformist socialist group. The Labour party to the
right of the Tribune group is defined by 1970s Broad Left
and Far Left activists as non-socialist. It is important to
remember that the student Broad Left is more committed to
fundamental change in the direction of greater equality than
is the national "moderate" left or the Labour party. Membership of the student Communist party, many of whom are
prepared, like European Communists, to work for change

through parliamentary processes, defines the center left position for student activists, whereas membership of the Communist party defines the Far Left for the British public and for many of the general, non-activist student body.

In contrast, the Far Left is well to the left of the student Communist party and includes student members of such groups as the Socialist Workers Party (S. W. P.), formerly International Socialists, and the International Marxist Group (I. M. G.).   The S. W. P. can perhaps be described, albiet with some qualifications to be examined later, as the descendant of the L. S. E. Socialist Society and other 1960s Far Left groups.   The activist Far Left in the 1970s, as in the 1960s, was committed to fundamental change in the direction of greater equality.   It differs from the Broad Left faction in that it envisages more basic change, demands the total elimination of capitalism and is prepared to accept violent means.   The L. S. E. Far Left also included self-styled anarchists and non-aligned activists committed to revolutionary socialism.

Klineberg's cross-cultural study of student political views in 1970 finds that for British students as a whole, 33 per cent define themselves as belonging to the moderate left. This is the faction, to the right of the Broad Left, that can be seen to have provided the less ideologically sophisticated rank-and-file supporters of 1970s activism.   Klineberg describes 12 per cent of the general student body as committed to Far Left views.   This figure, however, includes the 2 per cent of his sample who described themselves as Communists.   From the activist point of view these individuals would have belonged to the activist center left or Broad Left faction.

All of the above factions criticized the fees increases as being contrary to notions of racial equality and as likely to exacerbate economic inequality.   The Far Left leaders went further than this and argued that the fees increases were one part of expenditure cuts which harmed not only students but also the working class and the disadvantaged.   They stressed that the working class, the poor and students were paying the cost of a business recession generated by capitalism.   Thus for them increases were an example, not only of racial inequality, but also of the evils of the capitalist system, and its inherent class inequality.

There were a few other protests over the decade supporting class equality. As in the 1960s, a number of these took the form of disrupting the meetings of speakers unpopular for their economic beliefs. Such protests took place in the first half of the decade, as did another by L. S. E. students stressing class solidarity. Activists picketed the Law Courts in support of militant building workers who were appealing against prison sentences. Other meetings which had to be abandoned were concerned with racial inequality, and oppression overseas. Immigration rules were criticized, Eysenck was condemned for his views on race and, towards the end of the decade, there was a hunger strike at L. S. E. in connection with South Africa.

It is interesting to note, from Table I, the large number of protests following the overseas fees increases and expenditure cuts initiated by the Thatcher government in 1979. This would seem to support the analyses of Hoggart and Blackburn. It will be remembered that Hoggart feels the "bleak seventies" have made it difficult for a continuing left leadership to mobilize support. One might see the Thatcher government as likely to have affected leadership expectations about rank-and-file response and that response itself. Far Left activist leaders feel that any Tory government but particularly the Thatcher policies are committed to intensifying inequality, and will make more visible the extent of repression and inequality in society. Given this analysis, the leadership is likely to perceive an increase in mobilizable support and to redouble its effort to organize that potential support. The one-third of students found by Klineberg to be mild left, faced by the new Tory policies, are likely to be sufficiently opposed to censure such policies.

During the 1980 autumn term there has been a resurgence of interest in nuclear disarmament. Students formed a large proportion of participants in a rally held late in 1980. This recalls the 1960s concern with Vietnam and with international issues.

Political Belief and the Choice of Goals

This overview of protest in the 1970s does not reveal how the activists themselves felt their commitment to New Left political values to be. Nor does it demonstrate the extent and nature of similarities and differences between the way in which 1960s and 1970s commitment to participatory democracy and to equality was translated into political action.

Discussion now turns to an examination of a pilot study under-
taken at Essex in 1974 and of detailed research at L. S. E. in
1977. The main focus of the investigations was to try to determine the effect of leftwing political beliefs on political action. To this end an attempt was made to discover how key
activists felt the two political values were to them and the
extent to which commitment to these values was accompanied
by criticism of capitalism. A secondary objective was to
note the nature of discontinuities in the form in which protest
was expressed at the two periods.

The Essex confrontation began over grants but, after
the serving of a High Court Writ and the suspension of a number of "occupying" students, it became predominantly concerned with participation, student union autonomy, and the
legitimacy of university authority. The confrontations included a twenty-three day long sit-in, rent strikes, picketing
of essential supplies over a ten-week period, clashes with
police on the campus over the picketing, and some minor
damage to property. Data were collected during four day-
long visits to the university. Interviews with six Broad Left
leaders were conducted, questionnaires given to participants
and informal conversations held with students. While the
number of questionnaires returned was small (38), the data
permit some broad comparisons and generalizations.

The Essex Anarchist group was found to be a non-
homogeneous one that included some political nihilists. Therefore Essex Broad Left activists are contrasted with Essex
I. M. G. activists. The resulting comparisons are presented
tentatively, mainly as support for the more detailed findings
from the L. S. E. study. Differences between Essex Broad
Left and I. M. G. Far Left followed the trend revealed by
L. S. E. Broad Left and Far Left.

The L. S. E. 1977 confrontations began over the fees
increases to foreign students. They included a sixteen day
long occupation of the administrative offices, brought to a
close by police serving a High Court Writ. There were two
further, shorter occupations. The confrontations were finally brought to a close, as they were at Essex, by the advent of the summer exams and by the fact that clashes between Far Left and Broad· Left eroded much of the initial
rank-and-file support from ordinary activists.

At both universities presence of activism was associated with presence of commitment to participative democracy,

while absence of activism was associated with absence of
commitment to participative democracy--indeed with a rejection of notions of extreme decentralization of decision-
making. Although some L. S. E. Opponents used the term,
participative democracy, when further questions were asked,
it became clear that Opponents were referring to a very
representative and consultative form of democracy, rather
than to the highly decentralized notion of rank-and-file control advocated by the socialist activists. Rejection of the
notion of "equal say" for students can be seen in the following interview extract of a leading Opponent and member of
the rightwing student group, Federation of Conservative Students.

> I don't know what the hell students know about
> running a university. I think it would be disas-
> trous if students decided the running of the In-
> ternational Affairs department. (Cn/M/1)

The other Conservative Opponents of the confrontations at
L. S. E. expressed similar views. The Essex questionnaires
also revealed that the magnitude of disapproval among Opponents for the notion of "equal say" was almost identical
with the magnitude of activist approval expressed for this
notion, as can be seen from Table II.

The existence of approval of participative democracy,
on which Table II is based, was identified, in the case of
Essex activists from responses to set questionnaire items.
In the case of L. S. E. activists, the existence of approval
for participative democracy was inferred from interview comments, usually spontaneously introduced by activists themselves. These comments allocated good and bad moral marks
to events which activists felt aided or retarded the realization of participative democracy. Sometimes approval for the
value was expressed in response to a remark from the inter-
viewer. In either case, it is felt that such spontaneously
volunteered remarks revealed the existence, among L. S. E.
activists, of a genuine commitment to participative democracy. Indeed, one might argue that the value was being used
as an underlying moral principle, or "evaluative criterion. "

As both absence and presence of activism was strongly
associated with absence and presence of approval for participative democracy, one might feel that commitment to this
value constituted an important facilitating condition for the
occurrence of activism, particularly as at both universities,

TABLE II

Association of Presence and Absence of Approval of Participative Democracy with Presence and Absence of Activism at Essex University 1974, and at LSE, 1977

Activist Group Exhibiting Decreasing Levels of Activism	Total Numbers, LSE	Percentage Expressing Approval of Value	Total Numbers, Essex	Median Activism Score for Group	Percentage Expressing Approval of Value
Socialist Prime Initiators	4	+ 100 p. c.	6	(+ 100 p. c.)	+ 100 p. c.
Socialist Social Science Activists					
a) High Participants + Ex-High Participants	17	+ 82	16	(+ 79. 5)	+ 87
b) Enthusiastic Supporters	5	+ 80			
Physical Science and Math Socialist Activists	N/a*		8	(+ 75)	+ 75
Non-Socialist, Social Science Ordinary Supporters	4	+ 75	4	(+ 61)	+ 50
Opponents, Primarily Conservative**	6/36	- 80	7/41	(- 36)	- 70

*There was one activist at LSE from the Statistics Dept, he was an Ordinary supporter and, therefore, less involved in activism than the social science activists at LSE.

**N.B.: The percentages are given a minus sign to denote disapproval rather than approval of the value. Similarly, the negative activism score indicates average magnitude of rejection of direct action.

decreasing magnitudes of approval are associated with decreasing levels of activism. It could be said that this value endowed direct action with meaning and importance. In this case the value could be seen to have exerted an indirect causal influence on action.

It is now argued that, in the case of L. S. E. activists, there is some evidence to suggest that the value also exerted a more direct causal influence. Not only did L. S. E. activists approve and disapprove of events on the basis of their relationship to participative democracy, in addition, activist leaders used this value in a second and stronger sense. They used participative democracy to define the goals and degree of success of the occupation and, furthermore, described the day-to-day events of the confrontations in terms of their relevance to participative democracy. The value was being used in order to select what to include and omit in a description of the confrontations. One might say that the value was structuring perception of the events: it was being used as a "selective criterion." Interviews revealed that activists at L. S. E. also used the value, equality, in both the ways delineated above, i. e. , as an evaluative and as a selective criterion.

Vaughan and Archer argue that an ideology can influence action by specifying goals and selecting, from among the range available, particular means to that goal. It is now suggested that values which had been central to New Left ideology in the 1960s and that were still central to student socialist ideology in the 1970s (i. e. , commitment to participative democracy and to equality) causally influenced student political action. They did so due to their capacity to act as evaluative and selective criteria, which capacities resulted in the specification of goals for student political activity. For example, if a value has the capacity to act as evaluative criterion, or underlying moral principle, then it would seem likely that activists should choose that course of action which, other things being equal, conforms to the value. In this case, one can say that the value arbitrated choice of one goal from among a range of possible goals. To arbitrate choice of goal is to exert some degree of causal influence; a degree that is somewhat more direct than if the value simply endows action already taken with significance, as was argued could be the case on the basis of data in Table II. In the former case the value is one motive for action, among others. In the latter case the value legitimates action which it may, or may not, have motivated.

It is now suggested that a political value or belief, in the role of selective criterion, has an even more direct influence on selection of goals for action than has a political belief, in the role of evaluative criterion. This is because, before the moral principle and evaluative aspects of the belief can influence action towards supporting the confrontations, the latter must be perceived in a particular way.

Clearly, the confrontations could have been, and were, perceived in various ways. For example, Conservative Opponents felt that the fees campaign was an isolated and instrumental issue, not associated with other, wider, issues within or outside the L. S. E. In addition, though two-thirds of the Ordinary Supporters at L. S. E. approved of participative democracy, either within or outside the L. S. E. The pursuit of greater participative democracy, or rank-and-file control, was not part of the goal they had specified for action in the particular case of the fees occupation. In contrast, for socialist, particularly Broad Left socialist, activists, it did constitute a non-instrumental goal for action. Furthermore, the value, participative democracy, as argued earlier, did structure the socialists' perception of events and definitions of the situation represented by the confrontations. It did not structure the perception of the Ordinary Supporter, mildly left, activists. As it is in response to definitions of the situation that goals are selected and action is taken, one can argue that the value, acting as a selective criterion, exerted a distinct influence on the action of the socialist leaders. It exerted a more direct influence on the selection of goals for action than the influence exerted by the belief, in the role of evaluative criterion.

In making the above analytical distinction between the evaluative and perception structuring aspects of a value or belief, one should not, of course, overemphasize the separateness of the two aspects. The one implies the existence of the other: the two functions co-exist rather than exist separately. For example, Stevens argues that moral principles necessarily also have a perception structuring aspect. He suggests that "moral principles structure our internalized world, representing and generalizing about experience in the real world" and are thus "an integral part of symbolic thinking. " In other words, in evaluating reality, that reality is identified and, one might add, vice versa. The identifying, cognitive, perception-structuring aspects involve evaluative aspects, while evaluative aspects presuppose cognitive, perception-structuring aspects.

Discussion now turns to evidence of the perception structuring, goal selection capacities of commitment to participative democracy among leading Broad Left activists, while Table III, on the following page, shows the percentage of Far Left, as well as of Broad Left, leaders who used the value, participative democracy, as a selective criterion.

> <u>Interviewer</u>: What were the main issues of the occupation? The press says it was over fees increases. Do you agree?
>
> No. I think the reason why there was an occupation about that time, as opposed to other reactions to it, is to do with the lack of involvement of students in the way the School makes decisions.... Students should be on all the committees. So should all the trade unions. They should all be on. That's how decisions should be made. (BL/M/1: Prime Initiator)

In addition to his commitment to participative democracy and to his definition of participative democracy in terms of a collectivist autonomy, BL/M/1 shows that his commitment to participative democracy within the L. S. E. is echoed by approval of participative democracy in institutions outside L. S. E. He adopts the value as a universal principle.

> The question of the role of students in L. S. E. , what rights they have to be involved in decision-making, which is really what it comes down to.... Students have very little control over course content, methods of examination, etc.... Students have very little control over what any of the administrators at L. S. E. do, even though they are often the people who are administered to.... There are obvious parallels there anyway, in terms of the relationship between people who manage something and people who are managed by. If they feel drastically upset, they either leave or go on strike and here we had an occupation. (BL/M/1: Prime Initiator)
>
> Participatory structures are bound up with the fees issue. Neither the fees problem nor confrontation would have arisen if there had been proper participation on the part of the student body. (BL/F/1: High Participant and part-time Prime Initiator [10])

TABLE III

Numbers and Percentages of LSE Activists of Decreasing Levels of Activism Who Used the Value, Participative Democracy, as a Selective Criterion

Numbers of Individuals Out of Total in Each Category

Political Affiliation	Prime Initiators	High Participants	Ex-High Participants*	Enthusiastic Supporters	Ordinary Supporters	Opponents, Conservative, and Non-Socialist
Far Left	2/3	3/7	1/3	0/3		
Broad Left**	3/3	5/5	2/2	1/1		
Mild Left					0/4	
Conservative + Other Non-Socialist	—	—		—	—	0/6
Total Numbers	5/6	8/12	3/5	1/4	0/4	0/6

*Very active in 1975, 1976 but less active in 1977 during final year.
**There were two High Participants who took on temporary roles of part-time prime initiators. They are included in the prime initiator category to facilitate comparison with Far Left prime initiators.

As indicated above, Far Left leaders also used the value, participative democracy, usually referred to as rank-and-file control, as a selective criterion. However, as Table III shows, decreasing levels of activism among Far Left leaders were associated with decreasing propensities to use the value as a selective criterion, whereas 100 per cent of all of the Broad Left highly activist groups used this value as a selective criterion.

Table III shows that when socialist ideology is ignored, decreasing levels of activism are associated with decreasing propensities to use the value, participative democracy, as a selective criterion. However, as indicated earlier there was a difference between Broad Left and Far Left propensities to use the value in this way. In view of this, it is interesting to note that the Essex Far Left activists expressed a lower magnitude of approval for participative democracy than was expressed among Broad Left activists. Note that the following figures refer to percentages expressing approval, rather than to percentages using the value as a selective criterion. Among Essex Broad Left, 100 per cent approved of participative democracy within the university and 80-90 per cent disagreed with statements advocating hierarchical decisions associated with experts and bureaucratic rules in the wider society. Though 100 per cent of Essex Marxist activists approved of student participation (not surprising in view of the current confrontations with the authorities over disciplinary matters) only 75 per cent of them disagreed with statements that elicited disagreement from 80-90 per cent of the Broad Left Essex activists. This could indicate that participative democracy was a central value for Broad Left Essex activists whereas it was only a secondary value for Essex Far Left activists. At L. S. E. , as is partially revealed by Table III, participative democracy was a primary goal for the Broad Left but only a secondary goal for the Far Left. This difference is partially revealed because Table III shows that where 100 per cent of all Broad Left activists used the value as a selective criterion, this was not the case for Far Left activists. Not all of the leaders used the value in this way among the Far Left and those less involved in activism were less likely to use the value as a selective criterion.

The propensity of Far Left activists to regard participative democracy as a secondary goal can be seen from the following interview extract.

You've got to talk about student control of education

TABLE IV (a)

Percentage of LSE Activists Using the Value, Equality, as a Selective Criterion

Level of Activism	Number In Category	Proportion Using Value As Selective Criterion	Percentage Using Value as Selective Criterion %	Number In Category	Proportion Using Equality as Selective Criterion	Percentage Using Value As Selective Criterion %
	F A R L E F T			B R O A D L E F T		
PRIME INITIATORS	3	3/3	100	3*	2/3	67
HIGH PARTICIPANTS	7	5/7	71	5	1/5	20
EX-HIGH PARTICIPANTS	3	2/3	67	2	0/2	0
ENTHUSIASTIC SUPPORTERS	4	1/4	25	1	0/1	0
TOTAL NOS.	17	11/17	(65)	11	3/11	(27)

*Two part-time prime initiators are included in this category to facilitate comparison with Far Left prime initiators. The total number of activists is, therefore, increased to 28. This excludes the 4 Ordinary Supporters. None of the Ordinary Supporters used the value as selective criterion.

and all that, but to me that's just a minor thing.
That will never come about until the working class
actually changes things. These things are subsidi-
ary and that was the problem during the occupations.
(SWP/M/1: Prime Initiator)

Due to the fact that the Broad Left selected participative democracy as a primary goal, their attention was directed to events within the L. S. E. In contrast, the Far Left
located the primary goal of the confrontations outside the
L. S. E. and defined the pursuit of greater equality in the
wider society as the primary goal and an important precondition for the achieving of true rank-and-file control. The
following extracts indicate the extent to which commitment
to class equality defined for the Far Left the goals and success of the occupation and structured their perception of day
to day events in the confrontations.

From the point of view of a revolutionary socialist
I think it was a success. When people are involved
in this sort of collective activity you can generalize
their struggle further ... you say, look the government is doing these fees increases nationally ...
it's part of the government economic strategy, so
if you are against the fee increases, you are
against cuts in public expenditure.... They start
questioning why you need cuts. You need cuts to
shift the resources towards the manufacturing in-
dustries and all that, you know, in order to boost
the profits of the bosses. (SWP/M/1: Prime
Initiator)

If the School can get away with cuts in this area,
it will go on to cuts in other areas and you have
to be aware of the fact that it is not a limited,
localized attack. It is the spearhead of a generalized attack on students and the working class and
the poor--the government is using racism against
foreign students as a way to ease in this particular
cut and so weaken the struggle generally.... It is
only by launching a fight on the basis of clear socialist principles that you are going to be able to
fight effectively against the cuts. (IMG/F/1: High
Participant)

Table IV (a) shows percentages of Broad Left and Far
Left activists who used economic and class equality as a

TABLE IV (b)

Percentage of LSE Activists Using the Value, Equality, as an Evaluative Criterion Compared with Percentages of Essex Activists Expressing Approval of the Value. Percentage of LSE and Essex Opponents Expressing Disapproval of Equality*

| Level of Activism | LONDON SCHOOL OF ECONOMICS | | | | | | **ESSEX UNIVERSITY | | | | | |
	No. Far Left	%	No. Broad Left	%	No. Opponents	%	No. Far Left	%	No. Broad Left	%	No. Opponents	%
PRIME INITIATORS	3	+100	3	+100	6	(-100)	N/a	N/a	6	+100	7	(-70)
ALL HIGH PARTICIPANTS	10	+100	7	+50			4	+100	13	+80- / +90		
ENTHUSIASTIC SUPPORTERS	4	+100	1	0								
TOTAL NOS.	17		11		6		4		13		7	

*Plus signs denote the percentages approving of the value, or using it as an evaluative criterion. Minus signs denote the percentages disapproving of the value.

**The Essex activists are not sub-divided into High Participant and Enthusiastic Supporter categories.

N.B.: There were five apolitical, thus non-socialist, Essex activists. Of these 75 per cent expressed approval of equality. The Ordinary Supporters at LSE were mild left, therefore non-socialist, so not shown in the above Table. Of these 50 per cent expressed approval of equality. They did not use the value in the strongly approving sense of an evaluative criterion or underlying moral principle. Nor did the Essex non-socialist activists.

selective criterion. It will be seen that the lower the level
of activism, the less the propensity to use the value as a
selective criterion. In addition, at both Essex and L. S. E. ,
the Broad Left expresses a lower magnitude of approval for
equality than is expressed by the Far Left. At L. S. E. , the
propensity to use equality as a selective criterion does not
exist to any extent among Broad Left leaders below the activism level of prime initiator. It is felt that the association between decreasing levels of activism and decreasing
propensities to use the value as a selective criterion, indicates that the political value, equality, was exerting some
causal influence on action, through its capacity to act as selective criterion and specify goals for action. It is also felt
that the higher propensity among the Far Left than among
the Broad Left to use equality as a selective and as an evaluative criterion is related to the adoption of equality as its
primary goal by the Far Left. Table IV (b) shows the percentages of L. S. E. activists who used euqality as an evaluative criterion and compares them to the percentages of Essex activists who expressed approval for equality. Lastly,
it is felt that if Table III is compared with Tables IV (a) and
(b), it can be seen that not only the value, equality, but also
the value, participative democracy, exerted some causal influence on action and provided for the Broad Left a primary
goal whilst only providing for the Far Left a secondary goal.

In summary, it can be said that the two values, equality, particularly class equality, and participative democracy,
which were of central importance in New Left socialist ideology of the 1960s, remained important political values among
socialist activist leaders during the mid-1970s. Two case
studies reveal that commitment to equality varied with level
of activism and version of socialist ideology adopted. On
the whole, the higher the level of activism and the further
left the ideology, the greater the propensity to express commitment to this value. It was argued, further, that commitment to participative democracy also varied with the version
of the ideology and level of activism. Presence of Broad
Left ideology and higher levels of activism increased the propensity to approve of this value. These findings are being
interpreted as indicating that the two values had the capacity
to endow direct action with meaning. It was suggested that
among some of the activists, in particular some of the enthusiastic supporters at L. S. E. and possibly a large number
of those who completed the Essex questionnaires, the two
values acted more as legitimating criteria, enabling a continued participation in direct action, rather than acting as

motives that initiated action in the first place. It was suggested, however, that at L. S. E. , among the socialist activist
leaders, the two values acted as selective criteria and strong
underlying moral principles, causally influencing action by
specifying goals for action yet to be taken. Among socialist
leaders the values were both motives and legitimations.

Political Belief and the Choice of Means

It is now suggested that the two socialist ideologies not only
specified goals but also selected means to those ends, as
Vaughan argues ideologies can do.   Though detailed discussion is outside the scope of the present paper, it is argued
that the total ideology of the Broad and Far Left factions
helped to determine whether equality was defined as a primary or a secondary goal.   It is further argued that the two
socialist ideologies, focussed through their primary value,
specified not only goals but also the means to those goals
which best matched the definition of the situation presented
by the total ideology.   At both national and local university
political levels, means were selected that were already implicit in the analysis constructed by the total ideology.

For example, the advocates of an extreme Far Left
ideology, which shares some of the New Left belief in the
worth of all selves, tend to see the inherent inequality of
capitalism as an insurmountable obstacle, preventing all
"selves" from realizing their potentialities and from being
treated as of equal moral and economic "worth. "   One would
expect, therefore, that such an ideology should specify, as a
primary goal, the pursuit of equality and should define equality as a precondition for self-realizing, true, rank-and-file
control, as was the case.   At the level of national politics,
this analysis or definition of the situation perceives the problems of present society as intractable: intractable problems
imply the selection of strong measures, or militant means to
change society.   At the level of university politics, the specification of the need for widespread equality as a primary
goal, means that the attainment of participative democracy in
the university is defined as being of secondary importance.
In addition, if the main goal is the attainment of greater,
society-wide equality, then concessions from university authorities will tend to be defined as irrelevant, and events in
the university will tend to be defined as useful mainly as a
means of raising consciousness with regard to the primary
goal.   Given this analysis, advocates of the ideology could

be expected to adopt a policy of "no compromise" over activist demands, as was the case. Such a policy constitutes, by definition, inflexible, militant tactics at the level of political action in the university.

In contrast, though advocates of the Broad Left ideology tend to seek fundamental change, they also see much that is worth retaining in present society. One might describe this ideology as radical-reformist. A gradual approach to change is implicit in the definition of present society as containing much that is of worth: violent, rapid change would only destroy what should be preserved. A gradual approach to change implies that the final goal of fundamental change will be located in the future, when gradual, incremental change has had an opportunity to become considerable as well as cumulative. However, though widespread change might have to await the future, this does not mean that short range goals, pursuing greater equality in limited areas, are not feasible. Thus, it is not surprising that advocates of such an ideology should define the pursuit of greater equality in political decision-making in the university as a feasible, desirable, short-range goal. The pursuit of limited short-range goals implies the pursuit of goals of equality in practical, specific ways, as will be discussed further shortly.

A commitment to gradual change and to the pursuit of participative democracy as a short term goal imply moderate, flexible, tactics at both national and university levels, provided participative democracy is defined in terms of collectivist autonomy, as was seen to be the case earlier. This version of participative democracy implies that the will of all members of all affected groups should be ascertained and respected in reaching decisions. The process of ascertaining and respecting the will of all implies moderate, flexible means.

The above implications are of course logical rather than necessarily present empirically. In addition the two above ideologies are specified in ideal-typical terms. However, such ideal-type logical implications indicate how somewhat more vaguely articulated, empirically present, ideologies can select goals and means that match definitions of the situation presented by the ideology. Moreover, large portions of the above ideal-type ideologies were in fact, mentioned explicitly and hinted at implicitly by prime initiators and many high participant activists. This indicates a link be-

tween ideology, goal and means, via definitions of the situation, as far as socialist leaders were concerned.   Krech,
Crutchfield and Ballachey argue that leaders of small groups
"furnish the ideology of the group" and represent more
firmly and articulately the "beliefs, values and norms" of
rank-and-file members.   If this is so and if the leaders did
in fact advocate the main elements of the ideal-type ideology,
one might feel that the ideal-types above show how such
ideologies might specify means in the case of highly activist,
but rank-and-file members, who belong to the same small
groups as the socialist leaders.

     Clearly, an ideology does not operate in a vacuum.
Changed conditions in the mid-1970s led to goals of equality
and participative democracy being pursued in more practical
ways.   This was apparent in the discussion of changing issues of student protest over the decade and it has been mentioned briefly in the discussion above of the effect of ideologies on the selection of means to action.   Evidence of this
change has already been examined.   It can be seen in the
Broad Left pursuit of goals of greater decision-making equality in limited, practical areas.   It can also be seen, though
to a lesser extent, in the Far Left stress on expenditure
cuts and fees increases, and in the new stress that change
should be worked for together with the working class and
through trade unions.   This change, when compared with
1960s goals, represents a move to more practical, limited
ways of pursuing equality.   The move towards practical goals
has proceeded to the greatest extent among the apolitical
activists at Essex and the ordinary, mild left, supporters
at L. S. E.

     Accompanying the move towards more practical goals
has been a concomitant move away from the wish to pursue
these goals in the context of new forms of life.   One aspect
of this move away from a search for new forms of life is
the fact that at neither university did activists express a
commitment to counterculture values.   Earlier it was implied that, in the 1960s, elements of the counterculture values
suffused the political values.   As social conditions change
and counterculture values cease interpenetrating the political
values, the latter, by definition become more specific,
boundary-maintaining, limited, intensifying the propensity to
seek practical and limited goals.

     Another aspect of the move away from a search for
new forms of non-capitalist life is reflected in the fact that

at both universities there was a loss of faith in "student vanguardism" and a lessening of the outright, short-term, rejection of capitalism. Student vanguardism was the term for the 1960s belief that one small push from activists would usher in the new society. Accompanying the rejection of student vanguardism and the view that change would take longer, was a willingness to become involved in the political and occupational systems. This willingness to become involved in these aspects of present society is incompatible with an outright immediate rejection of capitalism. Most activists at both universities had voted and intended to vote again. All but one envisaged some form of job in the future. The one exception, an L. S. E. prime initiator anticipated periods of unemployment because she felt a capitalist society would make it difficult to find a congenial job.

It is important to stress, however, that the lessening of an outright and immediate rejection of capitalism does not mean that there was no longer any distaste for capitalism. At Essex, half the Marxist activists and a quarter of the Broad Left activists specified "capitalism" as a "system I dislike" in answer to an open-ended question asking if there was any reason common to their rejection of a range of possible jobs. At both universities the most popular jobs were those that occupied a niche apart from the capitalist mode of production: teaching, media, social work, particularly with small and independent anti-establishment agencies. At both universities the Far Left showed a greater preference for these jobs than the Broad Left or, rather, the Broad Left was relatively more likely to consider some jobs that fell within the capitalist mode of production, such as management in commerce and industry.

The relatively greater distaste among the Far Left leaders for capitalism might be interpreted as some evidence of the capacity of an ideology to act as barrier or protection against the full effect of changed social conditions. The greater distaste for capitalism is also a smaller move away from the wish for new forms of non-capitalist social arrangements. Thus one would expect the move away from a search for new non-capitalist life styles to increase the further away one moves from a Far Left ideology. This was indeed the case as has already been pointed out in the discussion of the move towards practical goals. As the two changes, the one towards practical goals and the other away from a search for new life styles are concomitant changes, one would expect evidence of the one to furnish evidence for the occurrence of the other.

Conclusion

Boudon argues that during the seventies among French students there has been a contraction of student activism. Those protests which have occurred have been concerned, he writes, with issues that are particularistic, corporatist and materialistic. This chapter finds that a similar change has occurred, to some extent, among British activists in the seventies.

An overview of numbers of protests in the 1970s, and of the main issues which precipitated such protests, shows that student activism has had less impact in England and that there has, indeed, been some change in the grievances which generate protest. There was very little direct action in the 1960s over particularistic, materialistic demands. In contrast in the 1970s a large proportion of all outbreaks of direct action have been over instrumental issues.

Accompanying the appearance of more materialistic concerns has been some modification in the configuration of politically active student groups. One might interpret the move towards more practical, instrumental goals as a move away from the idealistic leftwing concerns identified by Crouch and Hoggart among some 1960s activists. There has been a similar rightward shift in some sections of the student political leadership. For example, the rightwing Federation of Conservative Students has become important and has played an active role on the executive of a number of student unions. In addition, though the executive of the N. U. S. over the decade has contained Far Left and Broad Left members, from 1977 onwards the Far Left has no longer been the majority.

However, these changes in the composition of politically active students have been modifications rather than a sharp break with the 1960s. As in the 1960s, the 1970s have seen the continuing importance of reformist socialist (Broad Left) and of revolutionary socialist Far Left groups. The seventies have also seen a continuing clash between these two socialist factions, similar to the 1960s.

Overseas students, particularly those subscribing to the same revolutionary socialist beliefs which the British Far Left hold, have gained a different importance during the second half of the decade. In the late 1960s, Blackburn argues, foreign students furnished the British left leadership with a Marxist analysis or ideology. Due to the increase in overseas tuition fees, overseas students in the 1970s have formed their own distinct, separate activist group, rather than merging with the British leftwing leadership. In addition, British leftwing activists have, according to Blackburn, gained access to a "home grown" Anglo-Marxism. For this reason one must not too easily interpret the modification in the composition of activist groups as an overall shift to the right. There have also been significant developments on the left. In addition there have been important continuities.

For example, in the seventies as in the sixties, a significant proportion of the student body has continued to hold views sympathetic to the left, even though such views are not incorporated into a sophisticated leftwing ideology. This mild left orientation, at both periods, has been sufficient to generate support, among the student body, for grievances being pressed by the more ideologically sophisticated left leadership. Not surprisingly, therefore, such grievances have included, in the 1970s, a concern with the typical leftwing issues apparent in 1960s protests. As a result protests over class and racial inequality, inequality of educational and economic opportunity and over rank-and-file control or participative democracy have co-existed with protests over instrumental issues. In very recent times, during the first half of the 1980 autumn term there has been a revival of interest in nuclear disarmament, recalling the moral condemnation in the 1960s of issues relating to foreign policy.

However, though there has been a continuing commitment to concerns that were important to the New Left activists of the 1960s, such concerns have, in the 1970s, been expressed in more limited, practical ways. The wish to pursue these goals in the context of new non-capitalist life styles has changed. The search for new life styles in the 1960s can be described as a pursuit of goals that were cultural and universalistic. Boudon argues that French students have moved away from such universalistic cultural concerns. The same process is seen in the political views found among British activists as evidenced by the two case studies. These activists expressed a distaste for, rather than an outright, short-term, rejection of capitalism. One might see the modification in their attitude to capitalism as a result of the "bleak conditions" identified by Hoggart. These conditions and the accompanying pessimistic social climate of the 1970s lead activists to perceive change as more difficult to achieve and therefore a long term goal. Matching the view that change is a slower process is a willingness to become partially involved in the present society, through voting and through entering the occupational system. This, however, does not alter the fact that the distaste for capitalism was deeply felt.

It was suggested that the presence of this deep distaste, accompanied by a continuing wish for some form of non-capitalist social arrangements, indicates the capacity of socialist ideologies to act as a barrier against the full effect of changed conditions. The twin move away from a search for new life styles and towards more particularistic, practical goals, was found to have progressed to the greatest extent among apolitical activists and activists with a mild left orientation rather than a developed socialist ideology. It had progressed to a lesser extent among the Broad Left reformist socialists and to the least extent among Far Left activists with a developed revolutionary socialist ideology. At L. S. E., the S. W. P. activists advocated a highly voluntaristic, anarchistic version of Marxism and could perhaps, in this one institution anyway, be seen as descendants of the 1960s New Left activists.

Though it is outside the scope of this chapter, it is suggested that the discontinuities between 1960s and 1970s protest is strongly associated with changing economic and other conditions while the continuities are related to persisting structural and cultural factors. As the latter can be expected to continue to affect students in the 1980s, partly but not only through the effect exerted on early socialization by parental jobs, one might expect a continuing commitment, based on such structural factors, to notions of equality and rank-and-file control. Thus one might expect a resevoir of mobilizable support for protests when particular events falsify such values: an example would be the expenditure cuts of the present Thatcher government. One might also expect a resevoir of mobilizable support should leftwing expectations drift upwards. The recent election of the leftwing Tribune group supporter, Michael Foot, to the leadership of the Labour party might, given other events, result in a raising of student expectations about an increased drive to equality. Disappointment with the Wilson government in this respect was one influence identified by Crouch as facilitating 1960s protest. It is possible that a similar process could occur in the 1980s.

Notes

1. Crouch discusses the progress of the first confrontations
    of the 1960s pp. 33-80, whilst Ch. IV, particularly
    pp. 97-122, gives details of protest at other institu-
    tions, apart from LSE (see Crouch, 1970).

2. This estimate was printed in the "Times Educational
    Supplement," referred to by Crouch, op. cit. p. 115.
    There are approximately 38 universities, containing
    about two-thirds of students in higher education, and
    44 polytechnics in England. The universities offer a
    traditional, high-status education. The polytechnics
    offer more vocational and specialized courses and are
    considered to be second rank institutions.

3. Klineberg gives a brief summary of student protest in
    Britain during the 1960s. Appendix I, as part of his
    cross-cultural analysis of student political values at
    the end of the sixties and beginning of the seventies.
    (See Klineberg, 1979.)

4. Participation was seen as important in the attainment of
    a sense of community but participation in university
    committees was seen as irrelevant in the drive to
    equality and true rank-and-file control.

5. Hoggart writes that "the student movement ... stressed
    the importance of ideals beyond the immediate present
    [though not] in Britain since the late 1940s." See
    Occasional Papers, Society for Research into Higher
    Education, Annual Conference, 1978: Student Revolu-
    tion or Reform. (Ed.) Stewart Armstrong-Guilford.
    Also reprinted in Political Quarterly, No. 50, pp. 172-81.

6. These figures were derived from reports on activism
    carried by two newspapers, the leftwing "Morning
    Star" and the national, liberal daily "The Guardian."

7. To gain an idea of how widespread the protest was the
    number of institutions in the table can be compared
    with the 38 universities and 44 polytechnics in England
    (see note 2). These are listed in the Education Au-
    thorities Directory and Annual 1979, p. 958f. The
    figures for the universities count major universities,
    e.g., Oxford, Cambridge, London, as one. Each

separate college constituting the universities is not included in the total.

8. The total number of regular undergraduate, postgraduate, Diploma and Certificate regular students at LSE in selected years is as follows:

1966/67	1967/68	1976/77	1979/80
3,478	3,262	3,120	3,254

9. As the figures are derived from newspaper reports, the protests over limited, material demands could be under-represented if protests well outside London failed to be reported in the two newspapers. Despite this, however, the table gives a rough indication of number of protests and distribution of these by precipitating issue.

10. As the Essex interviews were found to be more revealing than the questionnaires, data on the L. S. E. 1977 protests were collected by long, unstructured tape-recorded interviews. Interviews were supplemented by periods of observation from mid-February to end of May, during which impromptu speeches in the occupied building were noted, groups of students working on posters, etc., were joined. Union meetings were attended and student bars and coffee bars visited in order to observe friendship patterns among the activists. It soon became clear that there were different levels of involvement in activism. Five activists were the prime initiators of action; four of whom were interviewed. The next most activist group, totalling seventeen, acted as "lieutenants." They directed and organized action and have been termed High Participants. Five other activists enthusiastically supported the confrontations but did not help organize the protests. These, together with four rank-and-file supporters, termed Ordinary Supporters, made up the thirty activists interviewed. The Ordinary Supporters attended the occupations and the Union policy meetings but, apart from this, they took a passive role. In addition there were long interviews with all six leading opponents of the confrontations.

   As far as the activist leaders are concerned, though not exhaustive, the L. S. E. coverage was extensive. Most High Participants were contacted:

the list of possible interviewees constructed from observation agreed with the names suggested by a range of activists. Though there is under-representation of Ordinary Supporters and of Enthusiastic Supporters, the main objective was to contrast leading activists and opponents. Most members of both these groups were compared, and it was found that commitment to the two political values varied systematically with group membership. Therefore, it is felt that, despite the under-representation of less activist groups, the L. S. E. data is of some use as a record of political commitment among the activist leadership, and of the way in which they affected political action.

Comparisons are made using percentages, which are considered to provide an adequate indication of differences between activist and non-activist groups. Lipset et al. present their findings in the form of percentages in the study "Union Democracy." Although the findings of the two studies cannot be generalized to all British student activists, it is felt that they reveal some general characteristics regarding the effect on their action of the ideologies advocated by student activist leaders. This is because, as indicated earlier, Essex and particularly L. S. E. have been taken as a model and symbol of activism by students since the 1960s. Thus one might see them as an ideal type applicable, to some degree, to other activists.

References

Becker, H. S. (1952). "Social-class variations in the teacher-pupil relationship," Journal of Educational Sociology 25(4): 451-65.

Bendix, R. (1963). Work and Authority in Industry; Ideologies of Management in the Course of Industralization. New York: Harper and Row.

Bernstein, B. (1970). "Elaborated and restricted codes, their social origins and some consequences," in Danziger, K. Readings in Child Socialization. Oxford: Pergamon.

Bernstein, B. (1973). Class Codes and Control. London: Routledge and Kegan Paul.

Blackburn, R. (1969). "A brief guide to bourgeois ideology," in Cockburn, A. , and Blackburn, R. (eds.) Student

Power. Problems, Diagnosis, Action. Baltimore: Penguin.

Blackburn, R. (1979). "Was this the birth of Anglo-Marxism?" The Times Higher Educational Supplement, 7 Dec., p. 11.

Boudon, R. (1979). "The 1970s in France: a period of student retreat" in Altbach, P. G. (ed.) Higher Education 8(6): 669-681.

Bradley, Ian. (1979). "The students turn right." Spectator, 23rd January, p. 16, 18.

Crouch, C. (1970). The Student Revolt. London: The Bodley Head.

Douglas, Mary (1973). ed. Rules and Meanings; The Anthropology of Everyday Knowledge. Selected Readings. Harmondsworth, Middx.: Penguin Education.

Fox, A. (1974). Beyond Contract: Work, Power and Trust Relations. London: Faber.

Frisk, T. (1970). "The nature and causes of student unrest," in Crick, B. and Robson, W. A. (eds.) Protest and Discontent. Harmondsworth, Middx.: Penguin Education.

Hoggart, R. (1979). "Student Politics 1968-78: the student movement and its effect in the universities." Political Quarterly, No. 50, April-June, pp. 172-81.

Klineberg, O., Zavoloni, M., Louis-Guérin, C. and Ben Brika, J. (1979). Student Values and Politics. A Cross Cultural Comparison. New York: The Free Press.

Krech, D., Crutchfield, R. S. and Ballachey, E. L. (1962). Individual in Society. New York: McGraw-Hill.

Lipset, S. M., Trow, M. A. and Coleman, J. S. (1956). Union Democracy; The Internal Politics of the International Typographical Union. Glencoe, Ill.: The Free Press.

Macpherson, C. B. (1962). The Political Theory of Possessive Individualism: Hobbes to Locke. Oxford: Clarendon Press.

Martin, David A. (1965). Pacificism: An Historical and Sociological Study. London: Routledge and Kegan Paul.

Martin, David A. (1973). Tracts Against the Times. Guildord: Lutterworth Press.

Newson, J. and E. (1965). Patterns of Infant Care in an Urban Community. Harmondsworth, Middx.: Penguin Books.

Stevens, R. (1975). "Making sense of society," Open University Social Science Foundation Course, Units 21-22. Milton Keynes: The Open University Press.

Vaughan, M. and Archer, M. S. (1971). Social Conflict and Educational Change in England and France 1789-1848. London: Cambridge University Press.

STUDENT ACTIVISM IN GREECE: A HISTORICAL AND EMPIRICAL ANALYSIS*

by George Psacharopoulos and
Andreas M. Kazamias

It is a widely held belief that student activism was one of the sparks that led to the downfall of a seven year military dictatorship in Greece. The Polytechneio students' uprising of November 1973 was the major open opposition to the regime that rules the country since 1967 and might have contributed to the collapse of the junta a few months later. In this chapter we give a historical background of student politics in Greece and present the results of a quantitative model attempting to explain present student activism. We also speculate on the future direction of student activism given the extension of educational opportunities to rural students.

Historical Background

In the Western societies, the years 1967-1969 are often taken to be an important landmark in the history of student activism [1]. In those same years Greece was under the iron grip of a military dictatorship (1967-1974) and the erstwhile volatile Greek students seemed to be totally unaffected by the ferment that shook Paris in May 1968, or caused the killings at Kent State University. Yet a few years later, in November 1973, a delayed reaction, as it were, struck with bloody vengeance at the regime of the colonels, causing a shake-up in its leadership and ominously heralding a new era in Greek student politics. A group of angry youths barricaded themselves behind the doors of the National Technical University (the Polytechneio) protesting against the oppressive rule of the junta and clamouring for "freedom, bread, and education."

*Reprinted by permission of the author and publisher from Higher Education, 9:1 (March 1980), pp. 127-138. Copyright ©1980 by the Elsevier Scientific Publishing Co., Amsterdam.

After their refusal to withdraw, army tanks smashed through the iron gates of the University and armed soldiers soon crushed the rebels, leaving behind several dead and wounded.

The events at the Polytechneio soon assumed symbolic significance as the expression of a popular stand against the curtailment of civil liberties, and more pertinently here, participation in and the rights to education.

It was not surprising therefore that when civilian government was restored in the summer of 1974 the students were among the first to demand the purging of the universities of junta or pro-junta professors, the abrogation of legislation that restricted their academic freedom, student participation in university governance, and generally the democratization and modernization of the educational system. The new government, representing a right-of-center political alignment headed by veteran politician Constantine Karamanlés [2], embarked upon a reformist program that encompassed all levels and types of education.

One of the several outcomes of this reformist activity [3] of most relevance here, was a "law-framework" (Nomos Plaisio) proposing changes in the structure and administration of Greek universities (AEI's). After going through several versions since the appearance of the first draft in 1975, it entered the state statutes in 1978 as Law 815, "On the Regulation of Subjects Pertaining to the Organization and Functioning of Highest Educational Institutions. "

From its inception, the Nomos Plaisio has been one of the most contentious aspects of the Greek educational reform movement of the last twenty years. The students never liked it in toto, least of all Law 815, which according to them left the much criticized and restrictive system of the professorial chair essentially unscathed, did not resolve the problem of university asylum or pupil participation in decision making, aimed at phasing out the teaching assistants, restricted the examination periods, etc. The Law was branded as "anti-pedagogical and anti-democratic. "

It was not, of course, the first time that Greek students had protested against government actions or policies affecting education or for that matter had taken part in the broader political life of the nation. The politicization of the Greek students and the universities dates back to the early years of the emergence of the Greek nation state in the

nineteenth century. In 1843, only six years after the establishment of the University of Athens (The Ottonian University
as the first higher educational institution was then called),
professors and students participated in the political upheavals
that forced King Otto to accept the first Greek constitution
and expel many of his Bavarian advisers [4]. Continuing
their protests against Otto's reign, students demonstrated
and clashed with the police in 1857, 1859, 1860 and in 1862
when Otto was forced to abdicate.

Subsequently there have been numerous other episodes
involving the universities, the police and the government.
Suffice to mention the bloody riots at the turn of the century
over the language question. In 1901 and 1903, students and
professors of the University of Athens were incited and mobilized against the translation of ancient Greek texts and the
Bible into the popular language (the demotiké) and in favour
of retaining the pure form (katharevousa). The results were
vandalism, bloody riots and the ultimate overthrow of the
government. One interesting characteristic of this activity
was its conservative orientation. Students supported the established language and were against progressive policies (see
Papapanos, 1970; and Tarrou, 1968).

Student activism in one form or another continued
intermittently in the decades since the events over the language question. After the brutal suppression of any form of
student activity outside the youth organization of the Metaxas
fascist dictatorship (1935-1940), different student organizations re-emerged in the fifties and sixties. Student activism
during this period was mainly directed towards the inadequa-
cies in their university education, although one must not for-
get the Lambrakis affair (Lambrakis, a leftist deputy and
favourite spokesman among students was assassinated in 1963
by rightist elements, the episode immortalized in "Z"). The
then Karamanlés government (1956-1963) suppressed, often
brutally, deviant student movements.

As with student activities of the sixties and seventies
in other countries, the ideological orientation of the Greek
student movement during these same decades, and more so
today, has been strongly toward the left of the political spectrum. Thus the most active and powerful groups since 1974
have been the socialist Panellēnios Agonistikē Syndikalistikē
Parataxi (PASP) and the two Communist organizations Pan-
spoudastikē Syndikalistikē Kinēsē (PSK) and Demokratikos
Agonas (DA). Each of these groups corresponds to "adult"

political opposition parties of the left: for PASP, the Pan-
hellenic Socialist Movement (PASOK), for PSK, the Communist Party of Greece (KKE) and for DA the Community Party
of Greece (Interior) [5].

Interestingly, the respective strength of the student
groups does not reflect the strength of the related adult political alignments, as the latter is gauged by parliamentary
representation. Since 1974 the right-of-center New Democracy has had an overall majority in the Greek Chamber of
Deputies (Voulé), but the equivalent student group, DAP, has
consistently and noticeably lagged behind the leftist groups
on university campuses.

Given the nature and ideological hue of the Greek
student movement, student activism has been directed
against most of the political, economic and social policies
(including the educational ones) of the post-junta "liberal"
Greek government. Thus the militant student leftist
groups have been critical of Greece's association with
NATO and the European Economic Community as well as her
economic ties with multinational corporations. From their
perspective, these policies continue to make Greece a "dependent" nation.

Students have protested against the recent reforms in
secondary and technical education, and have been especially
critical of several features of Nomos Plaisio as well as Law
815. They have all along called for the restoration of "university asylum, " real participation in university and faculty
governance, expansion of universities, changes in the numerus
clausus and methods of admissions into higher education, better buildings, equipment, welfare services, etc.

The nature and direction of the student movement in
Greece has been a constant source of concern and irritation
to the government, which, except for the short-lived Papan-
dreou government of 1964-1965 has been in the hands of right-
wing conservative parties. Since the restoration of civilian
rule in 1974, the militant student groups have been a powerful force affecting the actual functioning of the universities.
Through strikes, boycotts, rallies, and other pressure tactics
they have caused the cessation of classes, the intimidation of
professors, and currently, the obstruction of implementing
Law 815. University educational policy, in short, cannot and
does not ignore the student movement.

Despite its significance, there has hardly been any
systematic study historical, empirical or otherwise, of student activism in Greece. We hope that the present study
will arouse the interest not only of the Greeks, but also of
scholars of student politics in general.

Understanding Student Activism

Greece now has a population of 100,000 students (the country's population is 9 million) and is four times as large as
it was in the early sixties. In spite of the great expansion
in student numbers the numerus clausus continues to exist,
less than 20% of those who wish entry to a university institution being able to do so. Because of budgetary limitations
the expansion of student numbers was not accompanied by
the necessary expansion of lecture rooms and hiring of extra
professors. The increased student numbers were mainly directed at socio-political faculties and 2-year institutions of
technical education. The number of full professors increased
by less than 2-fold in the 1960-1976 period. As a result,
the student /teacher ratios stand at 90:1 regarding the main
teaching staff and 16:1 for all the teaching staff. There
exists a high proportion of working students and high non-
attendance rates because, among other things, of lack of
lecture rooms. Table I shows the composition of the student body in comparison with the occupational structure of
the labour force. In spite of the usual differences in representation by father's occupation (see last column) the fact
remains that a quarter of students have a father who is a
farmer and nearly as many have a father who is a manual
worker.

It was in this context that we conducted a survey in 1977
under the auspices of the Ministry of Education in order to
assess the profile of the student population in Greece. The
survey covered the Universities of Athens, Salonica, Patras
and Yannena, the School of Industrial Studies of Salonica,
the Athens Polytechneio, the Athens School of Economic and
Business Studies, the Herakleion KATEE (a post-secondary
but non-university status technical school) and the Herakleion
Teacher Training College [6]. The final usable sample size
was of the order of 1400 students mainly drawn from the
first and third year of studies.

Beyond those factual questions the survey questionnaire
contained a series of opinion probes by which one can assess

TABLE I

Distribution of Students by Father's Occupation and Comparison to the Occupational Distribution of the Labour Force

Father's occupation (1)	Students (2)	Labour force (3)	Difference (2) (3) (percentage)
Professionals	11. 7	6. 2	5. 5
Office workers	15. 8	8. 1	7. 5
Sales workers	14. 1	7. 7	6. 4
Manual workers	22. 9	32. 2	9. 3
Farmers	27. 6	37. 7	10. 1
Other	7. 9	8. 1	0. 2
Total	100. 0	100. 0	

Source: Col. 2 - Ministry of Education, unpublished material. Col. 3 - National Statistical Service of Greece (1971).

the degree of a student's attitude towards activism. Table II gives the percentage of students who agreed to a set of particular statements and also the fact that they voted in the last student elections. Preliminary factor analysis of the eight student attitudes in Table II revealed that the most important, if not explicit, factor loading corresponded to the second variable, namely the fact that a respondent agreed to the statement, "student political activity is the only hope for improvement in education. " Thus in what follows we shall name ACTIVISM the 0-1 dummy variable that has a value of 1 if a particular student agreed to the above statement and 0 otherwise [7].

The mean of this variable was equal to 0. 53, indicating that 53% of the students interviewed had a favourable attitude towards political activism. Table III presents the mean value of this variable disaggregated by particular student characteristics. Thus sex does not relate to student political activism as the 1% difference between males and females is not statistically significant. But there exist dramatic differences in student attitude towards political

TABLE II

Percentage of Students who Agreed to a Particular Statement

Statement	Percentage
Students should get mixed in politics for the benefit of education	53
Student political activism in the only hope for improvement in education	53
Student activism is desirable but students should not stick to a given party line	57
Without party support the student movement is bound to fail	40
Deep radical reforms are needed in post-secondary education	60
Universities should participate in community development	74
The university asylum is non-existent	30
Voted in student election	77

Source: 1977 Student Survey.

activism when considering other variables in Table III. For example:

- The younger the student the more active he or she is.
- Students from urban origins are more active than those from rural areas. The activism rate of those students who were born abroad is one of the lowest in this sample (30%).
- There exists a gradual increase in student activism as one moves up the father's income ladder.
- Students whose father was a university graduate have higher activism rates relative to the rest.
- Student activism is neatly stratified by the grade obtained at the last class of secondary school. Those who obtained a grade of 12 (the pass corresponding to 10) have double the activism rate of those with the top grade (20).

TABLE III

Mean Activism Rates by Selected Student Characteristics

Characteristic		Mean activity rate (Percentage)
Sex:	Males	53
	Females	54
Age:	19	58
	21	47
Place of birth:	Urban	56
	Rural	49
	Abroad	30
Father's income:	5-10000 drs/month	54
	10-15000 drs/month	57
	15-20000 drs/month	59
Father's education:	Primary school graduate	50
	Secondary school graduate	50
	University graduate	54
Secondary school grade:	12	61
	14	56
	16	50
	20	35
Institution and/or faculty:	Athens University, Theology	47
	Athens University, Law	58
	Athens University, Medicine	41
	Athens University, Mathematics	63
	University of Salonica, Geology	51
	University of Salonica, Dentistry	55
	Athens Polytechnic, Topography	55
	Patras University, Mathematics	37
	Yannena University, Mathematics	37
	Athens Business School (ASOEE)	53
	Salonica Industrial School	67
	Herakleion KATEE	69
	Herakleion Teacher Training	42
Year of study	First	56
	Second	54
	Third	48
	Fourth	37
Satisfied with his own progress:	Yes	45
	No	57

Source: 1977 Student Survey.

There exist interesting activism differences by kind of school and faculty:

- There exists less activism in the new provincial universities of Yannena and Patras relative to Athens.
- Low activism rates are observed among theology students (!) and prospective teachers.
- The highest activism rates are observed in the Athens Faculty of Mathematics, the Industrial Studies School of Salonica and especially the non-university status Herakleion Technical School.
- Activism decreases as a student progresses from one year to the next.
- Students who confess they are not satisfied with their own progress at the university have a much higher activism rate relative to the rest.

Table IV essentially documents the same information presented above using correlation analysis and alternative proxies for selected student characteristics, like father's income and father's education (measured by completed years of schooling).

TABLE IV

Zero-order Correlations Between Selected Sample Characteristics

Characteristics	Correlation coefficient
Urban origin and father's income	0. 354
Urban origin and father's education	0. 331
Father's education and father's income	0. 529
Secondary school grade and father's income	0. 248
Secondary school grade and father's education	0. 296
Father's income and attendance at Athens University	0. 138
Secondary school grade and attendance at Athens University	0. 304
Secondary school grade and activism	0. 026
Urban origin and activism	0. 138

Source: 1977 Student Survey.

A Path Model of the Determinants of Student Activism

From the above correlations, it is evident that more than one factor affects student activism in the sense that two or more earlier factors are highly associated with each other (e. g. father's education, father's income and urban origin).

The information raised, however, allows us to move from associations into a causal model by ordering happenings in time. Thus let us theorize along the following lines:

The region where the student was born is the most exogenous original factor. We expect this factor to act as a surrogate for a host of attitudinal, cultural and cognitive characteristics instilled in the student and his family that will determine later developments in life. For example, we expect an urban region of birth to be positively associated with (if not having earlier determined) the mother's level of education. In turn, mother's education is expected to determine the student's scholastic progress because of coaching, interest in his or her studies if not sheer encouragement. Finally, all three preceding factors, i. e. region, mother's education and scholastic progress are expected to affect the student's activism rate.

Figure 1 presents the results of fitting this recursive path model. "Urban origin" is measured by a 0-1 dummy variable, the 1 corresponding to the fact that a student was born in a city and 0 otherwise. "Mother's education" is measured by the number of completed years of schooling. "Bad progress" is measured by a 0-1 dummy variable, the 1 corresponding to the student confessing that he is not satisfied with his own progress at the university and 0 otherwise. Finally, "activism" has been measured by a 0-1 dummy variable, the 1 corresponding to the fact that the student agreed to the second statement in Table II.

The numbers on the arrows are standardized path coefficients. Their sign and size denote the way and relative strength one factor affects the next one in the theorized temporal causal sequence. Thus urban origin exerts a strong positive influence on student activism (0. 138) even when one corrects for mother's education and bad progress [8].

Urban origin also exerts indirect influences on student activism by positively affecting bad progress (upper loop of

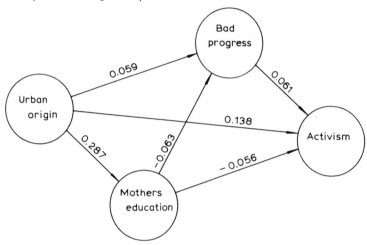

Fig. 1.   A path model of the determinants of student activism.

arrows in Fig. 1).   However, urban origin has a dampening
effect on student activism by positively and strongly (0. 287)
affecting mother's education, the latter negatively affecting
bad progress and student activism.

Discussion of the Results

Urban origin was found to be the major factor determining
student activism.   However, this variable acts as a surrogate
of many other cultural and attitudinal characteristics of the
population.   Urban students, in contrast to rural ones, are
exposed to a wider cognitive and cultural environment and see
more alternatives to social action.   At the same time they
have greater expectations from the educational system which,
in its present structure and orientation, cannot meet them.
Hence they are more likely to press for the kind of action
they think will change the system in accordance with their
expectations.

There is also some other evidence that students of
peasant origins tend to be more conservative.   For example,
in the elections for delegates to national conferences, the
DAP (the student faction closest to the New Democracy) drew
much support from students with peasant origins.

Activism is comparatively lower among theology and
teacher training students.   Possible explanations are:

(a) Students attending pedagogical academies generally come from lower socio-economic backgrounds and from rural areas, and, as noted above, rural students tend to be more conservative.

(b) Going to a pedagogical academy for many students is an avenue to social mobility. We expect that where a student perceives more chances for social mobility or where the occupational prospects are better visible activism would be lower. (Cf. also students in medicine.)

(c) Regarding theology students, the Church in Greece has been a very conservative institution. Students drawn to the priesthood would more likely be conservative and less active.

Medical students are less active mainly for the reasons listed above regarding mobility and occupational chances. Also medical students have tended to cast more votes for DAP, the New Democracy student faction.

Regarding KATEE students it should be remembered that ESEE (The National Union of Higher Education Students) came into existence after the fall of the junta in 1974. Many of the problems of these students stem from the establishment of KATEEs as yet an uncertain type of vocational institution in terms of occupational opportunities, guarantees and status. So attending a KATEE is fraught with ambivalences--and yet, given the numerus clausus, students are often obligated to go to a KATEE (it is something more than a secondary school). Added to this may be the criticism leveled against KATEEs that they are the product of the involvement of the World Bank and that they serve foreign capital interests. (This has been a point of criticism by PASP and PSK and both factions showed unusually high successes in the voting at Herakleion.)

To the extent the results generated above truly reflect students' attitudes they can be used to make some predictions regarding future student activity in Greece. Present government policies (or intended policies) include first, opening up of countryside campuses, second, elevating teacher training colleges to university status and third, channelling more students to KATEEs. If we extrapolate the results of our analysis, the first two policies will depress student activism. However, to the extent the promotion of KATEEs is successful, activism will increase.

Notes

1. For a historical and comparative perspective of student activism see Bowers and Bader (1977) and for a collection of essays on particular topics see Lipset and Altbach (1969) and Altbach (1970).

2. Constantine Karamanlēs was Prime Minister from 1956 to 1963 and leader of a conservative (rightist) political group called National Radical Union (ERE). From 1963-1974 he lived in self-exile in Paris. After the fall of the junta in 1974 he was called to restore civilian rule. Upon his return he formed a new party, which in actuality was centered in the nucleus of the older ERE. The new party, perhaps more reformist than its predecessor, was called New Democracy.

3. The reformist movement included two important laws-- 309 and 576--providing for the restructuring of general and technical/vocational education.

4. King Otto, previously Prince of Bavaria, was "given" to the nascent Greek state by the protecting powers (England, France, Russia). With his arrival came a coterie of Prussian advisers who exerted a powerful influence on him and the conduct of Greek affairs.

5. In Greece student groups are known as "parataxeis" (factions) and they are directly related to the political parties outside in the larger society. Two measures of the strength of the student groups are (a) their success in the biannual elections to university school councils. On both criteria the leftist factions (PASP, PSK and DA) have been the most successful in the elections of 1975, 1977 and 1979.

6. The initial sample design included several other institutions but the survey was boycotted by the local, mostly leftist oriented, student unions fearing that the returns might be used against the student body. We consider this boycotting an interesting "result" of the study.

7. Of course, the correlation of this variable with the others is very high, e.g., with first statement 0.387, with fourth statement 0.404, with fifth statement 0.281 and with sixth statement 0.306.

8. All coefficients are statistically significant at the 10%
   level of probability or better. Because the mean
   value of the ultimate dichotomous dependent variable
   is close to 0.5, ordinary least squares were used.
   We do not expect a maximum likelihood application,
   which would have been more appropriate in this case,
   to significantly alter the conclusions.

References

Altbach, P. (ed.) (1970). The Student Revolution: A Global
    Analysis. Bombay: Lalvani.
Bowers, W. J. and Bader, A. M. (1977). "Campus unrest,"
    in The Encyclopedia of Higher Education. Vol. 9,
    pp. 4275-4301.
Lipset, S. M. and Altbach, P. (1969). Students in Revolt.
    Boston: Houghton Mifflin.
National Statistical Service of Greece (1971). Population
    Census.
Papapanos, Costas (1970). "Historical Chronicle of our
    Highest Education." Athens: Pierce College,
    p. 419ff. (in Greek).
Tarrou, Demetrios, J. (1968). "Genesis, Origin and De-
    velopment of the National and Kapodistrian University,
    1837-1936." Ph.D. Thesis, New York University,
    p. 115ff.

We are grateful to Mina Typaldou for reading a first draft
of this paper and offering suggestions for improvement.

STUDENT POLITICS IN CONTEMPORARY LATIN AMERICA

by Daniel Levy

Just a decade ago, student politics was considered extremely important by policy-makers, media, and social scientists. Whatever happened since? The question, properly posed for much of the world, is particularly poignant for Latin America. This region, after all, has generally been regarded as the archetypical example, as hero or villain, of student activism. "Of all national or regional groups," Seymour Martin Lipset notes, "the students of Latin America have been the most significant politically for the longest period of time (Lipset, 1972, p. xxi). And during the 1960s Latin Americanists devoted a remarkable portion of their research to student politics. The student may even qualify as the area's most overstudied political actor of the 1960s, though there had been very little prior work. I will not analyze the literature here; there are some useful review essays (Peterson, 1970; Thomas and Craig, 1973) and regional overviews (Hennessy, 1967; Scott, 1967; Liebman, et al. , 1972). Suffice it to recall that the roots of political activism were explored in such matters as ideology, anti-americanism, the Cuban Revolution, antipathy to dictatorship, revulsion at inequality, unease about personal job prospects, gender, parental background, the generation gap, the youth culture, peer group socialization, lack of a sense of university community and extra-curricular activities, excessive academic rigidity, and also excessive academic laxity.

The contrast to the 1970s is like day and night. There has been very little additional study, at least since the very early 1970s. Part of the change obviously stems from the fact that much work had already been done. More importantly, the contemporary capitalist-authoritarian course of much of the region's politics, juxtaposed to the leftist or progressive tendencies of student politics, has cast grave doubt on whether students are really as significant in shaping national policies as many had assumed in the 1960s. Finally, in the 1970s, student activity itself tapered off in much, albeit certainly

far from all, of the region. Yet the academic pendulum has
swung so far back in the other direction that we have now
had a decade of too little study. Students do merit political
analysis. This becomes clear once we drop the image of
students frequently playing decisive roles in determining national policies, and instead focus more on matters such as
strong influence over higher education policy itself, political
recruitment, the generation of ideas, and legitimacy and disorder. The actual difference in student politics between the
1960s and 1970s was not one of day and night but only half
way around. And to the real extent that student politics did
decline in importance, we should understand why.

Although one could obviously deal with any number of
factors, such as the world-wide trend toward student depoliticization, I focus on two principal determinants of the degree
of Latin American student activism in the 1970s. One is
political regime type. The other is the private university/
public university distinction. The rise of highly repressive
authoritarian regimes and the astonishing growth of the private sector combine to account for much of the reduction in
student political activity.

Variation Among Political Regimes

The pitfalls of generalizing about Latin America nations are
reduced considerably if we disaggregate, forming distinct
categories. Kalman Silvert (1967, 381-83), for one, created
four categories based on level of societal development. After
playing practically no role in traditional societies, students
become most important in newly modernizing societies, before
losing relative strength in more developed societies and even
more in still more developed societies, the third and fourth
categories. Although obviously dated, the schema has held
up remarkably well, and I draw from it. Dissatisfied with
its tinge of developmental determinism, however, I propose
a new schema, based on political regime type. Although
level of development correlates with regime type to some degree, the correlation is not perfect. I do make one basic
development-related distinction, distinguishing my first and
second from my third and fourth categories. Regimes in the
latter are those which must respond to greater levels and
move diversified forms of mobilization and participation,
whether they respond by accommodation or repression. As
the overwhelming majority of Latin America's population is
found in categories three and four, it is the distinction be-

tween these categories that is in fact crucial. No assumption
is made here that category four encompasses more developed
nations than category three. Instead, by focusing on regime
type, we can make the absolutely essential distinction, for
the 1970s, between those regimes that have basically accom-
modated themselves to continued student activism and those
that have harshly repressed it.

The first category, the traditional, is the stable, authoritarian political regime, fundamentally unchanged for some
considerable time. Students play a very limited role either
in national or university politics (García Laguardia, 1977,
pp. 97-99). Embracing only two small countries, Haiti and
Paraguay, this is by far the least important category. The
second category encompasses the still narrowly-based but now
more vulnerable oligarchy, where the politics of change is
much in evidence. These regimes lack the long-standing
stability of those in category one. Students play their biggest
role here, raising demands now perhaps common elsewhere
but still quite radical at home. Because other societal institutions generally are weak, there is more "space" or leeway
for student influence. So although category two is not very
significant in terms of numbers, compared to categories
three and four, it is significant for the role that student activism can play. It is also important to analyze category
two, in direct contrast to categories three and four, because
category two is often wrongly stereotyped in popular images
as the Latin American modal form. In fact basically, the
"Central American mode" cases include El Salvador, Guatemala, Honduras, Nicaragua, and perhaps Panama, as well
as the Dominican Republic.

Reconciliation regimes are found in systems composed
of many more powerful groups than found in categories one
or two. These regimes (Anderson, 1967) may or may not
be democratic, but they are not headed by authoritarian mili-
taries bent on extended and extensive repressive rule. Even
where repression may characterize regime policy toward
lower sectors, it does not generally characterize regime policy toward the middle sectors that dominate higher education
(Levy 1980, pp. 148-50). Compared to category four, sufficient freedom is usually permitted for at least some student
political activity. Compared to category two, however, other
societal institutions now capture more space, so that student
activity plays a less decisive role in shaping national political
events. Labor unions, for example, now tend to be a more
organized, potent, force. Cases include Colombia, Costa

Rica, Ecuador, Mexico, Venezuela, probably Peru, and possibly Boliva.

The fourth category, the modern authoritarian (or "new" or "bureaucratic" authoritarian), is defined here by great repression of the relatively advanced degree of participation previously achieved (Collier, 1979; O'Donnell, 1978; Malloy, 1976). Here harsh repression is directed not only against lower sectors but also middle sectors, certainly including university students. Cases include Argentina, Brazil, Chile, and Uruguay. I shall also include Cuba, because there too an authoritarian regime severely circumscribes free student expression, but the regime's civilian and socialist character obviously could justify a separate regime category.

Problems with such a schema are obvious. Lines among categories are not absolutely clear or fixed. Political regimes have not remained unchanged throughout the 1970s. Certain cases could reasonably be placed in different modal-type categories. But the categorization allows us to identify and analyze the basic, contrasting, contemporary patterns of student politics. And most cases fall rather clearly into a given category [1]. I focus here only on categories two, three, and four, deleting category one.

Oligarchic regimes. The literature on student politics makes many romantic references to the student role in toppling dictators: Gómez and Pérez Jiménez in Venezuela, Ibáñez in Chile, Machado and Batista in Cuba, Uriburu and Perón in Argentina, Leguía in Peru, Trujillo in the Dominican Republic. In fact, the student role was generally complementary, not determinative. Where it has been and still can be most important, however, is where regimes rule over relatively undeveloped political systems. This is largely because the same amount of student activity that would be a nuisance in more complex systems is a danger here. Students can more easily form meaningful popular front alliances with other groups opposing oligarchical dictatorships. Peasants, workers, middle sectors, possibly even businessmen are potential allies. Prospects for such broad alliances diminish in the more developed systems; repression can prevent that. But activity is often intense, and very often significant when it is. In addition, students generally became more active in such countries as El Salvador, Guatemala, and Nicaragua in the 1970s than they had been in the 1960s.

An excellent example of student political influence came in Nicaragua toward the close of the decade. Students were in the forefront of the drive to oust the hated Somoza regime. The narrowness of Somoza's support base contrasted with the breadth of the popular alliance against him. Ruling circles in El Salvador and Guatemala feared a Central American domino effect. Guatemalan student activity, already prominent, linked with worker protests and immediately took on new verve and violence as the Nicaraguan situation unraveled. More important than any demonstration effects, however, were the comparatively similar political configurations among the oligarchic systems. Thus, violent student-government confrontation obviously predated Somoza's demise. In El Salvador, for example, the government took over the university in 1972, closed it for a year, and re-opened it under its own specially-appointed rector. Nonetheless, by 1974 there was great violence as students protested against the lack of intra-university democracy--and against the government's enthusiastic hosting of the quintessentially bourgeois Miss Universe pageant (Webre, 1979, pp. 185-89). Additional violent confrontations between students and government, in the ensuing years, served to stiffen student activists as major opponents of the ruling system. The General Student Assembly hailed the 1977 murder of the military-appointed right-wing rector, "a hated landlord and oligarch" (Latin American Political Report, 1977, p. 303). It is the oligarchic category that experiences the often violent political activity (Thomas and Craig, 1973, p. 85) too often facilely identified with Latin America as a whole.

Another striking feature of student politics in category two is the high degree of legalized participation in university governance sometimes found (though often abused) even under dictatorial regimes (Benjamin, 1965, 113-116; García Laguardia, 1977). More modern authoritarian regimes simply do not sanction anything similar.

Reconciliation Regimes. Student politics in the reconciliation category has less potential impact on national politics than in the oligarchic category. Yet it is significant compared to its forcibly limited role under modern authoritarian regimes. Neither the more democratic (e. g. , Venezuelan) nor more dictatorial (e. g. , Mexican) regimes in the reconciliation category have slammed the door shut on student politics, either because they do not choose to or because they cannot. Students form a potent pressure group.

A few caveats are indispensable. "Reconciliation, " as used here, should connote neither tranquility nor consensus. In fact, politics in category three nations are often quite competitive and conflictual. The regimes generally permit, sometimes actually may rest on, a relatively substantial degree of open contestation in the political arena (i. e. , compared to regimes in other categories). "Reconciliation" refers to the regime's acceptance as legitimate, even integral to the political process, of the rights of different groups actively to pursue their political ends, opposing other groups or indeed the State itself. All this obviously has to do with matters of degree. Thus, for example, the term "reconciliation" should not imply the absence of repression; reconciliation regimes do set limits to the amount and type of activism they will tolerate, particularly if students move beyond the campus to try to affect local or national as well as university policies. Such attempts, if successful, would give students in category three the sort of influence sometimes achieved by peers in category two [2]. Finally, we do not want to imply that most students in category three, or in any category for that matter, are activists; even during peak periods student activism has generally been spearheaded by minorities.

Clearly, student activity in the reconciliation cases had diminished somewhat by comparison with unprecedented activity in the 1960s. Internationally, a single year like 1968 may never been seen again. And it was Mexico, with the slaughter of perhaps 300 students, that shapes unforgettable memories of the year's and the decade's violence. So it is interesting to observe how different the 1970s would be (Levy, 1980, pp. 32-40). The regime worked hard at reconciliation. It gave unprecedented subsidies to the universities. It intensified its well-honed co-optation practices, holding out good positions for activists willing to work within the system. In 1976 it granted amnesty to students still imprisoned from 1968. By the close of the 1970s many former activists could be found working for the government. At the same time, the government certainly counted on the deterrent effect of the big stick. Its insidious role in the 1971 attack on National University (UNAM) student demonstrators was testimony to this. Significantly, however, this would mark the last major confrontation involving a loss of life at UNAM in the 1970s. The combined carrot and stick approach worked moderately well for the government. Students became markedly less active, reacting more than initiating, turning like their

U. S. counterparts more toward drugs (Estrada, 1973, p. 17).
Workers, not students, became UNAM's most active group
of the decade.   That antigovernment student activity was not
eradicated, however, was graphically shown in 1975 when
President Echeverría attempted an on-campus dialogue with
students.   He was ignominiously chased, and could only rant
furiously about fascist, CIA-supported students.   In 1979, to
celebrate the fiftieth anniversary of UNAM's autonomy, President López Portillo, quite without prior notice, slipped quickly
in and back out of the campus.

Once we relax comparisons to the 1960s, comparing
instead to contemporary affairs outside Latin America, or to
the region's own modern authoritarian cases, students in the
reconciliation cases still rank as highly active.   Leftist students have remained remarkably active in Ecuador's (public)
universities, for example, helping to elect marxist rectors
and to block stricter academic policies.   Politicization has
also persisted in Colombia, where the political regime has
been at once more democratic and more shaky than in Mexico; in fact, activity was as great as in the late 1960s (Lebot,
1976, pp. 65-68).   A major incident in 1971 at the Universidad del Valle left fifteen dead and led to solidarity movements
which then promoted a harsh government reaction.   Universities were closed, students and professors purged.   Despite
his high hopes for national unity, new President López Michel-
sen ran into immediate problems (1974) at the National University.   He had to insist on the resignation of the marxist
rector who had stood with his students in their dispute with
the government.   Throughout the 1970s student protests frus-
trated government-sponsored reforms.   Activists continued to
be importantly represented in guerrilla movements, such as
the M-19 group that took over the Dominican Republic's embassy in early 1980.   Such activity poses dilemmas for the
Colombian regime not totally unlike those faced by some Central American regimes: reformist reconciliation or hard-
line repression?   But such dilemmas are generally less severe for the reconciliation regimes.

An important stabilizing factor in the reconciliation
category is the recruitment link between student politics and
national politics.   Thus student politics, even while painfully
disruptive at times, also can be very functional for the status
quo.   Student leaders learn how to recruit, to form alliances,
to exert pressure, to make compromises, to deal in the political capital of power.   Their talent may be recognized and
ultimately rewarded with jobs by their part-time professors

(the bulk of the professioriate), who work in government or party positions (Camp, 1975; Smith, 1979). Some student leaders move directly from party posts in the university to party posts in the regional or national arena. Such links are found in some Mexican states, but they are much more pronounced in Venezuela, where the major national parties have greater legitimacy within the universities. The Venezuelan case now contrasts revealingly with the Chilean case, where the advent of authoritarianism has destroyed a similarly strong nexus between student and national politics. Free-wheeling student politics, in short, can be functional as well as disruptive for relatively permeable political regimes; it can only be dysfunctional or illogical for most of the oligarchic or modern authoritarian regimes.

Where students in category three wield their greatest power, often decisive power, is in intra-university policy. They generally enjoy considerable representation on governing bodies. Institutions like Venezuela's and Ecuador's Central Universities are highly politicized, with periodic elections for a host of student, faculty, and even some administrative positions, although officials have recently taken some measures to curb the student role by running institutions in more top-down fashtion (Pelczar, 1974, p. 62). Thus, for example, only in 1980 did Ecuador break a tradition that had held throughout the 1950s, 1960s and 1970s, in which the general assembly of students, professors, and workers elected marxist rectors to head the Central University (Scully, 1980, p. 15).

It is not institutionalized participation, however, that is the major source of student influence. It is the creation or threat of disorder. Indeed, officials have been more concerned and less able to curtail this sort of student influence. Some success has been achieved be decentralizing higher education, diminishing proportional enrollments in the giant national universities located in capital cities. But this has not reduced the absolute size of the nationals. And it has often merely transferred disorders to the provinces. While UNAM students became a less direct threat to the national government in the 1970s, students in Guerrero, Nuevo León, Oaxaca, Puebla, and Sinaloa shook state governments repeatedly. Frequently, student disorders actually reaped more reward than punishment; and it is hard to overstate the effect that inevitable student disorder has on forestalling tougher policies concerning curriculum, examinations, finance, degree requirements, or even professorial appointments (Levy, 1980, pp.

125-131, 150-154). An excellent example of the carrot-stick approach used by reconciliation regimes is found in the forcible 1977 police intervention against UNAM student demonstrations--followed by acquiescience to most of the students' demands. In some nations, notably Colombia and Venezuela, secondary school students have achieved similar influence through politicization, often with explicit solidarity from university students.

Obviously we must allow for variation within the broad reconciliation category. Costa Rica's universities, for example, rarely exhibit the degree of either leftism or disruption found in Colombia, Ecuador, Mexico, or Venezuela. Student protests, demonstrations, and propaganda are generally rather mild at the University of Costa Rica (the nation's only university until the 1970s). This is not to imply, however, that the nation's universities are unpoliticized. There is, in fact, terrific competition for virtually all administrative positions, from rector on down. Students enjoy twenty-five per cent participation in elections and on policy-making bodies. They also form a significant pressure group in national policies, in some instances blocking what they perceive as regressive tendencies (e. g. , extension of foreign economic penetration). As in Venezuela, there are strong links between student and national partisan politics. And also as in Venezuela, it is often hard to gauge the degree to which the former is influencing the latter or the latter is simply mobilizing the former to its ends. To make a general comparison to the norm in category three, Costa Rica's student activity has been less extremist but at least as politicized.

Far greater variation within the reconciliation category comes if we include Peruvian students. Peru has in fact been an ambiguous case, bordering precariously on the modern authoritarian category. Its 1968 military coup inaugurated a repressive authoritarian rule that remained in effect throughout the 1970s. The junta's 1969 law for higher education mandated drastic depoliticization of traditionally active students (Drysdale and Myers, 1975, pp. 286-291). Student participation in governing councils was eliminated, while much more authority was granted to top university administrators. During 1970 the regime tried hard to stick to some semblance of its plan. But already by 1971 it retreated in the face of great opposition, largely student. It then promulgated a much diluted plan allowing for some student participation. By the mid-1970s, the regime had given up even more ground. Although the ascension (1975) of conservative elements within the military assured authoritarian constraints for the decade's duration, a rather dramatic return to democracy inaugurated the 1980s. With the nation's last prejunta president restored to power, it seemed possible that Peru might stop teetering near the authoritarian category and once again fall squarely within the reconciliation category.

Modern Authoritarian Regimes

To whatever extent the literature on student politics in the 1960s remains relevant for the nations analyzed to this point, it is emphatically outdated for those nations in which modern authoritarian regimes have come to power. The immense importance of this fourth category is immediately clear from its size. It alone holds half of Latin America's population (50.0%, 1975) and a bigger percentage (56.8%, 1975) of its higher education population [3]. Of course repression of civilian politics in general, and student politics in particular, is nothing new in Latin America, and these authoritarian regimes have no monopoly on contemporary repression. Still, the thoroughness of repression (characteristically military repression), cast against a history of extensive participation, clearly warrants a distinct category.

Student politics becomes but a shadow of what it once was, and the contrast is especially startling because most of these nations had previously gone further than most others in both institutionalized and non-institutionalized student participation. Co-government had been pioneered in Argentina and then Uruguay, and had gained considerable ground in Chile with the University Reform of 1967. In some cases, especially the Chilean, student activity in both university and national politics accelerated dramatically in the years just prior to military takeover. The historic election of marxist Salvador Allende (1970), and the ensuing societal changes, led to large-scale student confrontations, principally pitting Christian Democrats against Communists, with considerable involvement of both more rightist and particularly more leftist groups. Other confrontations involved student demonstrations against the government or oppositely, against the government's opponents. Unprecedented politicization and polarization in student politics reflected, even contributed to, unprecedented politicization and polarization at the national political level, eventually culminating with the coup.

Paradoxically, then, systems in which student politics

develop the most sophisticated organizations and extensive involvement beyond the campus may become systems in which
student politics are most repressively restricted. Modern
authoritarian regimes ban all activity deemed extraneous to
a narrowly-defined student role, i. e. , to study. They ex-
pressly prohibit all student political activity, including meetings, publications, and free speech. Instead, they encourage
participation in non-political activities such as dances and
sports. They abolish political parties or push them into
"recess" so that constitutent student or youth contingents like-
wise die. They destroy venerable student organizations. All
this is part of a general coercive depoliticization of previously
highly politicized societies, epitomized by student activism.

The modern authoritarian regimes and their freshly-
appointed university officials have generally tried to build
some sort of controlled substitute for the vanquished independent student movements. As Philippe Schmitter (1971,
pp. 206-207) describes the Brazilian situation, the new authoritarian regime (1964) immediately repressed the existing
National Union of Students (UNE), and then attempted to substitute a National Student Directory (DNE)--forbidden from
engaging in political activity. The DNE would hold plenary
meetings only at the Education Ministry's behest. Its elections would be controlled by the university administration.
In return, the regime would give the DNE corporatist privileges: a monopoly on government subsidies, distributory
power over funds to affiliated groups, and a representational
monopoly on student participation. But the DNE could not
achieve legitimacy among the students, and the UNE remained
strong until the government abolished it. Thus, authoritarian
efforts failed to impose a viable substitute for the outlawed
student organization. Nonetheless, a series of "Institutional
Acts" severely repressed student activity until the mid-1970s
(Silva, 1979, p. 6).

After its 1973 takeover, Uruguay's military leadership
also tried to encourage a sympathetic student movement.
The fate of this idea was quickly sealed, however, when the
left handily defeated pro-government candidates in the September 1973 elections. Student organizations soon followed political parties, parliament, unions, and the free press into
oblivion. In September 1975, the government once again tried
for student cooperation, hoping now that obligatory voting
would do in an allegedly small minority of leftist activists.
Again the government lost badly. Again it responded with
increased repression (García Laguardia, 1977, p. 122).

Chilean authorities have not fared any better. To be sure, they carefully selected new student leaders who enjoyed their confidence. Nonetheless, they have had trouble even with some of these appointed representatives. The biggest problem, however, is that the "representatives" lack legitimacy among most students. A good test of student attitudes came in 1979, when officials decided to gamble on elections-- and saw their side garner only an embarassing 30%. Chilean students, like Uruguayan students, would not speak with the voice that government wanted to hear. Chilean officials also tried for a new institutionalization, praised as a "perfect system of indirect democracy," combining "representative democracy and depoliticization"; "participación sí, co-gobierno no. " But most students perceived that the new organization was imposed, that it made them objects more than participants. Showing remarkable courage, many students now joined in open demonstrations. As the 1970s ended, it was clear that Chilean students could not be completely silenced. In Argentina, by contrast, the regime has thus far concentrated on repression of former student activity without making comparable attempts to create new organizations.

It is of course in a radically different context, in Cuba, that an authoritarian regime has gone farthest in building a cooperative student movement. The history dates back to 1960 when Castro worked with revolutionary students to purge dissident personnel and to establish government-university unity. Student cooperation is sufficiently secure that students are safely given substantial representation compared to the situation in the capitalist-oriented modern authoritarian regimes. Cuba's students have served the State. They have been active in many official campaigns, such as literary campaigns. Their support is guaranteed by a combination of repression and allegiance, the latter reinforced by admissions standards aimed at helping the lower classes and giving consideration to "red" as well as "expert. " For our board purposes here, it can be said that the student movement remained active and loyal in the 1970s as it had in the 1960s. But even the Cuban regime has had some trouble with its students--scattered opposition, mostly just a lack of the prescribed active allegiance (Mesa-Laga, 1974, pp. 92-97).

Just as we saw for the third category, there is clearly important variation within the fourth category, even leaving aside the obviously exceptional case of Cuba. For example, compared to Argentina, Chile, or Uruguay, much greater reassertion of independent, anti-government, student activism

has occurred in Brazil. A student renaissance has clearly
gone hand-in-hand with the general abertura, or liberal
"opening up," of Brazilian politics. By the mid-1970s, exiled
dissidents such as Darcy Ribeiro, a prominent ex-rector,
were allowed to return to their homeland. In 1977, for the
first time in the entire decade, thousands of students took to
the streets and, with worker support, called for a general
amnesty (soon received), free elections, and a greater voice
in university governance. Student demonstrations have once
again become frequent, though limitations are still generally
tougher than those imposed by reconciliation regimes. By
1979, Brazilian students were meeting openly to reorganize
their union (UNE), despite the fact that it was still technically
illegal. And so, as the decade ended, Brazil fit a little less
squarely within the authoritarian category. In summary,
some of the category four cases, albeit in somewhat different
ways, suggest that while students are far less active under
modern authoritarian than reconciliation regimes, it still
would be wrong to overlook their significance. They have
formed one of the most visible centers of dissent where little other dissent is found. There is thus some, albeit limited, parallel with the oligarchic cases--even limited student
activity takes on importance because other groups are more
effectively repressed. The organization of student dissent,
after all, enjoys certain advantages in terms of youth, spirit,
physical concentration, legitimacy as representatives of the
national conscience, and relatively privileged social-economic
status. Student activists cannot topple modern authoritarian
regimes but they are perhaps more able than most other
groups to oppose them, embarrass them, and cause some
trouble for them.

Variation between Sectors

To this point, the analysis has focused on a system-level
variable, type of political regime. But student activism also
varies significantly within systems. The major factor affecting politicization at this level is the private-public distinction.

     Although public sector enrollments grew much more
than private sector enrollments in absolute terms in the 1960s,
privates grew much faster proportionally. In 1960 the private sector had roughly 11% of the enrollments, by 1970
roughly 23%; private gains continued into the 1970s and by
1975 the private sector captured roughly 34% of total higher
education enrollments! [4]. Much of this private growth is

accounted for by Brazil, but after deleting Brazil, the private
sector still had roughly 19% of the enrollments by 1975, compared to roughly 9% in 1960. Even where the private sector
has only maintained its proportion of systemic enrollments,
there has been substantial private sector growth, as Latin
America's systemic enrollments have grown in unprecedented
degree. In 1960 only 3.1% of the relevant cohort group was
in higher education, jumping to 6.8% by 1970 and 11.7% by
1975 (Wilkie, 1978, p. 119). The private sector has become
much more important than it ever was before.

Politicization versus Depoliticization

Evidence of far greater vitality in student politics in public
than private universities is overwhelming (Liebman et al. ,
1975, pp. 90-91; Silvert, 1967, p. 372; Trujillo, 1973). It
applies to Peru, to Mexico, to Venezuela, to the Dominican
Republic--the list can be extended throughout Latin America
with only the qualifications cited below. Co-government has
rarely found an institutional home in a private setting. Most
privates are governed from atop a much steeper organizational
hierarchy. Many are self-consciously patterned after the U. S.
model, purposefully and explicitly rejecting the Latin tradition
of student participation. Venezuela's privates, for example,
allow only indirect influence, not significant participation, and
are actually administered somewhat "like private enterprises"
(Albornoz, 1979, p. 134).

An even much wider gap opens between private and
public regarding the propensity to influence policy by the use
or threat of confrontation politics. Our earlier comments on
successful student opposition to academic rigor in reconciliation cases applies mostly to public universities. Many private universities have much tougher admissions, curricular,
and exam requirements, and of course impose the tuitions
that nearly always have been politically unfeasible in Latin
America's public universities.

In Colombia, for example, of the 2268 days lost to
different Colombian universities as a result of student activism between January 1966 and June 1971 (Rodríguez Forero,
1972, pp. 247-53), departmental (public provincial) universities lost most, followed by national public universities. Private universities, though most numerous, lost "only" 410
days. The two most prestigious privates lost only three
days (Javeriana) and seven days (Los Andes), respectively.

By comparison, the National University alone lost 128 days, and suffered the invasion of government troops. Some of its students joined guerrilla leader Camilio Tórres. In one official reaction, President Lleras Restrepo banned the National's student organization. Meanwhile, even the lesser disturbances at the Javeriana led the rector to close the offending Sociology faculty, citing the lack of jobs for its graduates and the university's financial difficulties. Private universities generally have tolerated much less student activism than have their public counterparts.

There are of course certain qualifications to the very strong generalization that private university students have been less politically active. One, still to be developed below, concerns the role of private sectors in the modern authoritarian cases. Another concerns intrasectoral variation. Some private universities have allowed significant student participation even where most private universities within the system have not. Such is the case with Colombia's Libre University in comparison with the University of the Andes or the Javeriana University (Liebman, et al., 1972, p. 92). It is the case with Mexico's Iberoamerican University in comparison with the University of the Americas or the Technical Institute of Monterrey. In other cases, of which Mexico's Autonomous University of Guadalajara is the best example, substantial student representation is encouraged but its ideological and social expression is very carefully regulated by the university administration. The major private-public difference usually lies less in the amount of sanctioned participation within university structures than in the latitude for disruptive action to force or obstruct certain university policies.

The Roots of Private Sector Depoliticization

It is not difficult to track down the roots of the fundamentally depoliticized nature of Latin America's private universities: Depoliticization was in fact one of the prime rationales for private sector growth. Chronologically, there is great overlap between Latin America's period of most intense politicization in public higher education and its most intense private enrollment growth. Whatever the region's tradition of politicized universities, the 1960s were clearly unprecedented. And the 1960s was the first decade in which more private (58) than public (50) universities were created, (Castellano, et al., 1976, pp. 103-105) except for the 1920s (which gave birth to but three privates and two publics). Private sector growth in the 1960s created for the 1970s a much larger sector in which student politics would be decidedly circumscribed.

Tracing private sector growth further back, we find that what is often referred to as the special Latin American propensity for student activism basically began with the 1918 Córdoba movement. Argentine students blazed a trail that would have an impact, albeit very variably, in much of Latin America. Newly but strongly represented middle-class students declared in favor of changes in the university and society. They were clearly more politically active than their their upper class peers had been (Scott, 1967, p. 406). Holding more leftist views, they would repeatedly advocate the overthrow of dictators, greater separation of Church and State, graduated income taxing, and socialism. The responsibility of the university to change society has remained a ubiquitous theme. Indeed, many of the region's most important progressive political movements have hatched themselves in the university. Among these are Costa Rica's National Liberation, Venezuela's Democratic Action Party, Peru's APRA and Chile's Christian Democracy. Key leaders of these movements, sometimes future presidents of the republic, began in student politics. Of course, student movements (let alone student bodies at large) have varied significantly in their ideologies, but leftism has dominated, compared to national politics beyond the campus.

A stunning irony of progressively-oriented public university student activity, however, is that it contributed critically to the rise of the despised private sector. Politicized movements won some victories within the public universities and even beyond, but they also energized forces pressing for private sector alternatives, forces which they often could not suppress.

Two results of politicized movements were changes in public university governance ... and then public university instability. The most crucial demand of the Córdoba movement was co-government, with one-third representation of students. In fact, sister movements achieved their goals only in some nations in some periods, over subsequent decades, but in the 1960s such movements led to more student participation in many Latin American nations, just as they did in many European ones. Both regions saw instability ensue, at least somewhat casually (Van de Graaff, et al., 1978). In Latin America, private sector alternatives existed or were created. Peru's 1960 University Law, for example, sanctioned the creation of privates as possible hedges against the results of its simultaneous enactment of many of the Córdoba reforms, including co-government, in the public universities (Bernales, 1972, pp. 147-8). From eight universities in 1960, Peru would have 33 in 1970. Whereas only one private university had existed in 1960, 12 existed by 1970, with politicization generally seen as the prime cause of growth (Roncagliolo 1970, pp. 90-1). Argentina offers another good case because private enrollments grew quickly in the 1960s from virtually zero to more than 10%. Again, politicization of public universities was crucial in fueling that growth (Graciarena 1972, pp. 73-4). Politicization became an especially potent factor when extremists gained control of the public universities reform movements.

The desire for depoliticization has not been the only determinant of private sector growth; it has generally gone hand-in-hand with others. This is especially true for the "second wave" of private university creation, in the 1960s and 1970s. The first wave, actually stretching back into the last century, but accelerated in the 1940s and 1950s, was fundamentally a religious reaction to public university secularism. Such a reaction often overlapped with a desire to escape politicization, often anti-Church or anti-tradition. But the data indicate that religion declined, depolitization grew, as the fundamental determinant of the second wave. Bolivia's, Panama's, and Paraguay's first and still only private universities are Catholic. Colombia's first three were, as were Ecuador's and Venezuela's first two, but a majority of their subsequent privates have been secular. Eleven of Brazil's first twelve private universities (created 1931-1961) were Catholic, and the other was Protestant; yet each of the next nine 1962-1970, was secular! The Dominican Republic's first private was Catholic (1962), but its next two have been secular. Chile's first private was Catholic (1888), but only one of its next five was. Peru's first private was Catholic (1917), but only one of the subsequent ten was (1958-1969). Five of Argentina's initial six privates were Catholic, but only five of the next seventeen were, resulting in a dual religious-secular private sector (Castellanos, et al., 1976, pp. 93-105; Consejo, 1978, p. 283). Latin American private higher education was becoming much more secular.

The second wave occurred partly because existing Catholic universities, reflecting changes after Vatican II, were themselves becoming politicized. Peru's first private university (Pontifical Catholic University), for example, became rather like its public counterparts in terms of student body, professors, academic programs, and even full participation with public universities in the national Federation of Peruvian students, complete with disruptive activities. If the Catholic University had been expected to remain pure and isolated from the political currents swirling in the publics it did not. It was natural, therefore, that private economic groups would look elsewhere for the personnel they needed. Business interests created a number of private institutions, such as the Pacific University (which dedicated itself to business administration) and the private sector doubled its proportional enrollments in the 1960s, despite record-breaking growth in the public sector (Roncagliolo, 1972, pp. 83-84; O. E. A. 1973, p. 220).

Such quests for depoliticization clearly have important economic and class components. Student strikes disrupt the efficient training of personnel required by the economy. More importantly, a politicized atmosphere is harmful to preparing the desired kind of reliable, disciplined human resources. Furthermore, politicization is disproportionally high in fields of study perceived as undesirable or overcrowded, such as law and sociology; many of the new privates try to orient themselves to fields such as business administration and accounting. The class component becomes relevant as public university student politicization involves unprecedented enrollment expansion to middle and even lower middle class groups, increased strains on resources, declining educational quality, and credential devaluation. This last factor means that the public university degree, once confined to a small elite, is now given more widely. Therefore, both demand and supply reactions emerge. Students from privileged strata demand a more tranquil, academically superior, and job-relevant education. Private enterprise, sometimes aided by the State, sometimes by international organizations or businesses, created private universities geared to depoliticization, efficiency, and quality. The depoliticized nature of these institutions would thus be underscored by both its original raison d'etre and an ensuing selection process that attracts students inclined toward a less politicized environment, students who often underscore their commitment by paying tuitions that most public university students could not or would not.

Private Sectors and Modern Authoritarian Regimes

The growth of private sectors has thus been explicitly aimed at providing a depoliticized alternative to student activism in the public sector.   As we have seen, modern authoritarianism has provided another depoliticizing alternative.   Therefore, privatization is not as crucial to depoliticization in the fourth as in other regime categories.   Modern authoritarian regimes simply do not tolerate independent student activism, regardless of sector.

In all category four cases, save Uruguay, the rise of authoritarianism played some role in diminishing private-public differences.   This was especially true of Argentina. Before 1976, public university students had generally been more active than their private counterparts; since 1976 activity has been minimal in both sectors.   But, in most category four cases, private-public differences were already comparatively limited even before authoritarianism took hold. Examining nation by nation, we see that two of the five modern authoritarian cases have no private sector whatsoever, so that authoritarian repression is clearly the bulwark against activism.   Uruguay never had a private sector.   Cuba has lacked a private-public distinction ever since the revolutionary regime quickly abolished existing private universities back in the early 1960s.

Years before Chile fell into the authoritarian category, private higher education there had already become the most "public" in all Latin America.   In fact, Chile is an exception that substantiates the generalization about the tendency of truly distinctive privates to have much less student political activity.   Chilean private universities had become relatively similar to public universities in terms of finance, goverance, and mission; and therefore private university students had become active.   Agitation for university reform actually began in private universities (1966)!   The private university (Concepción) most resembling the public University of Chile became a real center of left and extreme left activity until the 1973 coup.   The two Catholic universities, which maintained a somewhat greater degree of institutional distinctiveness from public universities, had somewhat less active student bodies, certainly much farther to the center and right (Chaparro, 1975).   Still, as in all the other nations where both private and public sectors operate, the implantation of authoritarian rule lessened the prior private-public distinction in political activity.

Brazil never developed the private-public pattern most common in Spanish America. Partly because the nation's private universities (1940s) arose so soon after its first public universities (1930s), the private sector has always been large--not a small, elitist, depoliticized alternative to a massive public sector. More importantly, the entire university system was still proportionally quite small in 1964, when the authoritarian regime assumed power. The regime insisted on maintaining a degree of exclusiveness in its public universities; but, as it could not deny the booming social demand for higher education, it tacitly encouraged tremendous private sector expansion. From 38% in 1964, the private sector grew to 55% in 1971 and 66% (O. E. A. , 1967, p. 162; OEA, 1979, p. 149). Because student activism was proscribed in the public sector, there was no need from the mid-1960s through the 1970s to create an elitist depoliticized private alternative [5].

Conclusion

Table 1 summarizes where our twenty cases lie according to both the system level and intersystem variables. Juxtaposed, the two variables basically account for the significant recent patterns of continuity and change in Latin American student politics.

We really lack the data and analysis to say much about the traditional category. Private sector enrollments are high and may provide some additional insurance against student activity, but the regimes basically proscribe such activity across the board. While oligarchic regimes generally also try to repress activism, frequently with success, students often constitute a much more potent force there. Private sectors therefore grow as major vehicles for depoliticization. Most oligarchies have substantial private sectors. So do most reconciliation systems. Only the two smallest reconciliation systems have relatively small private sectors. The very nature of reconciliation regimes makes generalized repression of public student activism a very difficult proposition, and so the private-public distinction is crucial. At first glance, the modern authoritarian category would seem to show a similar pattern. Three of its five nations have substantial private sectors. The key factor, however, is that these regimes do quash public sector activism. Thus the private-public distinction does not count for nearly as much as it does elsewhere. Table 1 summarizes only size, not degree

TABLE 1

Regime Type and Private Sector Size, 1975

Traditional	Oligarchy		Reconciliation		Modern Authoritarian	
	Small private sector*	Substantial private sector	Small private sector	Substantial private sector	Small private sector	Substantial private sector
Haiti 21% (1963)	Honduras 6% (1968)	Dominican Republic 21% (1969)	Bolivia 3% (1970)	Colombia 52% Ecuador 15%	Cuba 0%	Argentina 12%
		El Salvador 10%	Costa Rica 0%**	Mexico 14% (1970)		Brazil 65%
Paraguay 23%	Panama 6%	Guatemala 19% (1968)		Peru 32%	Uruguay 0%	Chile 35%
		Nicaragua 49% (1970)		Venezuela 17%		

Source: See Footnote No. 3.

*"Small" private sectors are those with less than 10% of the enrollments.

**Although our OAS data show no private sector, one in fact was opened in 1976, is growing rather rapidly.

of distinctiveness. Comparing those nations that have substantial private sectors, reconciliation cases show much greater private-public distinctiveness than modern authoritarian cases do. In fact, the comparison probably holds for all eight nations involved, with perhaps only Colombia and Argentina raising notable qualifications.

Taken together, then, the growth of authoritarianism and of private sectors account in very large degree for the changing face of student politics in the 1970s. Harshly authoritarian regimes have maintained or first gained power in many of Latin America's major nations, in fact comprising the bulk of the region's university enrollments. These regimes simply do not permit meaningful student participation in university governance, much less highly politicized activities beyond the campus. The ramifications of this authoritarianism for student politics are especially important because some of these regimes arose where students previously had been most active. Where such authoritarian regimes did not take hold, however, private universities offered a major alternative escape from highly politicized student activity.

While student activism declined significantly in the 1970s, it would be a mistake to conclude that a Latin American tradition has been consigned to history. Much depends on which nations and sectors we analyze. Only in the newly authoritarian systems has student politics changed drastically from the 1960s, though most other systems show some retreat from the unusual peaks of the late 1960s. While private sectors became much larger between 1960 and 1970, growing proportionally faster than their public counterparts, public sectors also expanded in unprecedented numbers. And except under some modern authoritarian regimes (in Argentina, Chile, Uruguay), public sectors continued growing in the 1970s. Therefore, despite losing proportional weight within their higher education systems, public sectors gained in absolute weight. One sees continuity as well as change in student politics in the 1960s and 1970s.

No one knows how politicized Latin America's students will be in the 1980s. Degrees and forms of student activity have varied both across and within systems. The four-part political regime categorization used in this article has purposefully avoided a deterministic orientation in which authoritarianism would be the tragic culminating point. Other nations may or may not move toward that category, and nations now within it may or may not remain there. Private sectors may or may not continue their proportional growth. Some private institutions may become more politicized over time than they were in their youth. Thus any news concerning the imminent death of Latin America's tradition of student political activism would be quite premature. What is true is that activism has recently been severely quarantined by growing private sectors and even more severely by the advent of modern authoritarian regimes.

The most important determinants of student political activism thus lie outside the student bodies themselves. Whatever role in shaping national policies one ascribes to student politics, an analysis of the 1970s clearly indicates that the shape of student politics is itself highly dependent on national policies. Student activity therefore reflects, and provides substantial illustrations of broader political patterns. Latin America's swing toward authoritarianism has combined with a swing toward privatization in higher education to produce new and varying patterns of student political activity [6].

Notes

1. Among the traditional twenty republics (omitting reference to Belize and some of the Caribbean) which I work with, Bolivia, Honduras, Panama, Peru and of course Cuba, are the hardest to place in my four categories. Bolivia for example, may have been placed in categories two or three for the 1970s (and may now waver between categories two and four for the early 1980s). An example of the time period problem is shown in the categorization of certain regimes as authoritarian despite their experiences early in the 1970s (Argentina 1972-5, Chile and Uruguay 1970-3). Where regimes have changed, I have categorized by the decade as a whole, emphasizing the contemporary.

2. While student politics at the national level may fit the reconciliation category, student politics in certain provinces may show many characteristics found under oligarchic regimes. Provincial regimes may be more narrowly based than national regimes; provincial students may be able to form alliances with non-university groups; student activism may well destabilize provincial governments, perhaps toppling governors. One good example occurred in the poor province of Oaxaca,

Mexico in 1977. Student protests received support
from many peasants and, after violent confrontation,
forced the governor's resignation. In such cases,
the federal government <u>may</u> intervene at some point
to impose a resolution more in keeping with reconciliation than oligarchic patterns.

3. Population data came from the Organization of American
   States (O. E. A. , 1979, p. 2). Higher education data
   came from the same source (pp. 149-55). Unfortunately, the latest available data for Bolivia (1969),
   Guatemala (1971) and Haiti (1966), predate 1975 and
   therefore these nations are slightly under-emphasized
   in our 1975 estimates. But the three nations together
   account for roughly only 1% of the Latin American
   enrollments; without these three, modern authoritarian
   regimes capture 57. 6% of 1975 enrollments.

4. The 1960 and 1970 O. E. A. data are found in Ocampo
   (1973, pp. 40-41). I have estimated the 1975 figures,
   drawing mostly from the O. E. A. 's 1975 data (1979,
   pp. 149-55). Data for the Dominican Republic, Honduras, Mexico, Nicaragua and Paraguay, however,
   did not give a private-public breakdown. I therefore
   computed private-public percentages from the latest
   O. E. A. recorded years (respectively, 1969, 1968,
   1970, and 1968), using these percentages to breakdown the 1975 figures. Such a procedure may well
   slightly underestimate private enrollments in 1975
   because the private sectors in each nation save Honduras had been growing proportionally prior to the
   years used and had larger private sectors than Latin
   America as a whole. For the three other nations
   that had no data at all I used the latest available
   O. E. A. years giving a private-public breakdown
   (Bolivia 1970, Guatemala 1968, Haiti 1963). These
   nations had relatively low private shares (though these
   may have grown) and so lack of up-to-date figures
   may produce a slight overestimation of 1975 private
   enrollments.

5. The primary function of Brazil's private sector is not
   to offer an alternative to a politicized public sector
   but to meet rapidly growing social demand for higher
   education. Brazil is thus unique in Latin America
   for having a <u>mass private</u> sector generally inferior
   academically to the public sector. But most other

Latin American nations have private sub-sectors
which similarly develop primarily to absorb excess
demand. Colombia is the only other case where private enrollments have climbed (slightly) over the
50% mark, but even there the elitist private sub-
sector is more prominent than in Brazil.

6. This is a slightly revised version of a paper which appears in the Canadian Journal of Political Science
   (June, 1980).

References

Albornoz, Orlando (1979). "Models of the Latin American
University," in Joseph Maier and Richard W. Weather-
head, eds., The Latin American University. Albu-
querque: University of New Mexico Press: 123-134.
Anderson, Charles (1967). Politics and Economic Change in
Latin America: The Governing of Restless Nations.
New York: Van Nostrand.
Benjamin, Harold (1965). Higher Education in the American
Republics. New York: McGraw-Hill.
Bernales, Enrique (1972). "Universidad y sistemas socio-
políticas: el caso de Perú," in Corporación Promo-
ción Universitaria, ed., La universidad latinoamericana: enfoques tipológicos. Santiago: C.P.U.:
135-81.
Camp, Roderic A. (1975). "The National School of Economics
and Public Life in Mexico," Latin American Research
Review 10: 137-51.
Castellanos, Juan F.; Hidalgo, Jesús; Huerta, Juan José;
Sosa, Ignacio (1976). Examen de una década: sociedad y universidad 1962-1971. Mexico City: Unión
de Universidades de América Latina.
Chaparro, Patricio E. (1975). "University Students' Activism
and Leadership in Two Chilean Universities." Unpub-
lished Ph.D. dissertation. University of North Caro-
lina.
Collier, David, ed. (1979). The New Authoritarianism in
Latin America. Princeton, N.J.: Princeton Univer-
sity Press.
Consejo de Rectores de las Universidades Privadas (1978).
20 años de universidades privadas en la República
Argentina. Buenos Aires: Editorial de Belgrano.
Drysdale, Robert and Myers, Robert (1975). "Continuity and
Change: Peruvian Education," in Abraham Lowenthal,

ed., The Peruvian Experiment. Princeton, N.J.: Princeton University Press: 254-301.

Estrada, Gerardo (1973). "La responsabildad política de los estudiantes," Revista mexicana de ciencias políticas 19: 17-20.

García Laguardia, Jorge Mario (1977). La autonomía universitaria en América Latina: Mito y realidad. Mexico City: UNAM.

Graciarena, Jorge (1972). "Los procesos de Reforma Universitaria y el cambio social en América Latina," in Corporación Promoción Universitaria, ed., La universidad latinoamericana: enfoques tipológicos. Santiago: C.P.U.: 61-80.

Hennessy, Alistair (1967). "University Students in National Politics," Claudio Véliz, ed., The Politics of Conformity in Latin America. London: Oxford University Press: 119-58.

Latin American Political Report (1977). "El Salvador: Killing at the University," 11:303.

Lebot, Ibon (1976). "El movimiento estudiantil durante el frente nacional (1958-1974)," Ideología y sociedad 19: 49-70.

Levy, Daniel (1980). University and Government in Mexico: Autonomy in an Authoritarian System. New York: Praeger.

Liebman, Arthur; Walker, Kenneth; Glazer Myron (1972). Latin American University Students: A Six Nation Study. Cambridge, Mass.: Howard University Press.

Lipset, Seymour Martin (1972). "Introduction," in Arthur Liebman, Kenneth N. Walker, Myron Glazer, Latin American University Students: A Six Nation Study. Cambridge, Mass.: Harvard University Press: xvii-xxvi.

Malloy, James, ed. (1976). Authoritarianism and Corporatism in Latin America. Pittsburgh, Pa.: Pittsburgh University Press.

Mesa-Lago, Carmelo (1974). Cuba in the 1970s: Pragmatism and Institutionalization. Albuquerque: University of New Mexico Press.

Ocampo Londoño, Alfonso (1973). Higher Education in Latin America: Current and Future. New York: International Council for Educational Development.

O'Donnell, Guillermo (1978). "Reflections on the Patterns of Change in the Bureaucratic-Authoritarian State." Latin American Research Review 13: 3-38.

Organización de los Estados Americanos (1967). América en cifras 1965: situación cultural. Washington, D.C.

Organización de los Estados Americanos (1979). América en cifras 1977: tomo 3. Washington, D. C.

Pelczar, Richard (1974). "University Reform in Latin America: The Case Colombia," in Philip G. Altbach, ed., University Reform. Cambridge, Mass.: Schenkman Publishing Co.: 42-64.

Peterson, John (1970). "Recent Research on Latin American University Students," Latin American Research Review 5: 37-56.

Rodríguez Forero, Jaime (1972). "Universidad y estructura socioeconómica: el caso de Colombia," in Corporación Promoción Universitaria, ed., La universidad latinoamericana: enfoques tipológicos. Santiago: C. P. U.: 209-74.

Roncagliolo Rafael (1970). "Estudiantes y política en Perú: datos para una discusión," in Corporación Promoción Universitaria, ed., Estudiantes y política. Santiago: C. P. U.

Schmitter, Philippe (1971). Interest Conflict and Political Change in Brazil. Stanford: Stanford University Press.

Scott, Robert E. (1967). "Student Political Activism in Latin America," in Seymour Martin Lipset and Philip G. Altbach, ed., Students in Revolt. Boston: Houghton Mifflin Company: 403-31.

Scully, Malcolm (1980). "Election of a Moderate Rector in Educador." The Chronicle of Higher Education, May 19.

Silva, Antonio da (1979). "Brazil: El movimiento estudiantil entre 1970 y 1977," OCLAE 13:4-19.

Silvert, Kalman (1967). "The University Student," in Peter G. Snow, ed., Government and Politics in Latin America. New York: Holt, Rinehart and Winston: 367-84.

Smith, Peter (1979). Labyrinths of Power: Political Recruitment in Twentieth Century Mexico. Princeton, N. J.: Princeton University Press.

Thomas, Dani and Craig, Richard (1973). "Student Dissent in Latin America: Toward a Comparative Analysis," Latin American Research Review 13: 71-96.

Trujillo, Julio César (1972). "Universidad y sistemas sociopolíticos: el caso de Ecuador;" in Corporación Promoción Universitaria, ed., La universidad latinoamericana: enfoques tipológicos. Santiago: C. P. U.: 182-208.

Van de Graaff, John; Clark, Burton; Furth, Dorotea; Goldschmidt, Dietrich; Wheeler, Donald (1978). Academic

Power: Patterns of Authority in Seven National Systems of Higher Education. New York: Praeger.

Webre, Stephen (1979). José Napoleón Duarte and the Christian Democratic Party in Salvadorean Politics. Baton Rouge, LA: LSU Press.

Wilkie, James, ed. (1978). Statistical Abstract of Latin America, volume 19. Los Angeles: UCLA.

The author wishes to give special acknowledgement to Jonathan Hartlyn, Orlando Albornoz and Philip G. Altbach for their helpful comments on an earlier draft. The Andrew W. Mellon Foundation has provided financial support.

SADHUS NO LONGER:
RECENT TRENDS IN INDIAN STUDENT ACTIVISM*

By N. Jayaram

The Pre-Emergency Scene

The history of student activism in India has been a chequered
one as part of the nationalist movement. It is often argued
that the nature and content of student activism have undergone
a qualitative change since Independence (Altbach, 1968a; p. 17,
Ross, 1969, p. 19). The crux of the argument runs as follows: while the pre-Independence student movement had a
single goal, namely, independence for India, and was linked
to the country's life and politics, the wave of student agitations since 1947 has not been directly political but has concerned local and non-ideological issues. Also, student agitations have become basically disruptive and lost the character
of a movement.

In the sixties, the colleges and universities were the
scene of student agitations. It is estimated that in 1966
there were 2,206 student demonstrations, of which 480 were
violent (Altbach, 1968a, p. 53). The prominent student agitations till 1968 have been recorded by Altbach (1968a), and the
Vishwa Yuvak Kendra (1973, pp. 59-98) has documented 59
student agitations which have obstructed the normal functioning of academic institutions during 1968.

A close examination of the series of student strikes
in Karnataka (Ross, 1969), Benares (Ray, 1977), Calcutta
(Dasgupta, 1974), and elsewhere (Vishwa Yuvak Kendra, 1973)
in the sixties, and in Delhi (Singhal, 1977) during the early
seventies highlights that in the sixties the student agitations
started gradually regaining an organized form. Student unions

*Reprinted by permission of the author and publisher from
Higher Education, 8:6 (November 1979), pp. 683-99. Copyright ©1979 by the Elsevier Scientific Publishing Co., Amsterdam.

came to be increasingly influenced by political parties though devoid of ideological fervour. But it was only in 1974 that the student agitations started manifesting characteristics of an articulated movement. It originated in Gujarat, spread to Bihar and was later transformed into a country-wide movement.

Gujarat: Navnirman Samiti

The rising inflation of the early seventies marked the turning point in the economic scene and paved the way for socio-political changes. It is reported that between 1971-72 and 1973-74 the per capita availability of food grains fell by 11 per cent and industrial production stagnated, and whereas the wholesale price index rose by 33 per cent, the per capita income declined by 4. 2 per cent. During 1972-73, prices of food grains, edible oil, vegetables and meat rose by 30 to more than 100 per cent. Such essential commodities as rice, wheat, cooking oil and kerosene became scarce (Hiro 1978: 255-257).

Spiralling prices and growing scarcity meant untold hardship to the people, who, especially in the urban areas, blamed the ruling Congress government for this and began expressing their discontent through rallies and strikes. The opposition political parties joined the protest. Instead of stopping the sliding of the living standards of the masses, the Congress government became defensive and resorted to the use of force to quell the protest. During the first half of 1973, the army was called out seventeen times to restore law and order--a record in post-Independence India (Race Today, Aug. 1975, p. 179). This only aggravated people's antagonism towards the government. This also marked the beginning of the systematic student movement directed against the Congress government, whose first phase occurred in Gujarat.

In December 1973, the resident students at an engineering college in Ahmadabad were asked to pay a 41 per cent higher mess bill the following month. The striking students turned violent and burnt public property. The Congress government in Gujarat resorted to ruthless handling of the situation. A large contingent of police was sent to quell the unrest. But this was counter-productive, as the police excesses further widened the existing alienation between the students and the people on the one hand and the government

on the other.   The movement spread like wildfire throughout
the state under the banner of Navnirman Samiti.   In the
course of four weeks of riots in January-February 1974, en-
gineered mainly by the students, the police had to open fire
on people 347 times, three times the annual average for the
country as a whole (Race Today, August 1975, p. 179).

All this led to the imposition of President's Rule in
Gujarat on February 2, 1974, but the assembly was kept in
suspended animation, with the hope of re-forming the Congress
government once the tension cooled down.   The strategy of
the central government betrayed its ulterior motives and another bout of agitation occurred demanding the dissolution of
the state assembly and the holding of fresh elections.   The
students evolved the novel technique of pressuring the legislative assembly members to resign their seats.   Seventeen
Congress members responded to the students' pressure and
resigned their seats.   On March 17, 1974 the state assembly
was dissolved.   This was a great achievement for the student
movement.

A latent consequence of this movement was the acquisition of a moral halo by the future Prime Minister, Morarji
Desai, who had joined the struggle started by the students,
and started on a fast unto death supporting the demand for
the dissolution of the state assembly.   He conveniently described the outcome of the students' struggle as a "victory
of the people's struggle."   While exhorting the students to
carry on their planned reconstruction work with courage and
conviction, he pleaded for non-violence.

"Here was youth power channelized to achieve something concrete--a phenomenon unthinkable till then" (Pandit,
1977, p. 142).   The government little realized that it was
facing the beginnings of a mass student movement.   It was
at this juncture that Jayaprakash Narayan realized the significance of student power.   The Gujarat incident provided
the inspiration that Narayan had been waiting for.

Bihar: Chhatra Sangharsha Samiti

Jayaprakash Narayan, an erstwhile non-violent leader, was
planning to lead a people's movement against what he described as widespread corruption in the country.   Encouraged
by the achievements of the student movement Navnirman
Samiti in Gujarat, Narayan gradually moulded students of
Bihar.

On March 18, 1974, the Governor of Bihar was due to address the Bihar legislature. Narayan and the students tried to prevent the governor and the legislators from reaching the legislature. The state government reacted with an excessive show of police force and the next two days witnessed unprecedented violence. The then Union Home Minister admitted that during those two days the police had opened fire nine times resulting in the death of eight and injury to seventy-two people.

In April 1974 a unique protest march called the Maun Julus took place. Volunteers of various non-violent groups were selected under oath to practice peace, silence, and thoughts of goodwill against the enemy. Led by Narayan they silently marched through the streets of Patna. It turned out to be an echo of the national conscience, and was described as "a deadening calm pregnant with typhoon."

In June 1974, Narayan called on the students to stay away from the classroom for one year so that they could fully devote themselves to the movement. This call was reiterated by the Chhatra Sangharsha Samiti which demanded the immediate closure of all the universities and colleges in Bihar. The state government was determined to hold the annual examinations, which had already been postponed once. The political atmosphere in the state was turning turbulent as the intermediate examination approached.

It is also important to note the alliances that were forged during this period. In Gujarat, the student wing of the right Jan Sangh combined with that of the Socialist Party to form the Navnirman Samiti, and the Congress (0) supported the Samiti. The same combination clicked in Bihar under the banner of Chhatra Sangharsha Samiti. The ultimate fruit of such a combination was the development of a united opposition political front, which became the Janata Party which later took power at the Centre and in a few north-Indian states. It is "a kind of political illogicality that went way beyond the rational understanding of those who had learnt to play politics only in the Western ways" (Pandit, 1977, p. 147).

By June 1975 the atmosphere was characterized by disenchantment and disillusionment. The central government grew increasingly repressive. The movement was spreading to other parts of the country. The popular reaction to the Congress rule was indicated by the fact that the party lost the Gujarat mid-term election in June 1975. On June 12,

1975 the fateful Allahabad High Court judgement was handed down declaring the election of Indira Gandhi, the then Prime Minister, to the Lok Sabha null and Void. The opposition was preparing to launch a national campaign to secure her resignation. But on June 26 the presidential proclamation declared a state of "Internal" Emergency.

The "Internal" Emergency and Supression of Student Activism

Whatever may be the explanation about the events leading to the Emergency, the period will go down in the history of India as a brutal and ignominious one. We shall confine ourselves to the plight of student activism during this period. Recognizing the disruptive potential of the student movement, Mrs. Gandhi's government dealt harshly with student activism and jailed many key student leaders.

The various measures taken by the Congress government to suppress student activism may be broadly categorized into direct and indirect. Among the direct measures, at the outset, the government arrested, detained, and tortured the student leaders belonging to or sympathetic to the opposition parties. In some universities, such as Delhi University, intelligence agents were enrolled as students to discover the secret structure of student activism and underground resistance. Students who were found to be in any way sympathetic to the opposition party or showing opposition to the ruling party or its programmes were blacklisted and thrown out of the college or university or denied admission.

Secondly, the students' unions were depoliticized. Elections for students' unions were banned, and directives were issued for the formation of student "associations" through nominations or indirect election. The functions of such "associations" were to be purely cultural. Finally the government propagated the idea of the "constructive role of students in the implementation of the '20 point' programme and national development."

While the foregoing dealt a death blow to the nascent student movement, other measures were instituted under the subterfuge of educational reforms. The universities were advised to semesterize courses starting with the first-degree level. Not only was the so called "semester system" a sham of the system working in the Western countries--as it involved a change neither in the content nor in the method of teaching, but only the multiplication of examinations and greater control over the students--but it was also introduced almost overnight with absolutely no preparation. Under the semester system, the students were constantly kept busy with course work and examinations, giving them little time to think about anything else.

Secondly, the government tried to appease the students belonging to the so called "Backward Classes" by proclaiming measures--like reservation of seats, concession in fees, etc. --in addition to the existing constitutional reservations and facilities for the benefit of students belonging to the Scheduled Castes and Tribes. This resulted in a discernible cleavage among the students whose interests now stood divided, and this had pernicious consequences for the student movement.

Finally, in some states, such as Maharashtra and Karnataka, the governments promulgated ordinances reorganizing the structure and functioning of universities, resulting in the curtailment of academic freedom within the autonomy of the universities on the one hand, and the increased governmental interference in, and the undemocratic functioning of the universities on the other hand.

Nehru University Under the Emergency

Jawaharlal Nehru University (JNU) in New Delhi is one of India's most prestigious universities. Focusing on post-graduate study and with a small and highly articulate student population, the university has been one of the most radical in India. It was not surprising that government repression was especially intense at JNU, starting with the arrest of sixty student leaders in July 1975, and continuing for the entire period of the Emergency. These arrests marked the birth of a resistance among the students, led mainly by the Students Federation of India (SFI), which engaged in underground activities. It kept a steady stream of handouts, bulletins, and other materials going in order to inform students of government actions and to keep the spirit of dissent alive.

With the onset of the Emergency, university authorities acted to restrict the Students' Union, which was somewhat unique in India in that it was completely independent of the university administration. Membership, which had been mandatory, was shifted to voluntary, thus weakening the organization. The university also imposed "norms of behaviour for students" without student input, and this was also condemned by the students. Finally, university authorities expelled a number of students who were sympathetic to opposition groups. The Students' Union called for a boycott of classes on August 22, 1975 and the faculty supported this boycott. While the boycott was almost completely successful, the university kept up its pressure and continued to deal harshly with dissidents. Another student strike was called in September, and this was also successful. University authorities called in the police and more student activists were arrested.

While most students supported the resistance and heeded the boycotts and strikes, the student community was not completely united. The All India Students' Federation (AISF), student group of the pro-Moscow Communist Party of India, which at the time supported the Emergency, denounced the resistance and advocated a return to normalcy on the campus. The continuing factional disputes between the leftist SFI and AISF no doubt played a role in this situation, which resulted in a loss of support for the AISF.

New university policies reduced the Students' Union to a cultural association, eliminated the democratic structure of the organization, provided academic authorities with power to nominate individuals for union positions, and in general changed the nature of the organization. The right of the union to protest university decisions was eliminated, and the union was provided with a staff advisor who had veto power over all decisions. The university took authority to dismiss any student from the union or from the university. After implementing these new regulations, the Registrar of the University informed the Students' Union leadership that they had been ousted and the existing union "derecognized."

The dissolution of the Students' Union meant success for the university authorities. On November 7, the "ex-president" of the Students' Union was expelled from the university for six months and on November 11 he was arrested and detained under the Maintenance of Internal Security Act.

In this situation, the AISF abruptly changed its stand. In its pamphlet entitled "The Truth About 'Resistance' " it vehemently criticized the SFI-led resistance, and accused the SFI of working against its candidate in the Delhi University Students' Union elections. It appealed to the honest section of the SFI-influenced students to "down with left opportunism"

and "professional hoodwinkers, " and return to the broad
democratic left movement.

Thus came to an end the saga of resistance which
nevertheless continued once the Emergency was lifted. It is
the commitment of the SFI to the resistance and the vacilla-
tion of the AISF during the Emergency that accounts for the
immense popularity of the former and the weakness of the
latter on the JNU campus today.

Suppression in Delhi University and Elsewhere

While the saga of suppression and resistance in JNU was
unique for its sophistication, the suppression of student activists in Delhi University and elsewhere was also significant.
The case of Hemant Kumar Vishnoi is noteworthy.   Vishnoi
was closely associated with the rightist Rashtriya Swayam
Sevak Sangh and the Akhil Bharatiya Vidyarthi Parishad (here-
after Vidyarthi Parishad), which had captured about seventy
percent of the students' unions in the university, and was the
target of government surveillance.   His election as Secretary
of the Delhi University Students' Union immediately caught
the attention of the government, since Vishnoi and his Vidyarthi Parishad associates had won the university elections
on issues involving the Gujarat-Bihar movement.

On the eve of the Emergency, Vishnoi was away in
Rhotak attending a students' camp.   On his return to Delhi
he had to go underground as he learnt that the President of
the Delhi University Students' Union had been arrested and
that the police were looking for him.   Since most of the
leaders had gone underground, it was difficult if not impossible for him to establish contact with his fellow Parishad
leaders.   A meeting with the General Secretary of the Vidyarthi Parishad resulted in rough plans of action.   The police,
however, sensed the situation; the underground office was
raided and the General Secretary of the Vidyarthi Parishad
was arrested.

On the eve of the reopening of colleges the police
rounded up about fifty leaders who were considered to be influential.   The Sangharsha Samiti issued a pamphlet condemn-
ing the arrests and urging the students to fight such repression and called upon them to observe July 25 as a "close-
the university demand day. "   With more policemen than students on the campus, July 25 and 26 proved to be days of

terror. In all 186 people were arrested, including some
120 college teachers.

In the light of the increasing difficulty and risk involved in communication a new method was evolved. Picnics
were organized in open places and parks where underground
people could meet and exchange information. At one such
"picnic," following information leakage, Vishnoi was arrested
along with other students. Then followed the inhuman third-
degree methods of torture of Vishnoi and his associates to
get secrets about the underground movement.

This, however, was not an isolated incident; the suppression of student leaders was almost a national phenomenon.

> Held under the Defence of India Rules, or Main-
> tenance of Internal Security Act, they [student
> leaders] came from universities and colleges--
> an incomplete list alone contains over one hundred
> institutions ... from one end of India to another
> (Selbourne, 1977, p. 166).

Thus, the largest and most valuable contribution to
the struggle of 1975-1977 came from the students and youth.
While the government apparently controlled and contained the
student unrest through repressive tactics and by creating a
fear psychosis in the community of students, the continuation
of such a trend only aggravated the latent anxiety and anger
of students. The pressure burst once Lok Sabha elections
were announced and student leaders released. A new wave
of student awareness was evident in early 1977. The students
took the election as a challenge and became involved in cam-
paigning for their respective parties. The students played a
crucial role in the defeat of the ruling Congress government
and the election of the first alternative government in the
political history of India since Independence.

The Rise and Fall of the Youth Congress

In any large and plural society it will be difficult to find a
political party without a youth wing. The youth wings act as
recruiting groups for the newly franchised young men looking
for a political party. They bridge the generation gap and
give a cosmopolitan character to the parent bodies. Further,
they may be the only source of uncontaminated--though often
naïve and inflexible--idealism for the party, serving as a

corrective to the cynicism and the will to compromise of the veteran members (Mehta, 1978, p. 73).

In a study of student politics in Delhi University, Oommen observed that since political parties believe in the slogan "catch them young, " they are eager to establish contacts with students and eventually "use" them for political purposes. The student leaders' perception that they cannot become "real" leaders unless they establish contacts with political parties facilitates the process of politicization (Oommen, 1974, p. 791). It is in this light that we should understand the emergence of the Youth Congress during the Emergency.

In the pre-Emergency days the Youth Congress was the rather weak youth wing of the Indian National Congress. It had very few members, lacked ideology, and had no voice in the parent body. Thus, as a pressure group it had virtually no impact. This hitherto dormant band got activized during the Emergency, as it provided the springboard for the assumption of power by Sanjay Gandhi, the then Prime Minister's son. With his sycophants hailing him as "the beacon of hope of an awakened India" and "the rising sun on the political horizon, " he in fact emerged as the second most powerful politician in the country during the Emergency.

Under his patronage the Youth Congress acquired undue recognition, and his mother--the Prime Minister--proclaimed at the Gauhati session of the All India Congress Committee that "the Youth Congress had taken the thunder out of the parent body's session. " The Congressmen who had watched this with apprehension were the first to be arrested during the Emergency.

Although never elected to a formal Youth Congress post, Sanjay Gandhi was coopted to its Executive Council, and then exercised almost dictatorial power in the organization. He increased the membership from 700, 000 to 6, 000, 000 by enrolling anyone under 35 who was willing to pay one rupee. Many, on seeing that the Youth Congress had power within the Congress hierarchy, were eager to join it. As one observer put it:

> The Youth Congress became 'an umbrella' organization which sheltered a variety of goondas, thugs, pickpockets, criminals--all the 'bad characters' and 'anti-social' elements police usually keep a record of (Mehta, 1978, p. 85).

Sanjay Gandhi cleverly committed the Youth Congress to a series of apolitical goals such as family planning, tree planting, abolition of caste and the dowry system, eradication of illiteracy and slum clearance. This was described as a "cultural revolution," but in fact the organization proved mainly to be a political weapon for Sanjay Gandhi in his various struggles within the government.

In due course it was recognized that the ultimate strategy of the Youth Congress under Sanjay Gandhi was to execute a coup in the ruling parent body. This was given concrete expression in 1977 at the time of the Lok Sabha election, when the Youth Congress put in a claim for 200 of the 540 seats. This raised doubts in the minds of veteran Congressmen and the sudden exit of the Methuselah of Indian politics, Jagjivan Ram, changed the situation overnight. The Congress party was reluctant to antagonize any more old stalwarts by inducting youth into the election. In the final analysis, the Youth Congress secured less than ten nominations and later lost them all.

Student Activism in the Post-Emergency Period

Contrary to expectations, the end of the Emergency did not bring peace and tranquility to the campus. According to an official estimate, there were 7,520 incidents of student unrest in 1977, of which 1,146 were violent. The corresponding figures for 1978 till August stood at 8,838 and 1,050 respectively. State-wise, student unrest was more pronounced in Uttar Pradesh (22%), Maharashtra (21%) and Bihar (13%). Moreover, the percentage of violent incidents was only 15 for the whole of 1977 whereas the corresponding percentage for the first eight months of 1978 was 18. What is the nature of student unrest in this period?

Marathwada Riots

An exceptional feature of Marathwada University in Maharashtra is the polarization of students along caste and community lines. On one side is the Nagasena Vana campus encompassing four colleges and hostels run by the People's Education Society started by Dr. B. R. Ambedkar, champion of the untouchables. Adjacent to it is the university campus proper. Over ninety per cent of the students on the Nagasena Vana campus are Harijans. While the government colleges reserve thirty-four percent of the seats for students belonging to the Scheduled Castes and Tribes, their number in private colleges is negligible according to the Annual Report of the University for 1977-1978.

In July 1978, the newly formed Janata and Rebel Congress coalition ministry in Maharashtra decided to rename the Marathwada University after Ambedkar. Whatever may be the motive behind this political decision, there followed riots which originating on the campus in Aurangabad spread like wildfire throughout the State.

On the campus, the renaming issue originated through a combination of the need to mark the fiftieth anniversary of Ambedkar's Mahad Satyagraha with a fitting memorial and certain personal manoeuvres. The campaign had lasted for over 18 months and was almost incident free. But the aggressiveness of Dalit Panther (a Harijan group) incited Vidhyarthi Kruthi Samiti. The issue of protective discrimination enlarged the renaming of the university into a symbolic act and it became a focus of a confrontation between the Harijans and the caste Hindus.

A ten-day-old state-wide strike which had resulted in loss of life and property was finally called off on August 6, 1978--even as violent incidents were reported for the first time from Bombay, Poona, Nanded, and Nagpur--on the assurance of the chief minister that no decision would be taken unless and until an amicable settlement acceptable to all concerned was found. There now prevails an uneasy calm in Marathwada University.

Pantnagar Incident

The Pantnagar Agricultural University was the only campus in Uttar Pradesh which the police had never entered to tackle law and order problems. But in April 1978, it saw a protracted and violent strike accompanied by an equally brutal and persistent police action. The incident originated as a farm workers' agitation and developed into a campus versus police affair.

The Pantnagar Karmachari Sangathan, which had been set up in October 1977 to represent the interests of nearly 8,000 migrant farm workers, submitted a memorandum to the vice-chancellor threatening to go on strike if their demands were not met. After two unsuccessful agreements, and the suspension of ninety workers, the Uttar Pradesh government declared any strike in the university illegal. The workers' retaliation resulted in the arrest of 100 workers and the posting of Provincial Armed Constabulary on the campus.

In March 1978, a procession of 6,000 demonstrators demanded among other things the repeal of the government decree declaring the strike illegal, the withdrawal of the constabulary from the campus, and the dismissal of the vice-chancellor. When the demands were not met, the strike was resumed and later turned violent. The constabulary opened fire on the strikers resulting in the death of fifty-one persons and injury to many more. The university was closed on the same day. In view of the prevailing tension, the university which was reopened on April 19, was closed again on May 5.

It appears that the rich farmers of the area were in-terested in scuttling the strike, as they apprehended that any hike in the wages of the university farm workers, would have repercussion on their own workers whom they had been ex-ploiting with strong-arm tactics. This was effectively coun-tered by the parties of the left, and some left-wing student leaders paid regular visits to Pantnagar to confer with the leaders of the strike.

With 1,100 head of cattle and 19,000 fowl uncared for, and cane and wheat crops likely to be ruined, the in-definite closure of the university by striking farm workers posed a threat of great physical and monetary loss to the university. However, the situation eased with the resigna-tion of the vice-chancellor in June 1978.

The Pantnagar incident is unique in several respects. The Action Committee of the university did not allow the strike to be politicized, and in fact, it explicitly requested the politicians to keep away from it. Moreover, the post-strike behaviour of Pantnagar students was exemplary. After the strike, but for the fullest cooperation extended by the students, hundreds of head of cattle would have perished, milk supply ceased, and sanitary arrangements on the cam-pus collapsed. Most important, the strike was initiated by the workers of the university and the students joined it, with the teachers following suit. Perhaps this is the first in-stance in which the intelligentsia came out of its closed cir-cle to join the workers' struggle, thus heralding a new trend in campus activism in the country.

Student Unrest in Other Parts of India

College students in Bangalore went on strike demanding among other things the institution of a judicial inquiry into the university affairs, removal of the vice-chancellor and removal of the police station from the university campus. In October the Harijan boarders of the university's Jnanabharati Men's Hostel demonstrated protesting against the "harrassment and discrimination" of hostel inmates by the chief warden. Students of a Christian women's college went on strike--for the first time in the history of the college--demanding democratic election to the students' union of the college.

● In Hyderabad, students went on strike in September 1978 demanding the resignation of a woman Minister for Women's Welfare, who had "degraded Indian women publicly." The vice-chancellor of Osmania University announced the closure of all the forty-five colleges in Hyderabad and Secunderabad for several weeks in view of the disturbed conditions on the campus resulting from clashes between two groups of students belonging to the Progressive Democratic Students' Union and the Vidyarthi Parishad.

● In 1979, students throughout Tamil Nadu went on strike in sympathy with striking teachers. In Pondicherry, about 4, 000 students organized a procession to protest against the proposal to merge Pondicherry with the neighbouring State of Tamil Nadu.

● In Bombay, the students of St. Xavier's College went on strike in 1977, against the continued attempts of the principal and the management to stifle free expression and democratic rights in the college. In August 1978, a strike against increased tuition charges culminated in the seizure of Bombay University by the students, whereby the university officials, including the vice-chancellor, were locked out of their offices.

● In Patna, the vice-chancellor's security guard opened fire when the law examinees started hurling chairs at him on September 12, 1978. The incident was sparked off when the squad detected the use of unfair means by the examinees, who later walked out of the examination hall with their question papers and answer books. In Bihar and Uttar Pradesh students agitating against the policy of protective discrimination in favour of the "Backward Classes" almost paralysed academic life for over six months.

There has been a sharp rise in student unrest in India since the end of the Emergency. In 1977, agitators in several universities demanded action against the "Emergency excesses." The reasons for a large number of recent agitations are non-academic. Besides politically motivated agitations, issues like restoration of democratic rights, protective discrimination, renaming of universities, alteration of state boundaries, police excesses, and purely local issues, such as bus fare increases, have disrupted the normal functioning of educational institutions.

The repeated occurrence of student unrest poses a major headache to the government and educational authorities. Intrusions by the police into a university campus has become a frequent occurrence and is no longer news. The two-day Conference of State Governors held in March 1979 has expressed grave concern at the growth of student indiscipline in the country and has called for firm steps to curb it.

Conclusion: Some Theoretical Considerations

It is not all surprising that a segment of a society's student population should be involved in activism that is militantly directed against the status quo.

> It can be strongly argued, as C. Wright Mills argued, that students are the one group who will continue to supply recruits for such causes, even when no other stratum is available. A completely inactive student body is a much more curious phenomenon historically than one which is involved to some degree in activism (Lipset, 1972, p. 263).

The explanations about the causes, content, and nature of student unrest are never the same or uniform in all the cases, because the manifestation of student unrest in any society is not ahistorical or isolated from its socio-economic milieu. Analyses of student unrest in India have highlighted various causes, from "high jinks" or the desire for "fun" (Ross, 1969, p. 17) on the one hand to acute politicization of academia (Ray, 1977, pp. 3-5) on the other. A recent survey of student indiscipline by the All India Committee of World Brotherhood lists the following causes:

> ... too much leisure time, political participation, sex problems, poor student-teacher relation, lack

of facilities for representation of complaint, anxiety over examination, student frustration (anxieties, separations from friends or family, hurt feelings, unsatisfied ambitions, financial difficulties), inade-quately handled student misbehaviour, and emotional immaturity (quoted in Jafar, 1977, pp. xv-xvi).

According to Singhal (1977, pp. 34-43), in addition to the economic factors, organizational climate and political inter-est in the campus, belief in agitational tactics and faith in violence, perception of political and governmental interfer-ence, and absence of a code of conduct are significant causal variables. Ghosh (1971) has argued that student unrest in the country is being deliberately fostered by certain foreign agencies.

As regards the form that the unrest takes, expression of resentment (both verbal and written); boycott of classes and walkout from examination halls; demonstrations, rallies and courting arrests; strikes, dharnas and gheraos; and dam-age to public property, assault and intimidation are found to be salient (Singhal, 1977, pp. 128-129). As Shils (1968b, pp. 5-6) points out, the students invariably attack discon-nected symbols like vice-chancellors, district collectors, police officers, post offices, railway stations, etc., rather than the center of the system, namely, the government or the regime.

Generally, student agitation fits into Shils' characteri-zation as a manifestation of juvenile delinquency (Shils, 1968a, 1968b). The manifestations are severe and recurrent as some impunity is always assured. But in the absence of of-ficial patronage and support, they tend to be unstable and short-lived (Altbach 1968b, p. 198).

This chapter observes that student unrest is not al-ways necessarily a manifestation of delinquency, and given certain conditions, it can develop into a concerted social movement. We have seen how the sixties witnessed a spate of student agitations, how in the early seventies the student agitations developed into a mass movement to be ruthlessly suppressed during the Emergency, and how, once the Emer-gency was lifted, the sixties' type of agitations have reap-peared. What accounts for this rhythmical alternation be-tween growth and decline of a student movement?

According to Smelser (1962), a society must be struc-

turally conducive to the development of the type of elementary
collective behaviour that will lead to a social movement before one can arise. In other words, the condition of the society must be such that new types of behaviour are possible,
or are likely to appear. He identifies the presence of structural strains accompanied by feelings of anxiety and frustration as characterizing such a situation. This situation must
have a common meaning for those who share the strain, so
that they are willing to act, and there must be a dramatic
event to precipitate action. Finally, there should be leaders
who are able to sustain the movement until it becomes formally organized. At every point in this development, the
instruments of social control, such as the government, the
police, or public opinion, may play a decisive role in lessening or increasing the activity. They may also be important in determining its length and severity.

We may supplement this structural theory of social
movement with an approach which stresses the role of specific politically relevant historical events as catalysts for
student movements. This approach seems to confirm the
views of those revolutionary theorists like Bakunin and Blan-
qui, who stressed the role of intellectuals and students as
the inspirers, leaders, and often mass troops of the revolution. In the light of these theoretical frameworks it is easy
to comprehend the origin and development of the student
movement in the pre-Emergency period and its evanescence
since then.

The Indian economy is characterized by a tension-
ridden imbalance: the educational output is not commensurate
with the absorptive capacity of the economy. Thus, between
1956 and 1974, the number of unemployed shot up from 5.3
million to over 15 million. The number of registered unemployed (only a fraction of the total) increased from 335,000
in 1951 to 9,315,000 in 1975--a twenty-eight-fold increase in
twenty-four years. Nearly half of the registered unemployed
had some educational qualification, including many with a university degree (quoted in Hiro, 1978, p. 85).

The ineffectiveness of the Constitution and the inability
of the ruling party to solve any of these problems, combined
with its incessant desire to remain in power, are glaringly
exposed by the fact that between 1951 and 1971, the Constitution was amended twenty-two times, on an average once
every eleven and one-half months. Between 1971 and 1974,
there were fifteen amendments, roughly one every eighty days.

Almost all these amendments had very little to do with the
welfare of the poeple and were basically designed to strength-
en the government's, particularly the ruling party's, position.

In 1974, the student movement was ably served by a
leadership which was both experienced and commanded respect.
Moreover, the movement started by the students developed
into a broader political movement with the government as its
target. Also important in this context were the dramatic
events of 1974-1975--such as police firings, imposition of
President's Rule in Gujarat without dissolving the state assembly, the defeat of the Congress party in the Gujarat mid-
term election, the Allahabad High Court judgement declaring
the election of Indira Gandhi to the Lok Sabha null and void,
etc.--which provided the necessary élan to the movement.

Given the course of events, the student movement
could have become full-blown. But, the government, realizing what was in store for it, ruthlessly crushed the movement during the Emergency. Student leaders were arrested,
detained, and tortured. Student unions were converted into
nominated associations for cultural activities. Resistance to
this suppression was systematically destroyed.

When the Emergency was lifted after the defeat of the
Congress party in the March 1977 Lok Sabha election, the
student movement had lost its raison d'être. But there were
innumerable student agitations resembling those of the sixties.
What are the prospects of the re-emergence of such a movement? The post-Emergency socio-economic scene being a
continuation of the pre-Emergency one, one should only expect the reappearance of such a movement. But whether this
expectation would materialize or not will depend on other conditions. In the first place, after joining hands in a movement and being responsible for the formation of a new government, the students seem to be obliged to refrain from any
attempt at resurrecting the movement, at least in the near
future. Even if they attempt it, it will not be blessed by
the political leaders who are in power.

Further, the various student and youth organizations
which were once united seem to be clearly divided. For example, in Bihar, the Chhatra Sangharsha Samiti, which had
led the 1974 movement, stands divided into four sometimes
feuding camps. Added to this is the parallel opposition force
of the left-wing student organizations like the AISF, the SFI
and the Bihar Students' Association. However, the left- and

right-wing opposition is not uniform throughout the country, or even in one state. In the recent JNU Students' Union election, the SFI and the AISF joined hands and this alliance was opposed by the Yuva Janata, whereas in the Delhi University Students' Union election, the SFI joined hands with the Yuva Janata to fight the Vidyarthi Parishad. But invariably the Congress-controlled National Students' Union of India and the Youth Congress are the weak enemies of both the left- and the other right-wing student organizations.

As it stands today, student unrest has the necessary infrastructure for its transformation into a movement, and the potentiality of students in this regard has been indubitably proved. Whether such a transformation takes place in the near future depends much on the role of instrumental conditions, which at the moment seem to be unfavourable.

References

Abraham, A. (1978). "A report from Marathwada." Economic and Political Weekly 13: 1536-1540.
Altbach, P. G. (1968a). "Student Politics and Higher Education in India," in P. G. Altbach, ed., Turmoil and Transition: Higher Education and Student Politics in India, pp. 17-73. Bombay: Lalvani Publishing House.
Altbach, P. G. (1968b). Student Politics in Bombay. Bombay: Asia Publishing House.
Amnesty International (1979). Summary of report on "Political imprisonment and torture in India," Economic and Political Weekly 14: 145, 147-150.
Banerjee, S. (1978). "JNU and the political power game," Economic and Political Weekly 13: 1542-1544.
Dasgupta, S. (1974). The Great Gherao of 1969 (A Case Study of Campus Violence and Protest Methods). New Delhi: Orient Longman.
Ghosh, S. K. (1971). "Student revolution in India," Quest 70: 51-54.
Hiro, D. (1978). Inside India Today. London: Routledge and Kegan Paul.
Jafar, S. M. (1977). Student Unrest in India: A Select Bibliography. Gurgaon (Haryana): Indian Documentation Service.
Lipset, S. M. (1972). Rebellion in the University (A History of Student Activism in America). London: Routledge and Kegan Paul.

Mankekar, D. R. and Mankekar, K. (1977). Decline and Fall of Indira Gandhi. New Delhi: Vision Books.

Mehta, V. (1978). The Sanjay Story--from Anand Bhavan to Amethi. Bombay: Jaico Publishing House.

Oommen, T. K. (1974). "Student politics in India: the case of Delhi University," Asian Survey 14: 777-794.

Pandit, C. S. (1977). End of an Era (The Rise and Fall of Indira Gandhi). New Delhi: Allied Publishers.

Ray, A. B. (1977). Students and Politics in India (The Role of Caste, Language and Region in an Indian University). New Delhi: Manohar Book Service.

Ross, A. D. (1969). Student Unrest in India--A Comparative Approach. Montreal: McGill-Queen's University Press.

Selbourne, D. (1977). An Eye to India--The Unmasking of a Tyranny. Harmondsworth: Penguin.

Sharma, D. (1977). The Janata (People's) Struggle. New Delhi: Philosophy and Social Action.

Sharma, U., ed. (1978). Violence Erupts. New Delhi: Radha Krishna Prakashan.

Shils, E. (1968a). "Indian Students: Rather Sadhus than Philistines," in P. G. Altbach, ed., Turmoil and Transition: Higher Education and Student Politics in India, pp. 74-92. Bombay: Lalvani Publishing House.

Shils, E. (1968b). "Students, Politics, and Universities in India," Introduction to P. G. Altbach, ed., Turmoil and Transition: Higher Education and Student Politics in India, pp. 1-13. Bombay: Lalvani Publishing House.

Singhal, S. (1977). Academic Leadership and Student Unrest. New Delhi: Newman Group of Publishers.

Smelser, N. J. (1962). Theory of Collective Behaviour. London: Routledge and Kegan Paul.

Vishwa Yuvak Kendra (1973). The Dynamics of Student Agitations. Bombay: Somaiya Publications.

DETERMINANTS OF THIRD WORLD STUDENT
POLITICAL ACTIVISM IN THE SEVENTIES:
THE CASE OF ZAMBIA[1]

by Y. G-M. Lulat

Introduction

A quick glance at the chapters in this book will reveal that
generally in the Western world, student political activism
has abated considerably in the Seventies. Certainly the level
of this activism reaches nowhere near the levels attained
during the decade of the Sixties. In comparison however,
student political activism in Third World nations still continues at a high level. Among the Third World nations that
have seen major student activism in the Seventies are: Brazil, Central African Republic, Chile, Ecuador, El Salvador,
Ethiopia, Ghana, India, Indonesia, Malaysia, Morocco, Nicaragua, South Africa, South Korea, Sri Lanka, Sudan, Tanzania, Thailand, and Zambia. What explanation can be offered for this continued, comparatively high level of student
political activism in the Seventies? This is a question that
this chapter attempts to address, by specifically examining the
case of one Third World country: Zambia.

Since a great deal of this student political activism in
Third World nations has tended, invariably, to be dominated
by political orientations inclined towards the left of the political spectrum, this chapter will also address this question.

The significance of these two questions arises of
course from the observation that students in Third World
nations (unlike in the Western world) have always been, and
continue to remain, a major political force. They exert,
from time to time, political influence in their countries that
is often far in excess of that warranged by their minority
status--in numerical terms. "Indeed...," as Altbach (1979,
p. 61) states, "it has only been in Third World nations that
students have successfully overthrown governments." "Thus
students," he continues, "are not only a force on the campus,

but they have very real potential to precipitate political change. " And in consequence, his observation more than a decade ago, is still as valid today as it was then: "it is of crucial importance that the student movement be thoroughly analysed if an important aspect of economic and political development in the new nations is to be understood. " (Altbach, 1966, p. 187).

In this chapter it will be argued that in Zambia, as in many other Third World nations, the endemic character of student political activism (and its radical orientation) is, in a major part, a function of the very situation of Zambia as a Third World nation [2]. That is, it is a former colonial country, existing on the periphery of the international capitalist economic system, and economically dependent on the metropolitan core. However, in isolating the factors that are pertinent to the continued, relatively high level of (radical) student political activism among Third World nations in the Seventies, the theoretical approach will be one that steers away from the major theoretical perspectives that have dominated the literature generally on student political activism in the Sixties, to an alternative theoretical perspective.

Past Perspectives on Student Political Activism

The literature on student political protest of the Sixties was dominated, as Burawoy (1976) points out, by two major theoretical perspectives in its effort to explain the dramatic rise of student political activism throughout the world: one theoretical perspective dwelt on structural factors that were isolated as pertinent to the causality of student political activism; while the other perspective dwelt on factors relating to student consciousness. Then there was also of course, the eclectic perspective that juxtaposed elements of both perspectives, without by any means integrating them into a theoretical whole.

Representatives of the first perspective included such names as Altbach (1966; 1969); Ben-David and Collins (1966); Boudon (1972); DuBois (1965); Finlay (1968); Lipset (1966; 1969); Moore and Hochschild (1968); Shils (1969); and Weinberg and Walker (1969). In adopting this perspective, in their studies of student political activism, they tended to look for variables such as those pertaining to the following: the disjuncture between universities and societies; disenchant-

ment with the ruling elite in contexts where students constitute potential members of this elite; high levels of governmental control and regulation of the educational system in
the context of low levels of national development; lack of institutionalized channels for meeting student grievances and
facilitating student political expression; archaic organizational
structures within educational institutions; national political
instability; highly repressive and authoritarian government
authority; social structural incongruity between students and
the political elite; the inherently critical role of the intellectuals; and so on.

As for those who leaned more towards, or wholly accepted, the consciousness perspective, the variables that they
were interested in were those pertaining, among others, to
the following: class background of the students; inter-genera-
tional incongruity of values; the family background of the students (whether liberal or authoritarian in character); politically provocative social definitions of students as a status
group; parental political ideologies; academic background;
"the stage of youth in the maturation process"; and processes
of political socialization of the youth.   Among the names that
could be associated with this perspective include: Aron (1972);
Bakke (1966); Bereday (1966); Block, Haan, and Smith (1972);
Eisenstadt (1972); Feuer (1972); Flacks (1972); Ghosh (1969);
Keniston (1972); and Mannheim (1972).

In identifying these perspectives, the point to note
here is that in adhering to one, to the exclusion of the other
of the two perspectives, the writers considerably weakened
the theoretical basis of their studies on student political activism.   In fact, one can go so far as to say that precisely
because of the failure in integrating and weaving together key
variables pertinent to both perspectives, the hallmark of the
literature on student activism in the Sixties has been, simply
put: theoretical sterility.   This has been especially so in
the case of cross-national studies.   As one authority on the
subject has commented recently after reviewing the literature
to date: "At present, there is no satisfactory 'theory' of
student political activism which covers a variety of national
settings, despite several efforts by social scientists to create
such a theory. "   (Altbach, 1979, p. 55).

It is in view of this that the theoretical approach in
this chapter turns to an alternative theoretical perspective:
that developed by Michael Burawoy (as a result of his dissatisfaction with the existing perspectives), while analyzing

the political confrontation between students and government in Zambia in 1971 [3]. In adopting Burawoy's theoretical framework (outlined in the section that follows) it must be pointed out however, that this chapter will seek to elaborate this framework further; this time in light of analysis of the second major confrontation between students and government in Zambia (which took place in 1976) [4]; and thereby facilitate explanation for the endemic and radical character of Third World student political activism.

An Alternative Theoretical Framework

In his analysis of the 1971 confrontation between Zambian students and their government, Burawoy (1976, p. 78) attempts to address the question that he feels has been inadequately answered by the literature of the Sixties on student political activism, namely: "Why, given the ostensible purpose of the university as an institution for the pursuit of research, teaching, and learning, does it so frequently become the focus of 'oppositional' political activity? Why are the students, whose defining activity is 'studying,' so easily politicized?" In response to this question, and in significant contrast to the theoretical approach adopted by the writers of the Sixties, Burawoy advances the thesis:

> That the university performs not just a single
> function but a multiplicity of functions and it is
> the relationship among these functions that deter-
> mines, at the structural level, the propensity to
> engage in political activity. Second, the political
> consciousness of the institution's members is deter-
> mined not merely by their roles within the univer-
> sity but by other roles they held in the past, hold
> in the present, or anticipate occupying in the fu-
> ture. Third, the outbreak of student protest must
> therefore be understood as the outcome of the inter-
> action of a specific student consciousness and the
> structural contradictions which inhere in the func-
> tions of the university. (p. 78).

Among the multiplicity of functions that the university performs, Burawoy states, there are three that are significant among Third World nations: the intrinsic function (training indigenous manpower); the symbolic function (the university symbolizing the attainment of the status of nationhood); and the solidary function (the university performing "an

integrative role supporting the dominant political organs and
abstaining from opposition to government positions. ") The
significant point about these functions is that they are inherently contradictory, and conflict-generating in character--
especially in the context of political systems characteristic
of Third World nations in general, which tend to be systems
with low levels of institutionalization and hence are unsuited
to the management of potential conflict. Thus for example,
the contradiction between the symbolic function and the intrinsic function was brought out during the 1971 student/gov-
ernment crisis, when it became clear that the university as
part of its symbolic function could not at one and the same
time be modeled on prestigious western universities (with
their emphasis on research, rather than teaching; and pos-
sessing firm traditions of university autonomy and academic
freedom), and yet remain closely in tune with the intrinsic
narrow function of training, as rapidly as possible, manpower for Zambianization of the expatriate-dominated bureaucracy, and the skilled labour market generally. This is because the latter function necessitated a considerable degree
of governmental control of the university. Thus not surprisingly, says Burawoy, the forcible closure of the university
was greeted ambivalently by many government ministers who
felt the closure would weaken the position of the university
as one of the nation's high status symbols, because it was
an attack on its autonomy and academic freedom.

Similarly, the contradiction between the symbolic function and the solidary function became obvious during the 1971
crisis, when violation of the solidary function, as a result of
the critical attitude of students on societal affairs (in this
particular case, Zambia's foreign policy)--attributable to the
symbolic function--"lead the university into confrontation with
the most powerful political institutions in the country...."
(p. 85).

Additionally, as Burawoy points out, "the symbolic
and intrinsic functions [came] into conflict with the solidary
function in respect of the freedom granted and the elite status
conferred upon students." That is, he explains "academic
freedom and university autonomy, signifying continuity with
the 'Western tradition,' together with its intrinsic function
as training students for incumbency in key positions in government, [had] themselves engendered the expression of dissatisfaction with the nation's progress and the conduct of the
nation's leadership." (p. 86).

Turning now to the other key aspect of the determinants of student political activism: student consciousness, Burawoy identifies the following variables as relevant to this consciousness among Zambian students: social mobility ("between different sub-systems of society") and physical mobility.

Social mobility can be divided into two forms of mobility: group mobility, "in which the 'group' expands into many new roles at the apex of the social structure"; and individual mobility (movement between classes). The former form of mobility is a result of Zambia achieving independence. To put it differently, in Zambia, "students are socially mobile within a population which is itself mobile due to the exodus of a colonial administration and the expansion of the occupational structure." (p. 91). Among the consequences of these two forms of mobility, says Burawoy, are (1) the development of a bourgeois consciousness among students who, as upper class aspirants, attempt to break away from involvement with lower classes to whom they are structurally bound via kinship and ethnic ties; (2) A perception by students that the political environment is hostile--because avenues of individual mobility, via elite recruitment, appear to be ambivalent towards the recruitment of students. This ambivalence is an outcome of the fact that in the case of a country such as Zambia, with its low levels of indigenous skilled manpower, coupled with its nascent status as an independent nation, upward mobility--especially within the government bureaucracy, a major employment sector--does not rest only on expertise, for experience, and loyalty to the party can also be, and often is, a substitute. As a consequence, says Burawoy, "tension over appropriate avenues of elite recruitment and legitimate arenas of participation underlay the confrontation between students and party during the [1971] July crisis" (p. 93).

Turning now to physical mobility, Burawoy states that student political consciousness is determined also by "relative deprivation to presently held status" and not merely anticipated status. And this he says is a function of the physical movement of students between the university campus (where students, because of the British civic model of the university, wield considerable influence, with student interests being accorded "singular importance in both formal and informal processes of decision-making"), and society at large (where students are "powerless" and are not given status commensurate with that held on campus.) As a consequence, says Burawoy,

"frustration in their expectations of their present role rein-
forces the anticipation of further frustration on graduation. "
(p. 92).

In concluding the outlay of his theoretical framework,
Burawoy goes on to state that when a crisis occurs between
the university and the government (such as that which occurred in 1971 in Zambia), it results in the activation "of hitherto latent contradictions, " and which in turn results "in the
imposition of a hierarchy of functions corresponding to the
interests of the most powerful pressure groups. " Thus he
explains with reference to the 1971 crisis:

> When students attacked the President publicly, dif-
> ferent interest groups entered the political arena,
> acting in accordance with their definition of the
> university. UNIP officials attacked the students
> for the latter's usurpation of the solidary function.
> "We cannot allow a state within a state, " read
> UNIP placards. Leading ministers and university
> faculty defended the university's autonomy and be-
> hind the scenes attempted to prevent the closure
> in the name of its symbolic function. Students,
> who regarded themselves as deprived incipient elite,
> emphasized the university's intrinsic function as
> grooming the "enlightened" leaders, teachers, and
> administrators of tomorrow. As a consequence of
> the violation of the "solidary function, " students
> compelled different groups to defend their concep-
> tion of the university and in this way contradictions
> gave rise to conflict. (p. 94).

Burawoy's analysis of the 1971 confrontation between
the university and government in Zambia demonstrated that
a fuller understanding of student protest in Third World nations, such as Zambia, required consideration of the dynamic
interrelationship between the structural contradictions of the
functions of the university, and the determinants of the character of student political consciousness. In the pages that
follow, analysis will focus on the second major confrontation
that took place between the university and the government
five years after the first major confrontation. Here the objective will be first, to demonstrate the validity of the theoretical framework developed by Borawoy by means of analysis
of additional data; and second, to further elaborate the theoretical framework, so as to include consideration of a second
set of structural contradictions--and their effect on student

political consciousness--that the 1976 confrontation highlighted. These contradictions principally relate to the dependent position of Third World nations, such as Zambia, within the world capitalist system. The proposal here will be that a fuller understanding of the continuation of student political protest-- and especially radical student political protest--in Third World countries such as Zambia requires consideration of the dynamic interrelationship between three sets of factors: first, those pertaining to the structural location of the university in society; second, those pertaining to the political consciousness of students (see above); and third, those pertaining to the very character of countries such as Zambia--as Third World countries.

The 1976 Confrontation and the Precipitation of Structural Contradictions

The 1976 confrontation between the university and the government was, like the previous 1971 confrontation, initially ignited by a student demonstration on a foreign policy matter pertaining to Southern Africa--the Civil War in the neighbouring country of Angola. In this demonstration however, the students for the first time chose to oppose the government's foreign policy on this matter, for largely ideological reasons --which itself added a new twist to the confrontation. Examination of the events of the 1976 confrontation reveals two points: first that, as in the 1971 confrontation, the 1976 confrontation brought to the surface once again some of the inherent structural contradictions of the university's position in society; and second, that student consciousness, unlike in 1971, was now qualitatively different [5]. These two points will now be considered in this and the subsequent section.

Besides the attack that the students launched on the nation's political leadership during the 1976 crisis, students also attacked two teaching staff members within the School of Humanities and Social Sciences--the Nigerian Dean of the school and a Zambian Political Science lecturer--accusing them of jeopardizing the security of the expatriate staff members, in the face of government arrests during the crisis [6]. The attack by students on these two staff members brought to the surface tension that had slowly been developing within the School of Humanities and Social Sciences, involving alleged racist behaviour on the part of the Dean, and some Zambian members of staff, such as the Zambian Political Science lecturer, towards expatriate lecturers. That there

existed considerable animosity between many, though certainly
not all, black and white lecturers in the School of Humanities
and Social Sciences, and which surfaced with the arrest, initially, of one of the British expatriate lecturers cannot be
doubted. A major part of this animosity, however, seemingly
can be credited to the fact that a dispute arose in 1975 over
whether the interdisciplinary general degree program (developed at the request of the Vice Chancellor in 1973) should be
continued or not. This general degree program was set up
on the understanding that the country required students who
were not narrow specialists, but possessors of broad-based
knowledge--capable of dealing with general development matters as well as being able to specialize in such interdisciplinary areas as rural development, administration, and so
on. The dispute was initiated by three Zambian lecturers
who had recently arrived from overseas following completion
of their post-graduate training. They felt that a general degree program with minimal course specialization did not suit
the needs of the country [sic] because it militated against
production of specialists and that it also acted against the
interests of those who wished to pursue post-graduate studies
overseas. In the course of the dispute the American expatriate Dean of the School had her contract terminated, and
she was replaced by the Nigerian Dean. The Nigerian Dean,
together with the Zambian Political Science lecturer, spearheaded the move towards the abolition of the interdisciplinary
fields of study and reintroduction of traditional specialized
fields of study. Here one observes the conflict between the
university's intrinsic function of producing manpower for development (supported by the expatriate lecturers), and the
symbolic function of serving as a prestigious institution of
learning, specializing in quality research and teaching--akin
to the major high-status Western universities, (supported by
the new, Western-trained Zambian lecturers).

At the time when the university was reopened on 19th
of May, in an address to Parliament, the then Minister of
Education, Fwanyanga Mulukita, stated that his Ministry would
reexamine the provisions of the University Act to see if measures could be taken to ensure that academic staff appointed
at the University comprised only those "who supported and
reflected the aspirations of the Nation. " He also went on
to state that the whole concept of academic freedom and institutional autonomy needed to be reexamined given that a developing country such as Zambia had many different priorities.
He stated that academic freedom and institutional autonomy
needed to be exercised "in accord with out national aspirations

and needs. " President Kaunda, in his speech at the Eighth
Graduation Ceremony of the University in Mulungushi Hall
on 11 December 1976, expressed similar sentiments: "I believe that in a developing country like Zambia, or in a developing situation, academic freedom and university autonomy
could be used usefully as a means to experiment and to lead,
rather than simply an enablement to follow blindly other people's practices. "

These statements by the Minister of Education and the
President point to the structural contradiction between the
solidary functions and the symbolic functions of the university.
Thus the symbolic functions of the university require retention of an institutional image as close as possible to that of
Western universities, including respect for such traditional
western university values as "academic freedom" and "institutional autonomy. " In fact, a number of statements issued
by both students and academic staff during the 1976 crisis
reflected this point. Thus the statement issued on 5 February 1976 by the Senior Staff Association on the detention of
the British expatriate lecturer read in part:

> Such action, imperils, by instilling insecurity and
> anxiety amongst us, the academic freedom of the
> entire University, teachers, students, research
> staff, workers, and other members of the com-
> munity.
>
> Furthermore, such action carries grave implica-
> tions for maintaining standards of excellence in
> the University:
>
> in teaching and in research;
> in developing graduates of high intellectual
> caliber;
> in retaining the services of staff of experi-
> ence and standing; and in recruiting staff
> from the international community.

(from the Senior Staff Association Resolution, 5th
February 1976)

Yet the solidary function requires that these values be
given less emphasis in light of the felt need to politically
mobilize all institutions in the nation--and this is especially
so in the context of a one-party state. A report that appeared in the Times of Zambia (19 May 1976), shortly after

the university reopened, headlines "UNZA to get Political Education, " further emphasizes this point. The report stated that the newly appointed Chairman of the University Council, Fwanyanga Mulikita (also a member of the Party's Central Committee) had said that a plan was being initiated to get all institutions of higher learning--including the University of Zambia--to undergo lessons in political education in order to bring them closer to the Party and government.

Another example of the contradiction between the symbolic function and the solidary function that the 1976 confrontation brought out was that pertaining to the large presence of expatriate lecturers. The symbolic function, requires their presence in large numbers; however, the solidary function calls for lecturers who are nationals who would be better capable of understanding and identifying with the aspirations, goals, and values of the country; and more importantly, whose role as an intelligentsia, critical of society, would be muted --or so the politicians believe.

This latter fact was clearly brought out by charges from politicians that expatriate lecturers were misleading students. An editorial in the government newspaper The Zambia Daily Mail (11 May 1976) that appeared a day after the university reopened reflected this sentiment. It read in part:

> ... There are, of course, lecturers who come to Africa to help the indigenous revolution gather force.
> But there are others who come as counter revolutionaries and reactionaries. These are the people that poison the minds of the young students and set father against son and the student against the leadership. ...
> The fact is that this country has never interfered in genuine academic freedom. Where the students have been at variance with leadership is when the students have tried to force their theories on the leadership.
> And the cause of this has always been the alien lecturer who comes to Zambia not to serve but to tell the country what to do. ...

The 1976 Confrontation and Student Consciousness

Turning to student consciousness, it is quite obvious, as

indicated earlier, that the 1976 confrontation revealed that it was of a different qualitative order from that manifested during the 1971 confrontation (see note No. 5). To be sure, some of the particularities of the political consciousness of the 1971 students were also evident among the 1976 students, revealing their contradictory character. For instance, the condescending attitude towards the "masses" was not entirely absent from utterances of the students during the 1976 confrontation, nor was the wholesale attack on the political leadership [7].

Yet it is also clear that a much more mature (that is less contradictory) consciousness has emerged among the students with regard to the political order in the country and internationally, as is indicated by considering the following: (1) Their opposition to the Zambian political leadership now does no longer seem to be restricted entirely to the questioning of the legitimacy of this leadership, but also includes the questioning of the premises that govern Zambian society. This is obvious from considering first, their reasons for supporting M. P. L. A. during the Angolan crisis, which were not based on a simple desire to adopt an anti-government stand no matter what. In explaining their reasons, as their statement on Angola indicated, they pointed to what they felt was the imperialist nature of the Angolan conflict--and that the role of Zambia in it was not only pro-imperialist but stemmed from the fact that it was a neo-colonial country itself [8].

(2) The need to form an alliance with the masses rather than adopting a patronizing attitude towards them if any meaningful change can be effected in the country is now increasingly becoming clear to students. This is revealed in their writings and also in their actions. For example in December 1977, when a University Workers' Union leader was sacked from his job by the University administration-- the students came out in full support of the Union and their strike action. Their joint activities, in support of the Workers' Union leader eventually led to the closure of the University for a short time by the administration and the expulsion of three student leaders. On that occasion the Students' Union issued a statement entitled "Working Class-Student Solidarity" which in part stated that there was "no division between workers and students" and therefore they were standing in solidarity with the working class, to whom they owed "their present position in society." The statement then attacked the university administration for its negative

246 / Lulat

approach to the grievances of the workers and their leader, and concluded by stating:

> We demand respect for the workers because with-
> out their labor even reactionaries who oppress and
> exploit the workers will feel their weight.... With-
> out their workers the clique cannot boast of their
> "PhDs. " We, as progressive forces like the work-
> ers, have reached a stage where we feel that it is
> not the PhD but revolutionary destination which
> matters.... [from the University of Zambia Stu-
> dent Union circular: "Working Class-Student Soli-
> darity" (14 December 1977)].

It should be noted that this support, on the part of the students, of the striking university workers stands in stark contrast to a similar situation a few years earlier, when students joined the administration in efforts to break another workers strike. (See Burawoy, 1976, p. 92).

(3) The ideological position of the students is clearly one that can be termed as socialist--and again it stands in stark contrast to the ideological position of the 1971 students, who were anything but socialist. This became clear not only during the 1976 confrontation but also on another occasion: the visit by a UNIP delegation in May 1977 with a conciliatory message from the Party. On that occasion the students re-iterated their opposition to affiliate with the Party; and at the same time severely criticized the Party's philosophy of Hu-manism in clearly socialist terms. Thus the campus news-paper UZ-Spokesman (30 May 1977) wrote:

> Students have done it again. They have said "no"
> to [affiliation with] U. N. I. P. They have refused
> to be part and parcel of vague ideologies and vague
> intentions. They have refused to look at the world
> in terms of the "animal in man" because like the
> forces of history have shown and will continue to
> show there is no such thing as evil interest in
> man. ...
> It is the type of society that man is born into
> that determined what he will be. Capitalist society,
> as such, dehumanizes man, it creates artificial
> values into him and develops in him an atomistic
> attitude toward others.... An ideology that seeks
> to clear up man without cleansing dirt which is
> outside the source of his moral uncleanliness, is

defeatist, apologetic and designed to turn man into
a dreamer. ...

The definite espousal of a socialist ideology by students received further confirmation on the occasion of a visit
to the University by the then U. S. Ambassador to the U. N.,
Andrew Young. Young commented following his address at
the University, and reported by the Daily Mail 27 May 1977,
that the only Soviet influence he had seen in Zambia was at
the University of Zambia where, it seemed to him, students
hold Marxist views of everything. In response to this com-
ment, UZ-Spokesman (30 May 1977) editorialized:

> ... Here we are engaged in independent analysis
> of events in any part of the world. We are free
> to use any ideological stand-point we feel like--
> nobody ever rams these down our throats. We
> think and decide on our own! Therefore to say
> our Marxist views of the material world are due
> to Soviet influence is gross simplification and dis-
> tortion of reality. ...
> If we seem to have Marxist views of everything
> it is because Marxism is a tool of analysis for the
> oppressed people. It is scientific and a product of
> long bitter developments of the capitalist system of
> production.

Determinants of Radical Student Political Consciousness

Having indicated the nature of student political consciousness,
as revealed by events of the 1976 confrontation between university and government, it remains now to point to its determinants, that is, to explain the emergence of a left-wing
(socialist) consciousness within the student body.

Before proceeding further however, a major caveat
is in order here. This new left-wing consciousness among
the students, as already hinted above, should not be considered as an all-pervasive consciousness encompassing all
students in the university. It is a consciousness that is
present very likely, only within those students from among
whom the student leadership (both formal and informal) is
drawn, namely: those who go beyond indicating simply political interest, that is the politically active. As for the rest
of the students their consciousness is, most probably, not
so dissimilar from that of the consciousness prevailing among

students in the 1971 confrontation, that is a consciousness that, for want of a better word, can be described as <u>campus populist</u> (see note No. 5)--except for the minority that <u>has definite</u> right-wing (bourgeois) consciousness. The explanation for the support that the majority of the students (that is, those with a <u>campus populist</u> consciousness) provide to the activities of <u>the left-wing student</u> leadership lies in the desire of the campus-populists to adopt anti-government stands for reasons mentioned earlier.

Therefore it is very likely that even today the determinants of the political consciousness of students identified by Burawoy (1976) such as structural involvement with poorer and unschooled kinsmen; ambiguity in avenues of elite recruitment; and relative deprivation with respect to presently held status generated by physical mobility, still holds true for the majority of the students. In consequence here, it is the emergence of the minority (albeit a very active minority) with a socialist consciousness--representing an entirely new kind of student consciousness in the history of the University of Zambia--that requires explanation.

It seems that the basis for the emergence of a left-wing or socialist-oriented political consciousness among those students who are politically active lies in specific socio-economic changes that have been taking place in the country at large as well as internationally since 1971. Principal among these changes of interest here, are the following: (1) The successes and victory of radical (Marxist-oriented) liberation movements in Southern Africa; (2) The development of state capitalism and the formation of an indigenous bourgeois class in Zambia; and (3) The failure to achieve economic development via diversification of the economy.

(1) The birth of what Rosberg and Callaghy (1979) term as the "second wave" of socialist African regimes in the mid-seventies represented by countries such as Angola, Guinea-Bissau, and Mozambique (that is, countries that had achieved independence through revolutionary struggle), brought onto the African scene for the first time the practice of government and politics that could be described as genuinely influenced by Marxism and Leninism. These second wave socialist regimes have not laid claims to an African uniqueness of their ideology as did the first wave socialist regimes (such as those of Nkrumah, Keita, and Nyerere) in their espousal of an ideology (if it could legitimately be called that) referred to as African Socialism. (See Friedland and

Rosberg, 1964). Rather the second wave socialists have ac-
knowledged the fact that theirs is an ideology that has its
roots in Marxism-Leninism; and as such their aspiration is
towards not African socialism but Scientific socialism. This
is evident for instance by tracing the historical development
of FRELIMO (of Mozambique) from a liberation movement to
a political party. Thus as Alpers (1979, p. 295) puts it,
"By the end of 1972, at the very latest, there can be little
doubt that FRELIMO was well along the path to transforming
itself into a socialist vanguard party with distinctively Marxist-
Leninist underpinnings." And by 1977 when the Third Congress was held in Maputo from 3-7 February, FRELIMO pro-
claimed itself as the Marxist-Leninist Vanguard Party of the
Working Class, with the goal of building scientific socialism
in Mozambique.

Similarly, in describing socialism in Angola, Kevin
Brown (1979, p. 297) emphasizes that, in his words, "Angolan
socialism as defined by the MPLA has little in common with
African Socialism." There are similarities in the aims of
the two types of socialism--for example, the restructuring of
former colonial societies into independent and egalitarian
nations--but the MPLA leadership has repeatedly made clear
its disdain for anything other than "Scientific Socialism."

The emergence of these left-wing Marxist-oriented
African regimes in the mid-seventies, following for most of
them a long and bitter but victorious armed revolutionary
struggle against colonialism had a tremendous impact upon
the thinking of African intellectuals and students--especially
those living in Southern Africa where the majority of these
regimes are to be found. It helped to radicalize them.
Many of these intellectuals and students, with the beginning
of the seventies, had become disillusioned with the so-called
ideology of African Socialism because of its lack of precision,
unity of ideas, analytical usefulness, and intellectual rigour.
More importantly perhaps, the disillusionment grew because
of its failure to provide the means to mobilize the peoples
of the African nations to defeat colonialism throughout the
continent on one hand, and on the other, to bring the continent out of its dependent state, through development. In
fact they realized that if anything, African Socialism had
served simply to legitimate the development of an African
bourgeoisie that was responsible for the continued exploitation of the African peoples by imperialist nations. As Au-
gustinho Neto, the former leader of MPLA explained when
pointing to the weaknesses of African Socialism:

> The so-called African Socialism doesn't take into
> account the universal character of the evolution of
> mankind. It does not take into account the pres-
> ence of social classes with opposing interests nor
> the implication of this. The so-called African So-
> cialism ... is based on a distorted conception of
> reality.... It exists generally in countries where
> a bourgeoisie flourished and which lives at the cost
> of the workers and peasants.... As for us, the
> only way to attain socialism is to abolish exploita-
> tion, to hand over the means or production to those
> who produce, and to insure the just distribution of
> the fruits of what they produce according to their
> work and according to their capacity. (Quoted in
> Kevin, 1979, p. 297).

Therefore, coming back to the left-wing students at
the University of Zambia, it is the introduction of Marxism
in Africa, and especially Southern Africa (a region within
which Zambia has for long played an important political role),
by Africans, via the dialectics of armed revolutionary struggle, that in large part explains the radical or socialist character of the consciousness of the political activists at the
University of Zambia. In other words, just as the Vietnam
War helped to radicalize students of advanced capitalist nations, the liberation struggle in Southern Africa--which it
should be pointed out has not yet ended--has helped to radicalize Zambian students, especially those who, while students,
witnessed the victories of Mozambique, Angola, and today
Zimbabwe. Of course, the Angolan Civil War--because of
its prolonged duration, its international character, and clear
ideological ramifications provided an important opportunity
and means for student activists to raise their political consciousness. It should be pointed out also that, as in the
case of the Vietnam War, the fact of United States involvement in Angola (albeit on a much smaller scale than in
Vietnam) and in Southern Africa generally helped to en-
hance further the radicalization of the students. This is indicated for instance by some of the pronouncements of the
students supporting MPLA during the Angolan crisis [9].

(2) The exit of formal colonial rule from what was
then called Northern Rhodesia on 24 October 1964 marked
the political victory of the new African elite (as opposed to
the traditional elite) that had emerged during the latter phase
of the expansion and consolidation of colonial rule in Zambia;
and which had begun, and led the nationalist struggle for

independence. The new African elite that inherited the State apparatus from the departing colonial bourgeoisie, was initially an unformed or amorphous stratum, lacking any clear characteristics of a class--and this of course was a function of the mode of its birth. This elite owed its birth to the imposition of colonial rule and the simultaneous intrusion of the capitalist mode of production. But note that this was a birth that was not <u>economically</u> determined but rather <u>politically</u> determined. <u>That is to say</u>, structural involvement of the new African elite in the new capitalist mode of production did not take the form of capitalist entrepreneurial activity on a scale commensurate with that of the colonial bourgeoisie. Rather, it was an involvement that was politically restricted (that is, artifically through discriminatory colonial laws) to the level of the instruments by which the reproduction of the capitalist mode of production is realized, in this instance specifically the colonial state apparatus; and note that even here, involvement was restricted to the lower levels of the echelon in the colonial state apparatus.

Not surprisingly, given this form of its birth, the African elite at the time of independence found that while it was now in possession of political power, it by and large lacked any economic power--that is, power attendant to the ownership and control of the means of production. Economic power was effectively retained in the hands of foreign capital. And in order to gain access to wealth, and thereby realize its long-held ambitions for both political and economic supremacy that had helped create and fuel the nationalist struggle, the new African elite turned to the state apparatus to aid it in achieving its ambitions. Specifically, the elite began to nationalize major means of production such as the copper-mines, and at the same time began to undertake on its own initiative, but in alliance with foreign capital via the state apparatus, major entrepreneurial activity in the form of State farms, State factories, and so on. Note however, that nationalization of the economy did not by any means imply a lesser role for foreign capital--on the contrary, foreign capital maintained and has continued to maintain its dominance in the economy via its monopoly over management expertise and technology on one hand, and on the other, easy access to capital, allowing it to go into partnership with the state.

The net consequences of this pattern of economic development in Zambia, where the state has become a major entrepreneur, have been (among others) as follows: It has allowed the African elite that took over power at the time of

independence to have access to surplus generated within the
economy by the activities of foreign capital (in alliance with
state capital). This access to surplus (that is, appropriation
of it) is facilitated through such mechanisms as maintaining
exorbitantly and artifically high salary levels for top bureau-
crats; outright stealing of public funds with no or minimal
disciplinary consequences; the use of graft; political repression of state workers' demands for higher wages; retention
of almost all the privileges that were enjoyed by former members of the colonial bourgeoisie such as chauffeur-driven
cars, subsidized or free housing, etc.; direction of foreign
exchange reserves toward imports of luxury goods (ranging
from expensive cars to exotic foods), redirection of public
investment funds to projects directly beneficial to themselves
(such as assembly plants for cars, TV sets, stereo systems,
etc.); and so on.

It has also allowed the continuation of the capitalist
mode of production, even though the state is the major owner
of the means of production. Symptomatic of this for instance,
besides the unchanged production relations, is that major investment decisions are almost always governed by the principle of profit.

As a consequence of this, the African elite of the Independence period has begun to evolve into a fairly well defined bourgeoisie, via first, its inheritance and control of
the state apparatus--which allows it to develop a state-
capitalist economy where it "owns" the means of production
collectively, and appropriates unpaid surplus labour individ-
ually--and second, via the individual appropriation of surplus
labour, it acquires the wherewithal to move into private enterprise. To be sure, this bourgeoisie is still numerically
small, but in alliance with foreign capital it is able to exert
considerable influence on the state apparatus so as often to
bring to nothing many of the populist "anti-capitalist" policies
that the Executive, notably the President, has attempted to
implement in Zambia.

The relevance of this, that is the formation of an indigenous bourgeoisie and the development of state capitalism,
to the student consciousness is threefold: job opportunities
for Zambian University graduates have continued to expand
(even in the face of economic stagnation since 1975--see
below) as a result of further expansion of state bureaucracy
necessitated by its direct role in the economy on one hand,
and on the other, the increased pace of Zambianization of

top positions of industrial and other echelons, that direct state intervention in the economy has facilitated. Thus the Zambian university student is not constrained from engaging in radical political activites by a bleak employment future (as is the case for instance among western nations).

It has led to a sharpening of contradictions, and this has provided ample ammunition for radical political activists to mount a severe criticism of Zambian society as it has been developing--especially from the perspective of pointing out the discrepancy between the rhetoric of the political leadership and the socio-economic reality (with particular reference to matters such as class-formation, the widening gap between the masses and the bourgeoisie, and so on). The implications of this for the political consciousness of the students is obvious.

(This following point, due to lack of concrete data, is purely speculative.) The formation of a bourgeoisie has probably meant that many of the students with parents in the professional/technical occupation bracket are actually coming from bourgeois backgrounds, and hence for these few, a university degree--unlike for the majority--does not necessarily imply upward mobility, since they have already achieved it. In this circumstance a group of students have emerged who are available for radical political activities because for these students, engagement in radical political activities does not hold so much risk, in terms of forfeiting potential mobility opportunities, as it does for the majority. The assumption here is that it is the student who has the most to lose who will be least inclined towards radical political activities.

(3) The nationalization of the major means of production by the state forced foreign capital to include the Zambian State bureaucracy in the appropriation of surplus generated by the activities of foreign capital but it did not loosen its grip on the economy. One consequence of this has been the fact that the presence of foreign capital has done little towards helping to diversify the mono-cultural (copper-mining) economy inherited at the time of Independence.

Zambia is one of the largest producers of copper in the world, ranking fourth after USA, USSR, and Chile. For a very long time, dating from the pre-Independence period to the present, copper mining (together with some other minerals) has been the mainstay of the economy. This is indicated by the fact that until the fall in copper prices in

1974, mineral exports accounted for more than 90% of the country's foreign exchange earnings, more than 50% of government revenue and some 15% of wage employment.

The consequences of this virtually total dependence on copper exports for revenue (internal and external) has been disastrous for the Zambian economy, for it not only encouraged the neglect of the countryside and the general diversification of the economy when there was relatively high revenue flowing from high copper prices during the period 1964 to 1974, but brought on an economic recession of crisis proportions when the revenue literally dried up through the fall in copper prices. Thus, as the Economic Report (Government/Zambia, January 1977, p. 16) puts it:

> Because of the predominant role of copper and foreign trade in the Zambian economy, the changes in terms of trade have an important bearing on the capacity of the nation to raise adequate resources for meeting the investment and consumption needs of the economy. From this point of view, the picture that emerges is somewhat sombre.

And how sombre the picture was, is gained by consideration of the following: As copper prices plummeted down to levels below production costs in the period 1975/76, the balance of payments surplus of K8.2 million and balance of trade surplus of K389.6 million in 1974 dropped to deficits of K144.2 million and K76.5 million, respectively, in 1975. The Government had to cut its recurrent expenditure by 13.9% and capital expenditure by 35% in 1976. Real Gross Domestic Produce (unadjusted for the terms of trade at 1965 prices) declined from a positive 5.6% change in 1974 over the preceding year to a negative 0.4% change in 1975.

In everyday terms this severe economic recession has translated itself into such consequences as closure of factories and massive lay-offs; shortages of essential spare parts for machinery and transport equipment; shortages of essential commodities such as salt, cooking oil, soap, etc.

These kinds of economic problems caused by the fall in copper prices have, needless to say, continued to this day. As a recent news report in Time Magazine (August 13, 1979, p. 25) noted:

While delegates to the Commonwealth Conference in

Lusaka enjoyed the best of everything, police in
Livingstone, 200 miles to the south-west, were
dispersing rioting crowds with tear gas and baton
charges after lines of people waiting to buy soap
and cooking oil got out of hand. In Lusaka itself,
laundry soap and detergents were in short supply;
toilet paper and cheese were unavailable; and milk
chocolate had become a rare luxury.

Now this state of affairs has given rise to two major
consequences for the political consciousness of the radical
students--both ultimately leading to a greater elevation of
this consciousness. The economic difficulties that have be-
fallen the country have provided additional ammunition for
radical students to mount further criticism of the performance of the government and the Party. Thus for example
Vasso (Vol. 3, No. 4, 1977/78), a campus newsmagazine,
commenting on the government-sponsored campaign to get
Zambians to eat Zambian (rather than imported) food wrote:

So much for the "Live Simply, eat Zambia dish"
campaign, but the question is Who must change
their eating habits. Is it the wretched of the
earth or the petty bourgeois roaders? A lot more
questions need to be asked....

The live simply, eat Zambian dish campaign is
just one of the many rhetorics Zambians have been
subjected to since independence. One hears of
such fallacies as "every able-bodied Zambian must
grow coffee." Ten years ago they chanted among
other fallacies that every Zambian will have an
egg and a pint of milk by 1970. Which people are
having the eggs and the pints of milk today?....

It is the ruling class who must change their eating
habits. They must stop importing Turkeys, Pea-
cock brains and British oysters for State functions.
They must turn to delele [okra], the President's
favourite dish. Next time the Youngs, Owens,
Rowlands, and that small man Ian Smith make their
frequent visits to Zambia, they must be served
with delele.

Given that the economic condition of the mass of Zambian people has further worsened (as a result of the economic
crisis), it has provided radical students with an opportunity

to express their solidarity with the masses in even more
strident terms than before.   (See for instance the editorial
in Scribe, (one of the campus newsmagazines) Volume 3,
no. 3, dated 18 January 1978 as well as the feature article
on the same subject).

Conclusion

In ending this chapter, it is necessary to reiterate the point
that the explanation for the rise of a radical political consciousness among student activists at the University of Zambia from around the mid-seventies lies on one hand, in the
particularities arising out of the dependent position of Zambia within the international capitalist system (discussed under
points 2 and 3 above), and on the other, its geo-political
position within Southern Africa (discussed under point 1
above).

It should be further added that this development of
radical consciousness among Zambian students stands in the
line with similar developments among many other Third
World nations.   The fact that this consciousness seems to
have emerged late in Zambia can perhaps be accounted for
by the fact that the University of Zambia is a very young institution, in comparative terms; and also by the fact that
many of the structural contradictions within the Zambian society and Polity had not yet surfaced.

In comparing the 1971 confrontation with the 1976
confrontation, it is clear that the major difference between
the two confrontations lies in the different character of the
political consciousness of the student activists of the two
confrontations.   In most other respects, the 1976 events took
a similar turn to those of 1971, thus pointing to the inherent
contradictory nature of the structural conditions of the university in a Third World setting--and in this regard they
vindicate the theoretical framework of analysis developed by
Burawoy (1976).   The only change (albeit an important
change) to the theoretical framework that consideration of
the 1976 confrontation has necessitated, is the elaboration
of the framework to facilitate analysis of the impact on student consciousness of the political-economic contradictions
arising out of the dependent position of Third World nations,
such as Zambia, within the international capitalist system.

As for the overall significance of this framework (as

it stands now), with respect to the study of student political
activism--whether it is in Third World nations or in Western
nations, the following observation is pertinent: while the actual descriptive specifics of student political activism will
vary from one country to another, analytical grip on the key
variables explaining this activism can be achieved and maintained only by means of the alternative theoretical framework
elaborated in this chapter. By means of this framework,
crude though it still remains, it is at least possible to attempt an explanation of student activism in a given country
or region, and predict its future course. This is something
that past theoretical perspectives (briefly outlined in the introduction) had not even remotely begun to do. All that they
had achieved was to collect a mass of data, and develop overviews that, in the words of Burawoy (1976, p. 96), "either
added up to a series of dislocated factors to be taken into
consideration or reduced to social-psychological generalizations
such as 'generational conflict,' 'the ethos of the expanding
ego and of a regime of plenitude' or prosaic assertions that
the university is inherently 'oppositional.' "

The alternative theoretical framework for the study of
student political activism elaborated in this chapter allows
one, in contrast to past theoretical perspectives, to develop
theses such as the one that follows: That the continued, comparatively high level of (radical) student political activism
among Third World nations in the seventies is an outcome of
a dialectical relationship between two factors: (1) The failure
to date to achieve meaningful levels of development among
these nations so as to enable them to wean themselves away
from dependence (of a self-undermining order) upon the nations of the metropolitan core. This failure is an outcome
of a host of complex and interrelated factors ranging from
historical ones pertaining to their mode of integration into
the world capitalist system, through to present-day activities
of international monopoly capital, on to development of specific social-structural configurations, and specific forms of
class-formation.

(2) The failure to achieve institutionalization of the
political process (an indirect result of the failure to achieve
development) to levels sufficient to contain potential systemic
(inter-institutional) conflict.

As a consequence of these two sets of factors in the
seventies among Third World nations, a radical student political consciousness has emerged (within the context of a gen-

eral disillusionment among Third World intelligentsia with past development ideologies and efforts); and at the same time intensification of inherent structural contradictions of the position of the university has proceeded space. The direct outcome of the dynamic interrelationship between these two factors in turn has been endemic (radical) student political activism.

Notes

1. This chapter could not have been written without the help of the following, to whom I owe special thanks: Philip G. Altbach; Michael Burawoy; Lionel Cliffe; Savitrie Masih-Das; and George Siemensma. Eileen Raines typed the final draft.

2. Some of the insights in this chapter were gained on the basis of my residence at the University of Zambia during the period covering both the 1971 and 1976 crises at the University.

3. The 1971 confrontation was born, ironically, out of a demonstration held by students at the French Embassy in support of government foreign policy on South Africa, and the relations that Western nations (such as France) had with that country. However, following the failure of the country's President, in joining the rest of the nation in supporting the students in their condemnation of police brutality--manifest during the course of the demonstration, and its eventual metamorphesis into a riot--the students proceeded to attack the President himself. They accused him of, among other things, hypocrisy in foreign policy matters--especially in relation to South Africa. This unprecedented action in the history of the country--never before had the President been publicly attacked by a section of the community--brought the students swift retribution from the government and the Party shortly afterwards. On the morning of 14th July, in the words of Burawoy (1976, p. 81), "at 4 a.m. ... the military, the para-military, riot police and ordinary police surrounded and invaded the campus. Fifteen hundred students were herded out of their rooms at gun point. The university was pronounced closed and the student leadership expelled." (For further details on this crisis see Burawoy, 1976; Legum, 1972; and Rothchild, 1971).

4. The 1976 confrontation also took place over a foreign policy matter: the Angolan civil war. On November 11,
1975, when the Portuguese finally left Angola, huge
anonymous posters appeared on the walls of the Central Dining Hall (where all residing students of the
Main Campus ate), outlining the ideological premises
and various aid sources of the rivals in the Angolan
Civil War, with the aim of pointing out that party that
could be considered as radical and progressive--and
hence worthy of student support. These posters attracted considerable attention, judging by the crowds
that milled around them and the comments profusely
scribbled over them by both those in support of MPLA
and those in support of UNITA/FNLA. The appearance
of these posters marked the first public incident on
campus indicating student interest and position on the
Angolan crisis. It quickly revealed that their position
was at variance with that of the government; and this
became formally clear following Zambia's refusal at
the OAU summit meeting in early January 1976 to
recognize MPLA as the legitimate government of Angola, when they staged a demonstration of January 15,
1976. This demonstration, which was held on campus
at the main entrance, took the form of a teach-in
exercise, and it facilitated the release of the official
statement of the students' union on the Angolan crisis,
which read in part as follows:

> Having recognized that the stand taken by our gov-
> ernment on the Angolan situation is extremely re-
> actionary and retrogressive, we the students of the
> University of Zambia, through our union, wish to
> dissociate ourselves completely from this oppor-
> tunist, hypocritical, imperialist and impossible
> stand.

> At one and the same time we wish to make our
> stand explicit--that without a speck of reservation
> we with full force support the anti-imperialist,
> therefore revolutionary MOVIMENTO POPULAR DE
> LIBERTO DE ANGOLA (M. P. L. A.)....

> ... It is indisputable that the Zambian government
> supports UNITA, a movement whose long standing
> treachery has been made explicit. This compels
> us to charge the Zambian ruling clique, headed by
> Dr. Kaunda "our beloved President" with CRIMINAL

TREACHERY. (From University of Zambia Student
Union: Statement on Angola, 15 January 1976).

Initially this demonstration provided little response from the government and the local news media
refrained from giving it any significant mention. However, veiled comments criticizing and deriding the
students from a number of MPs and other political
leaders did appear in Parliament and in the press
shortly after the demonstration was held. (See, for
instance Zambia Daily Mail of 19th January, and 26th
January 1976). These comments though, in turn generated harsh responses from the students. (See, for
example, University of Zambia Student Union circular:
"Open Letter to you Frank Chitambala, member of the
Central Committee, Chairman of the Rural Development Subcommittee of the same" (27 January 1976);
The Vanguard circular: "That Zambia Daily Mail
Editorial" (January 1976). Therefore, although there
was no immediate direct response from the government to the student demonstration of January 15th, a
veiled war of words was nonetheless very much in
evidence, precipitating on campus fairly intense political animation which further served as a prelude to
its eventual but drastic response on the 31st of January. On that day it took the unprecedented action of
arresting and detaining a British senior political lecturer, popular with students and housed on campus,
on grounds that he had allegedly instigated the student
demonstration (though this was not spelt out in so
many words). The arrest of the senior lecturer precipitated a deep crisis within the university amongst
both staff and students. The staff became very anx-
ious and concerned about its own security--especially
since no official explanation for the senior lecturer's
arrest was forthcoming.

The students on their part announced on 5th
of February a general strike, bringing the whole campus to a standstill. Four days later, following a number of incidents on campus, the Government, in its
turn responded: very early, on the morning of Mon-
day, 9 February, security forces that had earlier
over the weekend laid siege to the campus, sprayed
teargas into students' rooms forcing them out onto
the playing field where they were told that Government
had ordered that the university be closed, and that
they were to return home. That same morning two

more lecturers were arrested and some 17 students, and a fortnight later a Zambian Staff Development Fellow was picked up. The detention without trial of the lecturers and students lasted for some two weeks or so, while for others it was from a month to three months, and for three of them in particular it was close to a year. This unprecedented action on the part of the government attracted considerable attention--even outside the country, including the involvement of Amnesty International on behalf of the University detainees.

On their release from detention, the expatriate detainees were expelled from the country, while a number of the student detainees were expelled from the university, and the Staff Development Fellow was sacked. It should be noted that no evidence of Soviet involvement in the student disturbances, as alleged by the President in his speeches on two different occasions (February 15th and February 20th) was ever found--and all detainees were released without being charged or tried. The University was reopened on 10th May with a new Vice-Chancellor taking the helm.

5. Burawoy describes the nature of student consciousness of the 1971 students as follows:

> What is the precise content of student "oppositionalism"? It is not aimed at the premises which govern the organization of Zambian society but at the legitimacy of the nation's leadership....
>
> ... The idiom of Fanon is adopted to condemn the "exploitation of the common man at the hands of the native bourgeoisie," while the confidence Fanon placed in the peasant is rejected by the Zambian student. On the contrary the common man is portrayed as the innocent and helpless victim of opportunistic and self-serving politicians who must be replaced by enlightened and benign rulers. The glorification of the "common man" or "peasant" to be found in populist appeals of intellectuals in India and West Africa are not present among Zambian students. Rather they constitute a "modernizing elite" attempting to cast off a recent and ever present history of colonial oppression and they associate with villages only backwardness and ignorance. That "socialist" perspectives or even

rhetoric is conspicuous by its absence, in contrast
to students in other third world universities, reflects the proximity of the colonial order, a continuing intimacy with their rural roots and the availability of prestigious occupations as reflected in the
persistent need for expatriate personnel. (1976,
pp. 87-88)

6. In the statement issued on the occasion of the general
strike declared by students union on 5th February, the
students wrote, among other things:

... This university is harbouring some very undesirable lecturers who stand for everything that
is antithetical to what we have said so far. These
lecturers are bent on subverting the integrity of
this university for their own personal gains. They
are not only interfering with what is taught in other
courses but through intrigue and treachery are ex-
posing fellow lecturers to the dangers of being labelled by the government as subversive (as has
already happened in the case of one lecturer).
These lecturers are out and out enemies of the
true spirit of academic freedom.... [See also the
Vanguard circular "the Ndem-Mutukwa axis" (5th
February 1976)].

7. See for example the University of Zambia Students Union
Circular: "Open letter to you Comrade Frank Chitambala, Member of the Central Committee, Chairman
of the Rural Development Subcommittee of the same. "
(27 January 1976).

8. See the University of Zambia Student Union "Statement
on Angola" (15 January 1976).

9. Thus for example the Frantz Fanon Club Communique
on Angola, in describing UNITA's ally FNLA, stated
in part:

FNLA is the brain child of American multi-national
corporations which saw no future in the liberated
Angola under MPLA. It is clear that FNLA and
Roberto's assignment to Angola is not to liberate
the people but to further the interests of the U. S.
international monopoly Capital....
If Roberto [the FNLA leader] was standing for

a good cause, why does he ... get his financial
backing and arms from U.S. imperialists, the bar-
barous and shameless aggressor of modern times,
the main force of aggression and war, the right
leader of world reaction, the bulwark of modern
colonialism, the strangler of national liberation and
independence and disrupter of world peace? (from:
The Frantz Fanon Club circular: Communique in
support of MPLA--The Peoples Power, January
1976).

To take another example: recently U.S. involvement
in attempts to end the war in Zimbabwe brought forth
renewed attacks on the presence of the United States
in Southern Africa--and especially its black (former)
Ambassador: Andrew Young. Thus in response to
Young's visit to Southern Africa, a campus news
magazine: Right On (Volume 1, No. 10, June 1977)
wrote in part:

There is a tendency among the Middle Class Ne-
groes, who come to Africa, to spread reactionary
influence. These "Blacks" base their faulty ideology on their alley dog philosophy--"Get the dollar
if you can." They advise their African adversaries
that the problems of Africa could be easily settled
if only the African could keep his mouth shut and
do what the master--their master--says. In es-
sence what these sell-outs are all out to do is
(1) reduce the African revolution to a CIVIL RIGHTS
DEMAND; (2) sell to the Africans, for the conven-
ience of their masters, the bogus, reformist and
anti-popular ideology of NON-VIOLENCE in a violent situation; (3) buy time for their masters who
are now plundering the resources of mother Africa....

References

Alpers, Edward A. (1979). "The Struggle for Socialism in
    Mozambique, 1960-1972," in Carl G. Rosberg and
    Thomas M. Callaghy (eds.). Socialism in Sub-Saharan
    Africa--A New Assessment. Berkeley: University of
    California, Institute of International Studies, pp. 267-
    95.
Altbach, Philip G. (1966). "Students and Politics," Compara-
    tive Education Review 10 (June): 175-87.

Altbach, Philip G. (1969). "Student Politics and Higher Education in India, " in Seymour Martin Lipset and Philip G. Altbach (eds.). Students in Revolt. Boston: Houghton Mifflin, pp. 235-56.

Altbach, Philip G. (1979). Comparative Higher Education: Research Trends and Bibliography. London: Mansell Publishing.

Aron, Raymond (1972). "Student Rebellion: Vision of the Future or Echo from the Past, " in Anthony M. Orum (ed.). The Seeds of Politics: Youth and Politics in America. Englewood Cliffs, N. J. : Prentice Hall, pp. 327-42.

Bakke, E. Wight (1966). "Roots and Soil of Student Activism, " Comparative Education Review 10 (June): 163-74.

Ben-David, Joseph and Collins, Randall (1966). "A Comparative Study of Academic Freedom and Student Politics, " Comparative Education Review 10 (June): 220-49.

Bereday, George Z. F. (1966). "Student Unrest on Four Continents: Montreal, Ibadan, Warsaw, and Rangoon, " Comparative Education Review 10 (June): 188-204.

Block, Jeanne H; Haan, Norma; and Smith, M. Brewster (1972). "Socialization Correlates of Student Activism, " in Anthony M. Orum (ed.). The Seeds of Politics: Youth and Politics in America. Englewood Cliffs, N. J. : Prentice Hall, pp. 215-31.

Boudon, Raymond (1972). "Sources of Student Protest in France, " in Philip G. Altbach and Robert S. Laufer (eds.). The New Pilgrims: Youth Protest in Transition. N. Y. : David McKay, pp. 297-312.

Brown, Kevin (1979). "Angolan Socialism, " in Carl G. Rosberg and Thomas M. Callaghy (eds.). Socialism in Sub-Saharan Africa--A New Assessment. Berkeley: University of California, Institute of International Studies, pp. 296-321.

Burawoy, Michael (1976). "Consciousness and Contradiction: A Study of Student Protest in Zambia, " British Journal of Sociology 27 (No. 1): 78-97.

DuBois, Victor D. (1965). "The Student/Government Conflict in the Ivory Coast, " American University Field Staff Reports: West Africa Series 8 (No. 1): 11-24.

Eisenstadt, S. N. (1972). "Generational Conflict and Intellectual Antinomianism, " in Philip G. Altbach and Robert S. Laufer (eds.). The New Pilgrims: Youth Protest in Transition. N. Y. : David McKay, pp. 139-54.

Feuer, Lewis (1972). "The Sources and Traits of Student Movements," in Anthony M. Orum (ed.). The Seeds of Politics: Youth and Politics in America. Englewood Cliffs, N. J.: Prentice Hall, pp. 365-85.

Finlay, David J. (1968). "Students and Politics in Ghana," Daedalus 97 (Winter): 51-69.

Flacks, Richard (1972). "Young Intelligentsia in Revolt," in Anthony M. Orum (ed.). The Seeds of Politics: Youth and Politics in America. Englewood Cliffs, N. J.: Prentice Hall, pp. 258-70.

Friedland, William H. and Rosberg, Carl G. (eds.). (1964). African Socialism. Stanford, California: Stanford University Press for Hoover Institute on War, Revolution, and Peace.

Ghosh, S. K. (1969). The Student Challenge Round the World. Calcutta: Eastern Law House Private Ltd.

Government/Zambia. (January 1977). Economic Report 1976. Lusaka: Ministry of Development Planning.

Keniston, Kenneth (1972). "The Sources of Student Dissent," in Anthony M. Orum (ed.). The Seeds of Politics: Youth and Politics in America. Englewood Cliffs, N. J.: Prentice Hall, pp. 345-52.

Legum, Colin (1972). "The Year of the Students: A Survey of the African University Scene," in Colin Legum, (ed.). Africa Contemporary Record: Annual Survey and Documents 1971/72. London: Rex Collings, pp. A3-A30.

Lipset, Seymour Martin (1966). "University Students and Politics in Underdeveloped Countries," Comparative Education Review 10 (June): 132-62.

Lipset, Seymour Martin (1969). "Introduction: Students and Politics in Comparative Perspective," in Seymour Martin Lipset and Philip G. Altbach (eds.). Students in Revolt. Boston: Houghton Mifflin Company, pp. xv-xxxiv.

Mannheim, Karl (1972). "The Problem of Generations," in Philip G. Altbach and Robert S. Laufer (eds.). The New Pilgrims: Youth Protest in Transition. N. Y.: David McKay, pp. 101-38.

Moore, Clement H. and Hochschild, Arlie R. (1968). "Student Unions in North African Politics," Daedalus 97 (Winter): 21-50.

Rosberg, Carl G. and Callaghy, Thomas M. (eds.) (1979). Socialism in Sub-Saharan Africa--A New Assessment. Berkeley: University of California, Institute of International Studies.

Rothchild, Donald (1971). "The Beginning of Student Unrest

in Zambia, " Transition 8 (December): 66-74.

Scott, Robert E. (1969). "Student Political Activism in Latin America, " in Seymour Martin Lipset and Philip G. Altbach (eds.). Students in Revolt. Boston: Houghton Mifflin Company, pp. 403-31.

Shils, Edward (1969). "Dreams of Plentitude and Nightmares of Scarcity, " in Seymour Martin Lipset and Philip G. Altbach (eds.). Students in Revolt. Boston: Houghton Mifflin Company, pp. 1-34.

Weinberg, Ian and Walker, Kenneth N. (1969). "Student Politics and Political Systems: Toward a Typology, " American Journal of Sociology 75 (July): 77-96.

CONTRIBUTORS

PHILIP G. ALTBACH is Professor of Higher Education and
    Foundations of Education and Director of the Compara-
    tive Education Center at the State University of New
    York, Buffalo. He has written extensively on student
    activism, and is author of Student Politics in America
    (1974), The Student Internationals (1973), co-editor
    (with S. M. Lipset) of Students in Revolt (1968), edi-
    tor of Turmoil and Transition: Higher Education and
    Student Politics in India (1968) and other books.

RAYMOND BOUDON is Professor of Sociology at the Univer-
    sity of Paris-Sorbonne. He is the author of a number
    of books, most recently La logique du social (1979).

N. JAYARAM is Assistant Professor in the Department of
    Sociology, Bangalore University, India.

ANDREAS M. KAZAMIAS is Professor of Educational Policy
    Studies at the University of Wisconsin, Madison.

ARTHUR LEVINE is senior fellow at the Carnegie Foundation
    for the Advancement of Teaching in Washington, D. C.
    His most recent book is When Dreams & Heroes Died
    (1980).

CYRIL LEVITT is Assistant Professor of Sociology at McMas-
    ter University in Canada.

DANIEL C. LEVY is Research Associate at the Institution
    for Social and Policy Studies, Yale University. His
    most recent book is University and Government in
    Mexico (1980).

Y. G-M. LULAT is a doctoral student in the Department of
    Social Foundations of Education at the State University
    of New York, Buffalo.

GEORGE PSACHAROPOULOS teaches at the London School of

Economics and Political Science. His most recent book is Information in Educational Planning and Decision Making.

MICHIYA SHIMBORI is Professor of Sociology of Education, Hiroshima University, Japan. His most recent book is Scientific Community in Japan (1978).

GIANNI STATERA is Professor in the Institute of Sociology at the University of Rome, Italy.

WOLF-DIETRICH WEBLER is on the staff of Interdisciplinary Center for Higher Education at the University of Bielefeld, West Germany.

KEITH R. WILSON is a graduate student at the University of California, Berkeley.

PAMELA YETTRAM is on the teaching staff of the Open University, England.

INDEX

academic conditions   110, 123-124, 176-177
activism and egoism   59-66
African elites   250-252
Akhil Bharatiya Vidyarthi Parishad (India)   221, 227, 232
All-India Students Federation   220, 231
American student activism   16-35, 36-52; historical perspec-
     tives   17-20, 37; motivating forces   18, 32; organiza-
     tions   39, 65-66; religious factors   27; student jour-
     nalism   23; the 1960s   20, 29, 37; the 1970s   38, 45
attitudes   9, 15, 26, 40-43, 80, 107, 113-115, 123, 140,
     147-157, 165, 177-180, 246, 257

Baader-Meinhof Gant (West Germany)   107
Berkeley Student Revolt   3
British student activism   137-171

Canadian student activism   57-58, 61-63
causes for activism   108, 135, 140, 147, 166, 181-182,
     187-188, 192, 228-232, 245
CIA   192
Communist Party (England)   145-146
Communist Party (France)   77-78
Communist Party (Italy)   92, 94
conservative student groups   164, 221
Cordoba Reforms   5
counterculture and activism   140, 166

decline of activism   8-11, 28, 34, 97, 131, 186-187, 202,
     207, 234
Delhi University (India)   221-222
demographic factors   10, 30

economic factors and student activism   9, 30, 230, 252-253,
     255